Vegetarian

Vegetarian

This is a Parragon Publishing Book
This edition published in 2002

Parragon Publishing
Queen Street House
4 Queen Street
Bath BA1 1HE, UK

ISBN: 0-75257-956-8

Printed in China

NOTE

Unless otherwise stated, milk is assumed to be whole fat, eggs are large, and pepper
is freshly ground black pepper.

Recipes using uncooked eggs should be
avoided by infants, the elderly, pregnant women, and anyone
suffering from an illness.

Contents

Light Meals (continued)

Pasta, Grains & Pulses

Stir-Fries & Sautés

Casseroles & Bakes

Salads

Introduction

Vegetarian food need not be boring, as this inspirational cookbook will demonstrate! Packed full of delicious recipes that are nutritious and substantial, even the most diserning palate is sure to be satisfied.

Variety, of course, is the keynote to healthy eating, whatever the diet. As long as the day's meals contain a good mixture of different food types – carboydrates, proteins, and fats – a balanced diet and adequate supplies of essential vitamins and proteins are almost guarenteed. Typical dishes that are based on fresh vegetables, legumes, pasta, or rice, for example, also have the advantages of being low in fats, particularly saturated fats, and high in complex carbohydrates and fiber, resulting in a diet that is in tune with modern nutritional thinking.

Vegetables are an important source of vitamins, especially vitamin C. Green vegetables and legumes contain many B-group vitamins. Both carrots and dark green vegetables contain high levels of carotene, which is used by the body to manufacture vitamin A. Carrots also contain useful quantities of vitamins B3, C, and E. Vegetable oils contain vitamin E and most are also high in polyunsaturated fats. Vegetables are also a particularly good source of many essential minerals, especially calcium, iron, magnesium, and potassium.

There is a long and honorable tradition of the specific, healthgiving properties of different vegetables, which dates back at least as far as the Middle Ages. These qualities, once dismissed as old wives' tales, are now being recognized and valued again. Onions and garlic, for example, contain cycloallin, an anticoagulant that helps protect against heart disease. Garlic also contains a stong antibiotic, is thought to protect the body against some major diseases and also increases the absorption of many vitamins.

There is no question that a sensible vegetarian diet is at least as healthy as a sensible meat-eating diet and some nutritionalists maintain that it is better. However there are one or two particular points that are worth noting. Proteins are made up of 'building blocks' called amino acids and, while all those essential to the human body are easily obtained from most animal products, they are not always present in many vegetarian foods. A good mixed diet will prevent this from being a problem. For example, legumes are an excellent source of protein, but they do lack one essential amino acid called methionine. Grains, on the other hand, contain this amino acid, although they lack two others, trptophan and lysine. A dish that contains both rice and peas, a plate of hummus and pitta bread, or bowl of bean soup and slice of wholewheat toast, for example, will ensure that all the necessary first-class proteins are available to the body.

Dairy products are also a valuable source of protein, but they are high in fat. It is very easy for busy people to fall into the habit of basing rather a lot of meals around cheese, for example, resulting in an unhealthily high intake of cholesterol. Eaten in

Introduction

moderation, however, cheese is a very useful and versatile ingredient in the vegetarian diet. If you do use dairy products a lot, it may be worth considering buying low-fat types, such as skimmed or semi-skimmed milk, fromage frais and soft cheeses.

It is important to be aware that the body cannot absorb iron from vegetable sources unless vitamin C is ingested at the same meal. Although many vegetables also contain vitamin C, this is easily destroyed through cooking. Some raw fruit, a glass of fruit juice, or a side salad are simple and tasty solutions.

Vegans, who do not eat any dairy products, must be a little more scrupulous than straightforward vegetarians about ensuring that they obtain all the necessary nutrients. A lack of calcium, in particular, can be a problem, but this can be countered with a mineral supplement or by using calcium-enriched soya milk. A vegan diet can be just as healthy as a vegetarian or meat-eating one.

No foods can really be said to be bad for you, although some are best eaten in moderation. It is sensible to keep an eye on the quantities of butter, cream, high-fat cheese, dried fruits, oils, and unsalted nuts that you eat each day. Other popular vegetarian ingredients, such as grains, vegetables, legumes, fruit, bread, pasta, and noodles can be eaten more freely. All diets should include raw vegetables and fruit and these should comprise as much as 40 per cent of a vegetarian diet.

Finally, a hidden advantage to changing to a vegetarian diet is that, usually, it initially entails thinking in a more detailed way about all the things that you eat. This may extend across the whole spectrum of nutrition, including such things as your intake of salt, sugar, and refined foods. As a result, many long-term vegetarians have developed eating patterns that are among the healthiest in the world.

Vegetables

Vegetables are, of course, at the heart of a vegetarian diet, offering an almost endless choice of flavours and textures. Preparing and cooking them with care ensures that they may be enjoyed at their best and that they retain their full nutritional value.

Buying

The fresher vegetables are, the better. Nevertherless, some, such as root vegetables, can be stored for relatively long periods in a cool, dark place, and most will keep for two or three days in the salad drawer of the refrigerator. While supermarkets are very convenient and carry a wide range of good-quality vegetables, time spent finding a really high-quality supplier — possibly of organically-grown vegetables — will be repaid many times over in terms of flavour and nutritional value.

Whatever type you are buying, always look for unblemished and undamaged vegetables with no discoloration. Greens should have good color, with no wilting leaves, root vegetables should be firm and crisp, vegetable fruits, such as tomatoes and bell peppers, should not have soggy patches or wrinkled skin. No vegetables should ever look or smell stale.

Preparing

Use vegetables as soon as possible after buying them, but try not to prepare them much in advance of cooking. If they are left exposed to air or soaking in water, many vitamins and other valuable nutrients are leached out or destroyed.

The highest concentration of nutrients is in the layer directly under the skin, so if possible. avoid peeling them altogether. If they must be peeled, try to do it very thinly. A swivel vegetable peeler is a worthwhile investment. Also consider cooking potatoes, for example, in their skins — first scrubbing off any soil or dirt — and peeling them afterwards. The skin comes off in a much thinner layer than when they are peeled raw.

How thickly or thinly vegetables are sliced, or how large or small they are chopped will depend, to some extent, on the method of cooking and the individual recipe directions. However, remember that the smaller and finer the pieces, the greater the surface area from which nutrients can leach.

Basic Recipes

Fresh Vegetable Stock

1 cup shallots

1 large carrot, diced

1 celery stalk, chopped

½ fennel bulb

1 garlic clove

1 bay leaf

a few fresh parsley and tarragon sprigs

2 quarts water

pepper

1 Put all of the ingredients in a large saucepan and bring to a boil. Skim off the surface scum with a flat spoon and reduce to a gentle simmer. Partially cover and cook for 45 minutes. Leave to cool.

2 Line a strainer with clean cheesecloth and put over a jug or bowl. Pour the stock through the strainer. Discard the herbs and vegetables. Cover and store in small quantities in the refrigerator for up to 3 days.

Sesame Paste

3 tbsp sesame paste

6 tbsp water

2 tsp lemon juice

1 garlic clove, crushed

salt and pepper

1 Blend together the sesame seed paste and water.

2 Stir in the lemon juice and garlic. Season with salt and pepper to taste. The sesame paste is now ready to serve.

Sesame Dressing

2 tbsp sesame seed paste

2 tbsp cider vinegar

2 tbsp medium sherry

2 tbsp sesame oil

1 tbsp soy sauce

1 garlic clove, crushed

1 Put the sesame seed paste in a bowl and gradually mix in the vinegar and sherry until smooth. Add the sesame oil, soy sauce, and garlic and mix together thoroughly.

Béchamel Sauce

2½ cups of milk

4 cloves

1 bay leaf

pinch of freshly grated nutmeg

2 tbsp butter or margarine

2 tbsp all-purpose flour

salt and pepper

1 Put the milk in a saucepan and add the cloves, bay leaf, and nutmeg. Gradually bring to the boil. Remove from the heat and leave for 15 minutes.

2 Melt the butter or margarine in another saucepan and stir in the flour to make a roux. Cook, stirring, for 1 minute. Remove the pan from the heat.

3 Strain the milk and gradually blend into the roux. Return the pan to the heat and bring to a boil, stirring, until the sauce thickens. Season with salt and pepper to taste and add any flavorings.

Green Herb Dressing

¼ cup parsley

¼ cup mint

¼ cup chives

⅔ cup natural yogurt

salt and pepper

1 Remove the stalks from the parsley and mint and put the leaves in a blender or food processor.

2 Add the chives, garlic, and yogurt and salt and pepper to taste. Blend until smooth, then store in the refrigerator until needed.

Cucumber Dressing

1 cup natural yogurt

2 inch piece of cucumber, peeled

1 tbsp chopped fresh mint leaves

½ tsp grated lemon rind

pinch of superfine sugar

salt and pepper

1 Put the yogurt, cucumber, mint, lemon rind, sugar, and salt and pepper to taste in a blender or food processor and work until smooth. Alternatively, finely chop the cucumber and combine with the other ingredients. Serve chilled.

Warm Walnut Dressing

6 tbsp walnut oil

3 tbsp white wine vinegar

1 tbsp clear honey

1 tsp wholegrain mustard

1 garlic clove, sliced

salt and pepper

1 Put the oil, vinegar, honey, mustard, and salt and pepper to taste in a saucepan and whisk together.

2 Add the garlic and heat very gently for 3 minutes. Remove the garlic slices with a perforated spoon and discard. Pour the dressing over the salad and serve immediately.

Apple & Cider Vinegar Dressing

2 tbsp sunflower oil

2 tbsp concentrated apple juice

2 tbsp cider vinegar

1 tbsp Meaux mustard

1 garlic clove, crushed

salt and pepper

1 Put the oil, apple juice, cider vinegar, mustard, garlic, and salt and pepper to taste in a screw-top jar and shake vigorously until well-mixed.

Tomato Dressing

½ cup tomato juice

1 garlic clove, crushed

2 tbsp lemon juice

1 tbsp soy sauce

1 tsp clear honey

2 tbsp chopped chives

salt and pepper

1 Put the tomato juice, garlic, lemon juice, soy sauce, honey, chives, and salt and pepper to taste in a screw-top jar and shake vigorously until well-mixed.

How to Use This Book

Each recipe contains a wealth of useful information, including a breakdown of nutritional quantities, preparation, and cooking times, and level of difficulty. All of this information is explained in detail below.

The nutritional information provided for each recipe is per serving or per portion. Optional ingredients, variations, or serving suggestions have not been included in the calculations.

The number of chef's hats represents the difficulty of each recipe, ranging from easy (1 chef's hat) to difficult (5 chef's hats).

This amount of time represents the preparation of ingredients, including cooling, chilling, and soaking times.

This represents the cooking time.

The ingredients for each recipe are listed in the order that they are used.

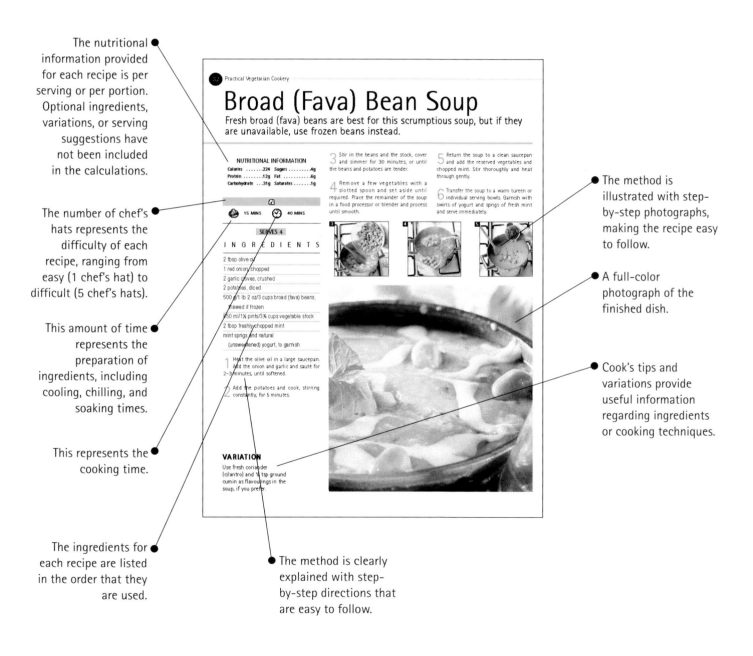

The method is illustrated with step-by-step photographs, making the recipe easy to follow.

A full-color photograph of the finished dish.

Cook's tips and variations provide useful information regarding ingredients or cooking techniques.

The method is clearly explained with step-by-step directions that are easy to follow.

Soups

Soup is easy to make but always produces delicious results. There is an enormous variety of soups which you can make with vegetables. They can be rich and creamy, thick and chunky, light and delicate, and hot, or chilled. The vegetables are often puréed to give a smooth consistency and thicken the soup, but you can also purée just some of

the mixture to give the soup more texture and interest. A wide range of ingredients can be used in addition to vegetables — legumes, grains, noodles, cheese, and yogurt all work well. You can also experiment with different substitutions if you don't have certain ingredients to hand. Whatever your preference, you're sure to enjoy the variety of tasty soups contained in this chapter. Serve with fresh, crusty bread for a truly delicious meal.

Winter Soup

A thick vegetable soup which is a delicious meal in itself. Serve the soup with thin shavings of Parmesan and warm ciabatta bread.

NUTRITIONAL INFORMATION

Calories 285	Sugars 11g	
Protein 16g	Fat 12g	
Carbohydrate ...29g	Saturates 3g	

 10 MINS   20 MINS

SERVES 4

I N G R E D I E N T S

2 tbsp olive oil

2 leeks, thinly sliced

2 zucchini, chopped

2 garlic cloves, crushed

14-oz cans chopped tomatoes

1 tbsp tomato paste

1 bay leaf

3¾ cups vegetable stock

14-oz can garbanzo
    beans, drained

8 oz spinach

1 oz Parmesan cheese,
    thinly shaved

salt and pepper

crusty bread, to serve

1 Heat the oil in a heavy-bottomed saucepan. Add the sliced leeks and zucchini and cook over a medium heat, stirring constantly, for 5 minutes.

2 Add the garlic, chopped tomatoes, tomato paste, bay leaf, vegetable stock, and garbanzo beans. Bring to the boil, lower the heat and simmer, stirring occasionally, for 5 minutes.

3 Shred the spinach finely, add to the soup and boil for 2 minutes. Season to taste with salt and pepper.

4 Remove the bay leaf. Pour into a soup tureen and sprinkle over the Parmesan. Serve with crusty bread.

Plum Tomato Soup

Homemade tomato soup is easy to make and always tastes better than bought varieties. Try this version with its Mediterranean influences.

NUTRITIONAL INFORMATION

Calories	402	Sugars	........14g
Protein	.........7g	Fat	..........32g
Carbohydrate	...16g	Saturates	.......3g

 20 MINS 30–35 MINS

SERVES 4

I N G R E D I E N T S

2 tbsp olive oil

2 red onions, chopped

2 celery stalks, chopped

1 carrot, chopped

1 lb 2 oz plum tomatoes, halved

3 cups vegetable stock

1 tbsp chopped oregano

1 tbsp chopped basil

⅔ cup dry white wine

2 tsp superfine sugar

1 cup hazelnuts, toasted

1 cup black or green olives

handful of basil leaves

1 tbsp olive oil

1 loaf ciabatta bread (Italian-style loaf)

salt and pepper

basil sprigs to garnish

1 Heat the oil in a large saucepan. Add the onions, celery, and carrot and fry over a low heat, stirring frequently, until soft, but not colored.

2 Add the tomatoes, stock, chopped herbs, wine, and sugar. Bring to the boil, cover and simmer for 20 minutes.

3 Place the toasted hazelnuts in a blender or food processor, together with the olives and basil leaves and process until thoroughly combined, but not too smooth. Alternatively, finely chop the nuts, olives, and basil leaves and pound them together in a mortar and pestle, then turn into a small bowl. Add the olive oil and process or beat thoroughly for a few seconds. Turn the mixture into a serving bowl.

4 Warm the ciabatta bread in a preheated oven, 375°F, for 3–4 minutes.

5 Process the soup in a blender or a food processor, or press through a strainer, until smooth, Check the seasoning. Ladle into warmed soup bowls and garnish with sprigs of basil. Slice the warm bread and spread with the olive and hazelnut paste. Serve with the soup.

Gazpacho

This Spanish soup is full of chopped and grated vegetables with a tomato paste base. It requires chilling, so prepare well in advance.

NUTRITIONAL INFORMATION

Calories 140   Sugars 12g
Protein . . . . .3g   Fat 9g
Carbohydrate . . .13g   Saturates 1g

6½ HOURS   0 MINS

SERVES 4

INGREDIENTS

½ small cucumber

½ small green bell pepper, seeded and
    very finely chopped

1 lb 2 oz ripe tomatoes, peeled or
    14-oz can chopped tomatoes

½ onion, coarsely chopped

2–3 garlic cloves, crushed

3 tbsp olive oil

2 tbsp white wine vinegar

1–2 tbsp lemon or lime juice

2 tbsp tomato paste

scant 2 cups tomato juice

salt and pepper

TO SERVE

chopped green bell pepper

thinly sliced onion rings

garlic croûtons

1 Coarsely grate the cucumber into a large bowl and add the chopped green bell pepper.

2 Process the tomatoes, onion, and garlic in a food processor or blender, then add the oil, vinegar, lemon or lime juice, and tomato paste and process until smooth. Alternatively, finely chop the tomatoes and finely grate the onion, then mix both with the garlic, oil, vinegar, lemon or lime juice, and tomato paste.

3 Add the tomato mixture to the bowl and mix well, then add the tomato juice and mix again.

4 Season to taste, cover the bowl with plastic wrap and chill thoroughly — for at least 6 hours and preferably longer so that the flavors have time to meld together.

5 Prepare the side dishes of green bell pepper, onion rings, and garlic croûtons, and arrange in individual serving bowls.

6 Ladle the soup into bowls, preferably from a soup tureen set on the table with the side dishes placed around it. Hand the dishes around to allow the guests to help themselves.

Gardener's Broth

This hearty soup uses a variety of green vegetables with a flavouring of ground coriander. A finishing touch of thinly sliced leeks adds texture.

NUTRITIONAL INFORMATION

Calories ....169 Sugars 5g
Protein ....4g Fat 13g
Carbohydrate ....8g Saturates 5g

10 MINS   45 MINS

SERVES 6

INGREDIENTS

3 tbsp butter

1 onion, chopped

1–2 garlic cloves, crushed

1 large leek

8 oz Brussels sprouts

4½ oz green or string beans

1½ quarts/5 cups vegetable stock

1 cup frozen peas

1 tbsp lemon juice

½ tsp ground coriander

4 tbsp heavy cream

salt and pepper

MELBA TOAST

4–6 slices white bread

1 Melt the butter in a saucepan. Add the onion and garlic and fry over a low heat, stirring occasionally, until they begin to soften, but not color.

2 Slice the white part of the leek very thinly and reserve; slice the remaining leek. Slice the Brussels sprouts and thinly slice the beans.

3 Add the green part of the leeks, the Brussels sprouts, and beans to the saucepan. Add the stock and bring to the boil. Simmer for 10 minutes.

4 Add the frozen peas, seasoning, lemon juice, and coriander and continue to simmer for 10–15 minutes, until the vegetables are tender.

5 Cool the soup a little, then press through a strainer or process in a food processor or blender until smooth. Pour into a clean pan.

6 Add the reserved slices of leek to the soup, bring back to the boil and simmer for about 5 minutes, until the leek is tender. Adjust the seasoning, stir in the cream and reheat gently.

7 To make the melba toast, toast the bread on both sides under a preheated broiler. Cut horizontally through the slices, then toast the uncooked sides until they curl up. Serve immediately with the soup.

Speedy Beet Soup

Quick and easy to prepare in a microwave oven, this deep red soup of puréed beets and potatoes makes a stunning first course.

NUTRITIONAL INFORMATION

Calories 120   Sugars 11g
Protein . . . . .4g   Fat 2g
Carbohydrate . . .22g   Saturates 1g

  20 MINS   30 MINS

SERVES 6

I N G R E D I E N T S

1 onion, chopped

12 oz potatoes, diced

1 small cooking apple, peeled,
    cored, and grated

3 tbsp water

1 tsp cumin seeds

1 lb 2 oz cooked beets,
    peeled and diced

1 bay leaf

pinch of dried thyme

1 tsp lemon juice

2½ cups hot vegetable stock

4 tbsp soured cream

salt and pepper

dill sprigs, to garnish

1 Place the onion, potatoes, apple, and water in a large bowl. Cover and cook on HIGH power for 10 minutes.

2 Stir in the cumin seeds and cook on HIGH power for 1 minute.

3 Stir in the beets, bay leaf, thyme, lemon juice, and hot vegetable stock. Cover and cook on HIGH power for 12 minutes, stirring halfway through the cooking time.

4 Leave to stand, uncovered, for 5 minutes. Remove and discard the bay leaf. Strain the vegetables and reserve the liquid. Process the vegetables with a little of the reserved liquid in a food processor or blender until they are smooth and creamy. Alternatively, either mash the vegetables with a potato masher or press them through a strainer with the back of a wooden spoon.

5 Pour the vegetable purée into a clean bowl with the reserved liquid and mix well. Season to taste. Cover and cook on HIGH power for 4–5 minutes, until the soup is piping hot.

6 Serve the soup in warmed bowls. Swirl 1 tablespoon of soured cream into each serving and garnish with a few sprigs of fresh dill.

Pumpkin Soup

This is an American classic that has now become popular worldwide.
When pumpkin is out of season use butternut squash in its place.

NUTRITIONAL INFORMATION

Calories	112	Sugars	7g
Protein	4g	Fat	7g
Carbohydrate	8g	Saturates	2g

 10 MINS 30 MINS

SERVES 6

INGREDIENTS

2 lb 4 oz pumpkin

3 tbsp butter or margarine

1 onion, sliced thinly

1 garlic clove, crushed

3½ cups vegetable stock

½ tsp ground ginger

1 tbsp lemon juice

3–4 thinly pared strips of orange
  rind (optional)

1–2 bay leaves or 1 bouquet garni

1¼ cups milk

salt and pepper

TO GARNISH

4–6 tablespoons light or heavy cream,
  natural yogurt or fromage blanc

snipped chives

1 Peel the pumpkin, remove the seeds and then cut the flesh into 1 inch cubes.

2 Melt the butter or margarine in a large, heavy-bottomed saucepan. Add the onion and garlic and fry over a low heat until soft but not colored.

3 Add the pumpkin and toss with the onion for 2–3 minutes.

4 Add the stock and bring to the boil over a medium heat. Season to taste with salt and pepper and add the ginger, lemon juice, strips of orange rind, if using, and bay leaves or bouquet garni. Cover and simmer over a low heat for about 20 minutes, until the pumpkin is tender.

5 Discard the orange rind, if using, and the bay leaves or bouquet garni. Cool the soup slightly, then press through a strainer or process in a food processor until smooth. Pour into a clean saucepan.

6 Add the milk and reheat gently. Adjust the seasoning. Garnish with a swirl of cream, natural yogurt or fromage blanc and snipped chives, and serve.

Bell Pepper & Chili Soup

This soup has a real Mediterranean flavor, using sweet red bell peppers, tomato, chili, and basil. It is great served with an olive bread.

NUTRITIONAL INFORMATION

Calories 55   Sugars 10g
Protein . . . . .2g   Fat 0.5g
Carbohydrate . . . .11g   Saturates 0.1g

 10 MINS   25 MINS

SERVES 4

I N G R E D I E N T S

8 oz red bell peppers,
   seeded and sliced

1 onion, sliced

2 garlic cloves, crushed

1 green chili, chopped

1½ cups passata (sieved tomatoes)

2½ cups vegetable stock

2 tbsp chopped basil

basil sprigs, to garnish

1 Put the bell peppers in a large saucepan with the onion, garlic, and chili. Add the passata (sieved tomatoes) and vegetable stock and bring to the boil, stirring well.

2 Reduce the heat to a simmer and cook for 20 minutes, or until the bell peppers have softened. Drain, reserving the liquid and vegetables separately.

3 Press the vegetables through a strainer with the back of a spoon. Alternatively, process in a food processor until smooth.

4 Return the vegetable paste to a clean saucepan with the reserved cooking liquid. Add the basil and heat through until hot. Garnish the soup with fresh basil sprigs and serve immediately.

VARIATION

This soup is also delicious served cold with ⅔ cup of unsweetened yogurt swirled into it.

Avocado & Mint Soup

A rich and creamy pale green soup made with avocados and enhanced by a touch of chopped mint. Serve chilled in summer or hot in winter.

NUTRITIONAL INFORMATION

Calories 199   Sugars 3g
Protein ....3g   Fat 18g
Carbohydrate ....7g   Saturates 6g

15 MINS   35 MINS

SERVES 6

INGREDIENTS

3 tbsp butter or margarine

6 scallions, sliced

1 garlic clove, crushed

¼ cup all-purpose flour

2½ cups vegetable stock

2 ripe avocados

2–3 tsp lemon juice

pinch of grated lemon rind

⅔ cup milk

⅔ cup light cream

1–1½ tbsp chopped mint

salt and pepper

mint sprigs, to garnish

MINTED GARLIC BREAD

½ cup butter

1–2 tbsp chopped mint

1–2 garlic cloves, crushed

1 whole wheat or
   white French bread stick

1 Melt the butter or margarine in a large, heavy-bottomed saucepan. Add the scallions and garlic clove and fry over a low heat, stirring occasionally, for about 3 minutes, until soft and translucent.

2 Stir in the flour and cook, stirring, for 1–2 minutes. Gradually stir in the stock, then bring to the boil. Simmer gently while preparing the avocados.

3 Peel the avocados, discard the pits, and chop coarsely. Add to the soup with the lemon juice and rind, and seasoning. Cover and simmer for about 10 minutes, until tender.

4 Cool the soup slightly, then press through a strainer with the back of a spoon or process in a food processor or blender until a smooth paste forms. Pour into a bowl.

5 Stir in the milk and cream, adjust the seasoning, then stir in the mint. Cover and chill thoroughly.

6 To make the minted garlic bread, soften the butter and beat in the mint and garlic. Cut the loaf into slanting slices but leave a hinge on the bottom crust. Spread each slice with the butter and reassemble the loaf. Wrap in foil and place in a preheated oven, 350°F, for about 15 minutes.

7 Serve the soup garnished with a sprig of mint and accompanied by the minted garlic bread.

Minted Pea & Yogurt Soup

A deliciously refreshing, summery soup that is full of goodness. It is also extremely tasty served chilled.

NUTRITIONAL INFORMATION

Calories ....208 Sugars 9g
Protein ....10g Fat 7g
Carbohydrate ...26g Saturates 2g

15 MINS   25 MINS

SERVES 6

INGREDIENTS

2 tbsp vegetable ghee or sunflower oil

2 onions, coarsely chopped

8 oz potato, coarsely chopped

2 garlic cloves, crushed

1 inch gingerroot, chopped

1 tsp ground coriander

1 tsp ground cumin

1 tbsp all-purpose flour

3½ cups vegetable stock

1 lb 2 oz frozen peas

2-3 tbsp chopped mint

salt and pepper

⅔ cup strained Greek yogurt,
    plus extra to serve

½ tsp cornstarch

1¼ cups milk

mint sprigs, to garnish

1 Heat the vegetable ghee or sunflower oil in a saucepan, add the onions and potato and cook over a low heat, stirring occasionally, for about 3 minutes, until the onion is soft and translucent.

2 Stir in the garlic, ginger, coriander, cumin, and flour and cook, stirring constantly, for 1 minute.

3 Add the vegetable stock, peas, and the chopped mint and bring to the boil, stirring. Reduce the heat, cover and simmer gently for 15 minutes, or until the vegetables are tender.

4 Process the soup in batches, in a blender or food processor. Return the mixture to the pan and season with salt and pepper to taste. Blend the yogurt with the cornstarch to a smooth paste and stir into the soup.

5 Add the milk and bring almost to a boil, stirring constantly. Cook very gently for 2 minutes. Serve the soup hot, garnished with the mint sprigs and a swirl of extra yogurt.

Stilton & Walnut Soup

Full of flavour, this rich and creamy soup is very simple to make and utterly delicious to eat.

NUTRITIONAL INFORMATION

Calories ....392 Sugars 8g
Protein ....15g Fat 30g
Carbohydrate ...15g Saturates 16g

 10 MINS ⏱ 30 MINS

SERVES 4

INGREDIENTS

4 tbsp butter

2 shallots, chopped

3 celery stalks, chopped

1 garlic clove, crushed

2 tbsp all-purpose flour

2½ cups vegetable stock

1¼ cups milk

1½ cups blue Stilton cheese,
    crumbled, plus extra to garnish

2 tbsp walnut halves, roughly chopped

⅔ cup unsweetened yogurt

salt and pepper

chopped celery leaves, to garnish

1 Melt the butter in a large, heavy-bottomed saucepan and stirfry the shallots, celery, and garlic, stirring occasionally, for 2–3 minutes, until soft.

2 Lower the heat, add the flour, and cook, stirring constantly, for 30 seconds.

3 Gradually stir in the vegetable stock and milk and bring to a boil.

4 Reduce the heat to a gentle simmer and add the crumbled blue Stilton cheese and walnut halves. Cover and simmer for 20 minutes.

5 Stir in the yogurt and heat through for a further 2 minutes without boiling.

6 Season the soup to taste with salt and pepper, then transfer to a warm soup tureen or individual serving bowls, garnish with chopped celery leaves, and extra crumbled blue Stilton cheese, and serve at once.

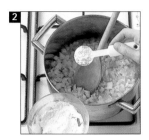

COOK'S TIP

As well as adding protein, vitamins, and useful fats to the diet, nuts add important flavor and texture to vegetarian meals.

Thick Onion Soup

A delicious creamy soup with grated carrot and parsley for texture and color. Serve with crusty cheese biscuits for a hearty lunch.

NUTRITIONAL INFORMATION

Calories 277   Sugars 12g
Protein . . . . .6g   Fat 20g
Carbohydrate . . .19g   Saturates 8g

20 MINS   1HR 10 MINS

SERVES 6

INGREDIENTS

5 tbsp butter

1 lb 2 oz onions, finely chopped

1 garlic clove, crushed

6 tbsp all-purpose flour

2½ cups vegetable stock

2½ cups milk

2–3 tsp lemon or lime juice

good pinch of ground allspice

1 bay leaf

1 carrot, coarsely grated

4–6 tbsp heavy cream

2 tbsp chopped parsley

salt and pepper

CHEESE BISCUITS

2 cups malted wheat or
  whole wheat flour

2 tsp baking powder

¼ cup butter

4 tbsp grated Parmesan cheese

1 egg, beaten

⅓ cup milk

1 Melt the butter in a saucepan and fry the onions and garlic over a low heat, stirring frequently, for 10–15 minutes, until soft, but not colored. Stir in the flour and cook, stirring, for 1 minute, then gradually stir in the stock and bring to a boil, stirring frequently. Add the milk, then bring back to a boil.

2 Season to taste with salt and pepper and add 2 teaspoons of the lemon or lime juice, the allspice, and bay leaf. Cover and simmer for about 25 minutes until the vegetables are tender. Discard the bay leaf.

3 Meanwhile, make the biscuits. Combine the flour, baking powder, and seasoning and rub in the butter until the

mixture resembles fine breadcrumbs. Stir in 3 tablespoons of the cheese, the egg, and enough milk to mix to a soft dough.

4 Shape into a bar about ¾ inch thick. Place on a floured baking sheet and mark into slices. Sprinkle with the remaining cheese and bake in a preheated oven, 425°F, for about 20 minutes, until risen and golden brown.

5 Stir the carrot into the soup and simmer for 2–3 minutes. Add more lemon or lime juice, if necessary. Stir in the cream and reheat. Garnish and serve with the warm biscuits.

Curried Parsnip Soup

Parsnips make a delicious soup as they have a slightly sweet flavor. In this recipe, spices are added to complement this sweetness.

NUTRITIONAL INFORMATION

Calories 152   Sugars 7g
Protein ....3g   Fat 8g
Carbohydrate ...18g   Saturates 3g

 10 MINS   35 MINS

SERVES 4

I N G R E D I E N T S

1 tbsp vegetable oil

1 tbsp butter

1 red onion, chopped

3 parsnips, chopped

2 garlic cloves, crushed

2 tsp garam masala

½ tsp cayenne pepper

1 tbsp all-purpose flour

3¾ cups vegetable stock

grated rind and juice of 1 lemon

salt and pepper

lemon rind, to garnish

1 Heat the oil and butter in a large saucepan until the butter has melted. Add the onion, parsnips, and garlic and stirfry, stirring frequently, for about 5–7 minutes, until the vegetables have softened, but not colored.

2 Add the garam masala and cayenne pepper and cook, stirring constantly, for 30 seconds. Sprinkle in the flour, mixing well and cook, stirring constantly, for a further 30 seconds.

3 Stir in the stock, lemon rind, and juice and bring to a boil. Reduce the heat and simmer for 20 minutes.

4 Remove some of the vegetable pieces with a draining spoon and reserve until required. Process the remaining soup and vegetables in a food processor or blender for about 1 minute, or until a smooth paste. Alternatively, press the vegetables through a strainer with the back of a wooden spoon.

5 Return the soup to a clean saucepan and stir in the reserved vegetables. Heat the soup through for 2 minutes until piping hot.

6 Season to taste with salt and pepper, then transfer to soup bowls, garnish with grated lemon rind and serve.

Fava Bean Soup

Fresh fava beans are best for this delicious soup, but if they are unavailable, use frozen beans instead.

NUTRITIONAL INFORMATION

Calories	224	Sugars	.........4g
Protein	........12g	Fat	...........6g
Carbohydrate	...31g	Saturates	.......1g

 15 MINS   40 MINS

SERVES 4

INGREDIENTS

2 tbsp olive oil

1 red onion, chopped

2 garlic cloves, crushed

2 potatoes, diced

3 cups fava beans, thawed if frozen

3¾ cups vegetable stock

2 tbsp freshly chopped mint

mint sprigs and unsweetened yogurt,
  to garnish

1 Heat the olive oil in a large saucepan. Add the onion and garlic and stirfry for 2–3 minutes, until softened.

2 Add the potatoes and cook, stirring constantly, for 5 minutes.

3 Stir in the beans and the stock, cover and simmer for 30 minutes, or until the beans and potatoes are tender.

4 Remove a few vegetables with a draining spoon and set aside until required. Place the remainder of the soup in a food processor or blender and process until smooth.

5 Return the soup to a clean saucepan and add the reserved vegetables and chopped mint. Stir thoroughly and heat through gently.

6 Transfer the soup to a warm tureen or individual serving bowls. Garnish with swirls of yogurt and sprigs of fresh mint and serve immediately.

VARIATION

Use fresh cilantro and ½ tsp ground cumin as flavorings in the soup, if you prefer.

Spinach & Mascarpone Soup

Spinach is the basis for this delicious soup, which has creamy mascarpone cheese stirred through it to give it a wonderful texture.

NUTRITIONAL INFORMATION

Calories . . . . . . .402 Sugars 2g
Protein . . . . .11g Fat 36g
Carbohydrate . . .10g Saturates 21g

15 MINS   30 MINS

SERVES 4

INGREDIENTS

¼ cup butter

1 bunch scallions, trimmed and chopped

2 celery stalks, chopped

3 cups spinach or sorrel, or
    3 bunches watercress

3½ cups vegetable stock

1 cup mascarpone cheese

1 tbsp olive oil

2 slices thick-cut bread, cut into cubes

½ tsp caraway seeds

salt and pepper

sesame bread sticks, to serve

1 Melt half the butter in a very large saucepan. Add the scallions and celery, and cook over a medium heat, stirring frequently, for about 5 minutes, until softened.

2 Pack the spinach, sorrel, or watercress into the saucepan. Add the stock and bring to a boil, then reduce the heat, cover and simmer for 15–20 minutes.

3 Transfer the soup to a blender or food processor and process until smooth. Alternatively, rub it through a strainer. Return to the saucepan.

4 Add the mascarpone to the soup and heat gently, stirring constantly, until smooth and blended. Season to taste with salt and pepper.

5 Heat the remaining butter with the oil in a skillet. Add the bread cubes and fry, turning frequently, until golden brown, adding the caraway seeds towards the end of cooking, so that they do not burn.

6 Ladle the soup into warmed bowls. Sprinkle with the croûtons and serve with the sesame bread sticks.

VARIATION

Any leafy vegetable can be used to make this soup to give variations to the flavor. For anyone who grows their own vegetables, it is the perfect recipe for experimenting with a glut of produce. Try young beet leaves or surplus lettuces for a change.

Leek, Potato, & Carrot Soup

A quick chunky soup, ideal for a snack or a quick lunch. The leftovers can be puréed to make one portion of creamed soup for the next day.

NUTRITIONAL INFORMATION

Calories	156	Sugars	.........7g
Protein	.........4g	Fat	...........6g
Carbohydrate	...22g	Saturates	.....0.7g

 10 MINS   25 MINS

SERVES 2

I N G R E D I E N T S

1 leek, about 6 oz

1 tbsp sunflower oil

1 garlic clove, crushed

3 cups vegetable stock

1 bay leaf

¼ tsp ground cumin

1 cup potatoes, diced

1 cup coarsely grated carrot

salt and pepper

chopped parsley, to garnish

P U R E E D   S O U P

5–6 tbsp milk

1–2 tbsp heavy cream, crème
  blanc or soured cream

1 Trim off and discard some of the coarse green part of the leek, then slice thinly and rinse thoroughly in cold water. Drain well.

2 Heat the sunflower oil in a heavy-bottomed saucepan. Add the leek and garlic, and fry over a low heat for about 2–3 minutes, until soft, but barely colored. Add the vegetable stock, bay leaf, and cumin, and season to taste with salt and pepper. Bring the mixture to a boil, stirring constantly.

3 Add the diced potato to the saucepan, cover and simmer over a low heat for 10–15 minutes until the potato is just tender, but not broken up.

4 Add the grated carrot and simmer for a further 2–3 minutes. Adjust the seasoning, discard the bay leaf, and serve sprinkled liberally with chopped parsley.

5 To make a puréed soup, first process the leftovers (about half the original soup) in a blender or food processor, or press through a strainer until smooth and then return to a clean saucepan with the milk. Bring to a boil and simmer for 2–3 minutes. Adjust the seasoning and stir in the cream or crème blanc before serving sprinkled with chopped parsley.

Broccoli & Potato Soup

This creamy soup has a delightful pale green coloring and rich flavor from the blend of tender broccoli and blue cheese.

NUTRITIONAL INFORMATION

Calories	452	Sugars	.........4g
Protein	........14g	Fat	..........35g
Carbohydrate	...20g	Saturates	......19g

 5-10 MINS   40 MINS

SERVES 4

INGREDIENTS

2 tbsp olive oil

2 potatoes, diced

1 onion, diced

8 oz broccoli florets

4½ oz blue cheese, crumbled

4½ cups vegetable stock

⅔ cup heavy cream

pinch of paprika

salt and pepper

1 Heat the oil in a large saucepan. Add the potatoes and onion. Stirfry, stirring constantly, for 5 minutes.

2 Reserve a few broccoli florets for the garnish and add the remaining broccoli to the pan. Add the cheese and vegetable stock.

COOK'S TIP

This soup freezes very successfully. Follow the method described here up to step 4, and freeze the soup after it has been puréed. Add the cream and paprika just before serving. Garnish and serve.

3 Bring to a boil, then reduce the heat, cover the pan and simmer for 25 minutes, until the potatoes are tender.

4 Transfer the soup to a food processor or blender in batches and process until the mixture is smooth. Alternatively, press the vegetables through a strainer with the back of a wooden spoon.

5 Return the paste to a clean saucepan and stir in the heavy cream and a pinch of paprika. Season to taste with salt and pepper.

6 Blanch the reserved broccoli florets in a little boiling water for about 2 minutes, then lift them out of the pan with a draining spoon.

7 Pour the soup into warmed individual bowls and garnish with the broccoli florets and a sprinkling of paprika. Serve immediately.

Potato & Field Pea Soup

Split green peas are sweeter than other varieties of split pea and reduce down to a purée when cooked, which acts as a thickener in soups.

NUTRITIONAL INFORMATION

Calories 260   Sugars 5g
Protein . . . . .11g   Fat 10g
Carbohydrate . . .32g   Saturates 3g

 5–10 MINS   45 MINS

SERVES 4

INGREDIENTS

2 tbsp vegetable oil

2 unpeeled mealy potatoes, diced

2 onions, diced

2¾ oz split green peas

1 litre/1¾ pints/4½ cups vegetable stock

5 tbsp grated Gruyère cheese

salt and pepper

CROUTONS

3 tbsp butter

1 garlic clove, crushed

1 tbsp chopped parsley

1 thick slice white bread, cubed

1 Heat the vegetable oil in a large saucepan. Add the potatoes and onions and stirfry over a low heat, stirring constantly, for about 5 minutes.

VARIATION

For a richly colored soup, red lentils could be used instead of split green peas. Add a large pinch of brown sugar to the recipe for extra sweetness if red lentils are used.

2 Add the split green peas to the pan and stir to mix together well.

3 Pour the vegetable stock into the pan and bring to the boil. Reduce the heat to low and simmer for 35 minutes, until the potatoes are tender and the split peas cooked.

4 Meanwhile, make the croûtons. Melt the butter in a skillet. Add the garlic, parsley and bread cubes and cook, turning

frequently, for about 2 minutes, until the bread cubes are golden brown on all sides.

5 Stir the grated cheese into the soup and season to taste with salt and pepper. Heat gently until the cheese is starting to melt.

6 Pour the soup into warmed individual bowls and sprinkle the croûtons on top. Serve at once.

Indian Potato & Pea Soup

A slightly hot and spicy Indian flavor is given to this soup with the use of garam masala, chili, cumin, and cilantro.

NUTRITIONAL INFORMATION

Calories 153	Sugars 6g	
Protein 6g	Fat 6g	
Carbohydrate ...18g	Saturates 1g	

 10 MINS   35 MINS

SERVES 4

I N G R E D I E N T S

2 tbsp vegetable oil

8 oz mealy potatoes, diced

1 large onion, chopped

2 garlic cloves, crushed

1 tsp garam masala

1 tsp ground coriander

1 tsp ground cumin

3¾ cups vegetable stock

1 red chili, chopped

scant 1 cup frozen peas

4 tbsp unsweetened yogurt

salt and pepper

chopped cilantro,
   to garnish

warm bread, to serve

VARIATION

For slightly less heat, seed the chili before adding it to the soup. Always wash your hands after handling chilies as they contain volatile oils that can irritate the skin and make your eyes burn if you touch your face.

1 Heat the vegetable oil in a large saucepan. Add the potatoes, onion, and garlic and stirfry over a low heat, stirring constantly, for about 5 minutes.

2 Add the garam masala, ground coriander, and cumin and cook, stirring constantly, for 1 minute.

3 Stir in the vegetable stock and chopped red chili and bring the mixture to a boil. Reduce the heat, cover the pan and simmer for 20 minutes, until the potatoes begin to break down.

4 Add the peas and cook for a further 5 minutes. Stir in the yogurt and season to taste with salt and pepper.

5 Pour into warmed soup bowls, garnish with chopped fresh cilantro, and serve hot with warm bread.

Cauliflower & Broccoli Soup

Full of flavor, this creamy cauliflower and broccoli soup is simple to make and absolutely delicious to eat.

NUTRITIONAL INFORMATION

Calories	378	Sugars	........14g
Protein	........18g	Fat	..........26g
Carbohydrate	...20g	Saturates	.......7g

10 MINS   35 MINS

SERVES 4

I N G R E D I E N T S

3 tbsp vegetable oil

1 red onion, chopped

2 garlic cloves, crushed

10½ oz cauliflower florets

10½ oz broccoli florets

1 tbsp all-purpose flour

2½ cups milk

1¼ cups vegetable stock

¾ cup Gruyère cheese, grated

pinch of paprika

⅔ cup light cream

paprika and Gruyère cheese shavings,
   to garnish

1 Heat the oil in a large, heavy-bottomed saucepan. Add the onion, garlic, cauliflower florets and broccoli florets and stirfry over a low heat, stirring constantly, for 3–4 minutes. Add the flour and cook, stirring constantly for 1 minute.

2 Gradually stir in the milk and stock and bring to a boil, stirring constantly. Reduce the heat and simmer for 20 minutes.

3 Remove about a quarter of the vegetables with a draining spoon and set aside. Put the remaining soup in a food processor or blender and process for about 30 seconds, until smooth. Alternatively, press the vegetables through a strainer with the back of a wooden spoon. Transfer the soup to a clean saucepan.

4 Return the reserved vegetable pieces to the soup. Stir in the grated cheese, paprika, and light cream and heat through over a low heat, without boiling, for 2–3 minutes, or until the cheese starts to melt.

5 Transfer to warmed individual serving bowls, garnish with shavings of Gruyère, and dust with paprika and serve immediately.

COOK'S TIP

The soup must not start to boil after the cream has been added, otherwise it will curdle. Use unsweetened yogurt instead of the cream if preferred, but again do not allow it to boil.

Asparagus Soup

Fresh asparagus is now available for most of the year, so this soup can be made at any time. It can also be made using canned asparagus.

NUTRITIONAL INFORMATION

Calories 196   Sugars 7g
Protein . . . . .7g   Fat 12g
Carbohydrate . . .15g   Saturates 4g

 5–10 MINS   55 MINS

SERVES 6

INGREDIENTS

1 bunch asparagus, about 12 oz,
  or 2 packs mini asparagus,
  about 5½ oz each

3 cups vegetable stock

¼ cup butter or margarine

1 onion, chopped

3 tbsp all-purpose flour

¼ tsp ground coriander

1 tbsp lemon juice

2 cups milk

4–6 tbsp heavy or light cream

salt and pepper

1 Wash and trim the asparagus, discarding the woody part of the stem. Cut the remainder into short lengths, keeping a few tips for garnish. Mini asparagus does not need to be trimmed.

2 Cook the tips in the minimum of boiling salted water for 5–10 minutes. Drain and set aside.

3 Put the asparagus in a saucepan with the stock, bring to the boil, cover, and simmer for about 20 minutes, until soft. Drain and reserve the stock.

4 Melt the butter or margarine in a saucepan. Add the onion and fry over a low heat until soft, but only barely colored. Stir in the flour and cook for 1 minute, then gradually whisk in the reserved stock and bring to a boil.

5 Simmer for 2–3 minutes, until thickened, then stir in the cooked asparagus, seasoning, coriander, and lemon juice. Simmer for 10 minutes, then cool a little, and either press through a strainer or process in a blender or food processor until smooth.

6 Pour into a clean pan, add the milk, and reserved asparagus tips, and bring to the boil. Simmer for 2 minutes. Stir in the cream, reheat gently, and serve.

COOK'S TIP

If using canned asparagus, drain off the liquid and use as part of the measured stock. Remove a few small asparagus tips for garnish and chop the remainder. Continue as above.

Jerusalem Artichoke Soup

Jerusalem artichokes are native to North America, but are also grown in Europe. They have a nutty flavor which combines well with orange.

NUTRITIONAL INFORMATION

Calories 211   Sugars 17g
Protein . . . . .7g   Fat 8g
Carbohydrate . . .29g   Saturates 4g

 10 MINS   30 MINS

SERVES 4

I N G R E D I E N T S

1½ lb Jerusalem artichokes

5 tbsp orange juice

2 tbsp butter

1 leek, chopped

1 garlic clove, crushed

1¼ cups vegetable stock

⅔ cup milk

2 tbsp chopped cilantro

⅔ cup unsweetened yogurt

grated orange peel, to garnish

1 Rinse the Jerusalem artichokes and place in a large saucepan with 2 tablespoons of the orange juice and enough water to cover. Bring to a boil, reduce the heat, and cook for 20 minutes, or until the artichokes are tender.

2 Drain the artichokes, reserving 2 cups of the cooking liquid. Leave the artichokes to cool, then peel and place in a large bowl. Mash the flesh with a potato masher.

3 Melt the butter in a large saucepan. Add the leek and garlic and fry over a low heat, stirring frequently, for 2–3 minutes, until the leek is soft.

4 Stir in the mashed artichoke, stock, milk, remaining orange juice, and reserved cooking water. Bring to a boil, then simmer for 2–3 minutes.

5 Remove a few pieces of leek with a draining spoon and reserve. Process the remainder in a food processor for 1 minute until smooth. Alternatively, press through a strainer with the back of a spoon.

6 Return the soup to a clean saucepan and stir in the reserved leeks, cilantro, and yogurt and heat through. Transfer to individual soup bowls, garnish with orange peel and serve.

Avocado & Vegetable Soup

Avocado has a rich flavor and color which makes a creamy flavored soup. It is best served chilled, but may be eaten warm as well.

NUTRITIONAL INFORMATION

Calories	167	Sugars	.........5g
Protein	.........4g	Fat	..........13g
Carbohydrate	....8g	Saturates	.......3g

15 MINS   10 MINS

SERVES 4

I N G R E D I E N T S

1 large, ripe avocado

2 tbsp lemon juice

1 tbsp vegetable oil

½ cup canned corn, drained

2 tomatoes, peeled, and seeded

1 garlic clove, crushed

1 leek, chopped

1 red chili, chopped

2 cups vegetable stock

⅔ cup milk

shredded leek, to garnish

1 Peel the avocado and mash the flesh with a fork, stir in the lemon juice, and reserve until required.

2 Heat the oil in a large saucepan. Add the corn, tomatoes, garlic, leek, and chili and stirfry over a low heat for 2–3 minutes, or until the vegetables have softened.

3 Put half the vegetable mixture in a food processor or blender, together with the mashed avocado and process until smooth. Transfer the mixture to a clean saucepan.

4 Add the vegetable stock, milk, and reserved vegetables and cook over a low heat for 3–4 minutes, until hot. Transfer to a warmed individual serving bowls, garnish with shredded leek, and serve immediately.

COOK'S TIP

If serving chilled, transfer from the food processor to a bowl, stir in the vegetable stock and milk, cover, and chill in the refrigerator for at least 4 hours.

Vichyssoise

This is a classic creamy soup made from potatoes and leeks. To achieve the delicate pale color, be sure to use only the white parts of the leeks.

NUTRITIONAL INFORMATION

Calories 208   Sugars 5g
Protein . . . . .5g   Fat 12g
Carbohydrate . . .20g   Saturates 6g

 10 MINS   40 MINS

SERVES 6

I N G R E D I E N T S

3 large leeks

3 tbsp butter or margarine

1 onion, thinly sliced

1 lb 2 oz potatoes, chopped

3½ cups vegetable stock

2 tsp lemon juice

pinch of ground nutmeg

¼ tsp ground coriander

1 bay leaf

1 egg yolk

⅔ cup light cream

salt and white pepper

TO GARNISH

freshly snipped chives

1 Trim the leeks and remove most of the green part. Slice the white part of the leeks very finely.

2 Melt the butter or margarine in a saucepan. Add the leeks and onion and fry, stirring occasionally, for about 5 minutes without browning.

3 Add the potatoes, vegetable stock, lemon juice, nutmeg, coriander, and bay leaf to the skillet, season to taste with salt and pepper, and bring to a boil. Cover and simmer for about 30 minutes, until all the vegetables are very soft.

4 Cool the soup a little, remove and discard the bay leaf, and then press through a strainer or process in a food processor, or blender until smooth. Pour into a clean pan.

5 Blend the egg yolk into the cream, add a little of the soup to the mixture and then whisk it all back into the soup and reheat gently, without boiling. Adjust the seasoning to taste. Cool and then chill thoroughly in the refrigerator.

6 Serve the soup sprinkled with freshly snipped chives.

Vegetable & Corn Chowder

This is a really filling soup, which should be served before a light main course. It is easy to prepare and filled with flavor.

NUTRITIONAL INFORMATION

Calories ....378 Sugars 20g
Protein ....16g Fat 13g
Carbohydrate ...52g Saturates 6g

15 MINS   30 MINS

SERVES 4

INGREDIENTS

1 tbsp vegetable oil

1 red onion, diced

1 red bell pepper, seeded, and diced

3 garlic cloves, crushed

1 large potato, diced

2 tbsp all-purpose flour

2½ cups milk

1¼ cups vegetable stock

1¾ oz broccoli florets

3 cups canned corn, drained

¾ cup hard cheese, grated

salt and pepper

1 tbsp chopped cilantro,
   to garnish

COOK'S TIP

Vegetarian cheeses are made with rennets of non-animal origin, using microbial or fungal enzymes.

1 Heat the oil in a large saucepan. Add the onion, bell pepper, garlic, and potato and stirfry over a low heat, stirring frequently, for 2–3 minutes.

2 Stir in the flour and cook, stirring for 30 seconds. Gradually stir in the milk and stock.

3 Add the broccoli and corn. Bring the mixture to a boil, stirring constantly, then reduce the heat and simmer for about 20 minutes, or until all the vegetables are tender.

4 Stir in ½ cup of the cheese until it melts.

5 Season and spoon the chowder into a warm soup tureen. Garnish with the remaining cheese and the cilantro and serve.

Dal Soup

Dal is the name given to a delicious Indian lentil dish. This soup is a variation of the theme — it is made with red lentils and curry powder.

NUTRITIONAL INFORMATION

Calories 284   Sugars 13g
Protein . . . . .16g   Fat 9g
Carbohydrate . . .38g   Saturates 5g

5 MINS   40 MINS

SERVES 4

INGREDIENTS

2 tbsp butter

2 garlic cloves, crushed

1 onion, chopped

½ tsp turmeric

1 tsp garam masala

¼ tsp chili powder

1 tsp ground cumin

2 lb 4 oz canned, chopped
    tomatoes, drained

1 cup red lentils

2 tsp lemon juice

2½ cups vegetable stock

1¼ cups coconut milk

salt and pepper

chopped cilantro and lemon
    slices, to garnish

naan bread, to serve

1 Melt the butter in a large saucepan. Add the garlic and onion and stirfry, stirring, for 2–3 minutes. Add the turmeric, garam masala, chili powder, and cumin and cook for a further 30 seconds.

2 Stir in the tomatoes, red lentils, lemon juice, vegetable stock, and coconut milk and bring to a boil.

3 Reduce the heat to low and simmer the soup, uncovered, for about 25–30 minutes, until the lentils are tender and cooked.

4 Season to taste with salt and pepper and ladle the soup into a warm tureen. Garnish with chopped cilantro and lemon slices and serve immediately with warm naan bread.

COOK'S TIP

You can buy cans of coconut milk from supermarkets and delicatessens. It can also be made by grating creamed coconut, which comes in the form of a solid bar, and then mixing it with water.

Spicy Dal & Carrot Soup

This nutritious soup uses split red lentils and carrots as the two main ingredients and includes a selection of spices to give it a kick.

NUTRITIONAL INFORMATION

Calories 173   Sugars 11g
Protein ....9g   Fat 5g
Carbohydrate ...24g   Saturates 1g

 15 MINS   45 MINS

SERVES 6

I N G R E D I E N T S

4½ oz split red lentils

5 cups vegetable stock

12 oz carrots, sliced

2 onions, chopped

8 oz can chopped tomatoes

2 garlic cloves, chopped

2 tbsp vegetable ghee or oil

1 tsp ground cumin

1 tsp ground coriander

1 fresh green chili, seeded and chopped,
    or 1 tsp minced chili

½ tsp ground turmeric

1 tbsp lemon juice

salt

1¼ cups milk

2 tbsp chopped cilantro

unsweetened yogurt, to serve

1 Place the lentils in a strainer and rinse well under cold running water. Drain and place in a large saucepan, together with 3½ cups of the stock, the carrots, onions, tomatoes, and garlic. Bring the mixture to a boil, reduce the heat, cover and simmer for 30 minutes or until the vegetables and lentils are tender.

2 Meanwhile, heat the ghee or oil in a small pan. Add the cumin, ground coriander, chili, and turmeric and fry over a low heat for 1 minute. Remove from the heat and stir in the lemon juice. Season with salt to taste.

3 Process the soup in batches in a blender or food processor. Return the soup to the saucepan, add the spice mixture, and the remaining 1¼ cups stock and simmer over a low heat for 10 minutes.

4 Add the milk, taste, and adjust the seasoning, if necessary. Stir in the chopped cilantro and reheat gently. Serve hot with a swirl of yogurt.

Bean Soup

Beans feature widely in Mexican cooking, and here pinto beans are used to give an interesting texture. Pinto beans require soaking overnight.

NUTRITIONAL INFORMATION

Calories 188   Sugars 9g
Protein ....13g   Fat 1g
Carbohydrate ...33g   Saturates 0.3g

 20 MINS   3 HOURS

SERVES 4

INGREDIENTS

6 oz pinto beans

6 cups water

6–8 oz carrots, finely chopped

1 large onion, finely chopped

2–3 garlic cloves, crushed

½–1 chili, seeded and finely chopped

5 cups vegetable stock

2 tomatoes, peeled, and finely chopped

2 celery stalks, very thinly sliced

salt and pepper

1 tbsp chopped cilantro (optional)

CROUTONS

3 slices white bread, crusts removed

oil, for deep-frying

1–2 garlic cloves, crushed

1 Soak the beans overnight in cold water; drain and place in a saucepan with the water. Bring to a boil and boil vigorously for 10 minutes. Lower the heat, cover and simmer for 2 hours, or until the beans are tender.

2 Add the carrots, onion, garlic, chili, and stock and bring back to a boil. Cover and simmer for a further 30 minutes, until very tender.

3 Remove half the beans and vegetables with the cooking juices and press through a strainer or process in a food processor or blender until smooth.

4 Return the bean paste to the saucepan and add the tomatoes and celery. Simmer for 10–15 minutes, or until the celery is just tender, adding a little more stock, or water if necessary.

5 Meanwhile, make the croutons. Dice the bread. Heat the oil with the garlic in a small skillet and fry the croutons until golden brown. Drain on paper towels.

6 Season the soup and stir in the chopped cilantro, if using. Transfer to a warm tureen and serve immediately with the croutons.

 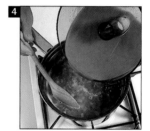 

VARIATION

Pinto beans are widely available, but if you cannot find them or you wish to vary the recipe, you can use cannellini beans or black-eyed peas as an alternative.

Indian Bean Soup

A thick and hearty soup, nourishing, and substantial enough to serve as a main meal with whole wheat bread.

NUTRITIONAL INFORMATION

Calories	237	Sugars	........9g
Protein	.........9g	Fat	...........9g
Carbohydrate	...33g	Saturates	.......1g

20 MINS   50 MINS

SERVES 6

I N G R E D I E N T S

4 tbsp vegetable ghee or vegetable oil

2 onions, peeled, and chopped

1½ cups potato, cut into chunks

1½ cups parsnip, cut into chunks

1½ cups turnip or rutabaga, cut
    into chunks

2 celery sticks, sliced

2 zucchini, sliced

1 green bell pepper, seeded, and cut into
    ½ inch pieces

2 garlic cloves, crushed

2 tsp ground coriander

1 tbsp paprika

1 tbsp mild curry paste

5 cups vegetable stock

salt

14 oz can black-eye peas,
    drained, and rinsed

chopped cilantro, to garnish (optional)

1 Heat the ghee or oil in a saucepan, add all the prepared vegetables, except the zucchini and green bell pepper, and cook over a moderate heat, stirring frequently, for 5 minutes. Add the garlic, ground coriander, paprika, and curry paste and cook, stirring constantly, for 1 minute.

2 Stir in the stock and season with salt to taste. Bring to a boil, cover and simmer over a low heat, stirring occasionally, for 25 minutes.

3 Stir in the black-eye peas, sliced zucchini, and green bell pepper, cover, and continue cooking for a further 15 minutes, or until all the vegetables are tender.

4 Process 1¼ cups of the soup mixture (about 2 ladlefuls) in a food processor or blender. Return the mixture to the soup in the saucepan and reheat until very hot. Sprinkle with chopped cilantro, if using and serve hot.

Mixed Bean Soup

This is a really hearty soup, filled with color, flavor, and goodness, which may be adapted to any vegetables that you have to hand.

NUTRITIONAL INFORMATION

Calories 190	Sugars 9g
Protein 10g	Fat 4g
Carbohydrate ...30g	Saturates 0.5g

 10 MINS   40 MINS

SERVES 4

INGREDIENTS

1 tbsp vegetable oil

1 red onion, halved and sliced

3½ oz potato, diced

1 carrot, diced

1 leek, sliced

1 green chili, sliced

3 garlic cloves, crushed

1 tsp ground coriander

1 tsp cayenne pepper

4 cups vegetable stock

1 lb mixed canned beans,
   such as red kidney, borlotti, black eye,
   or small navy, drained

salt and pepper

2 tbsp chopped cilantro, to garnish

COOK'S TIP

Serve this soup with slices of warm corn bread or a cheese loaf.

1   Heat the vegetable oil in a large saucepan. Add the onion, potato, carrot, and leek and stirfry, stirring constantly, for about 2 minutes, until the vegetables are slightly softened.

2   Add the sliced chili and crushed garlic and cook for a further 1 minute.

3   Stir in the ground coriander, cayenne pepper, and the vegetable stock.

4   Bring the soup to a boil, reduce the heat, and cook for 20 minutes, or until the vegetables are tender.

5   Stir in the beans, season well with salt and pepper, and cook, stirring occasionally, for a further 10 minutes.

6   Transfer the soup to a warm tureen or individual bowls, garnish with chopped cilantro, and serve.

Cream Cheese & Herb Soup

Make the most of homegrown herbs to create this wonderfully creamy soup with its marvelous gardenfresh fragrance.

NUTRITIONAL INFORMATION

Calories 275	Sugars 5g	
Protein 7g	Fat 22g	
Carbohydrate ...14g	Saturates 11g	

 15 MINS   35 MINS

SERVES 4

INGREDIENTS

2 tbsp butter or margarine

2 onions, chopped

3½ cups vegetable stock

1 oz coarsely chopped mixed
   herbs, such as parsley, chives, thyme,
   basil, and oregano

7 oz full-fat soft cheese

1 tbsp cornstarch

1 tbsp milk

chopped chives, to garnish

1 Melt the butter or margarine in a large, heavy-bottomed saucepan. Add the onions and fry over a medium heat for 2 minutes, then cover and turn the heat to low. Continue to cook the onions for 5 minutes, then remove the lid.

2 Add the vegetable stock and herbs to the saucepan. Bring to a boil over a moderate heat. Lower the heat, cover and simmer gently for 20 minutes.

3 Remove the saucepan from the heat. Transfer the soup to a food processor or blender and process for about 15 seconds, until smooth. Alternatively, press it through a strainer with the back of a wooden spoon. Return the soup to the saucepan.

4 Reserve a little of the cheese for garnish. Spoon the remaining cheese into the soup and whisk until it has melted and is incorporated.

5 Mix the cornstarch with the milk to a paste, then stir the mixture into the soup. Heat, stirring constantly, until thickened and smooth.

6 Pour the soup into warmed individual bowls. Spoon some of the reserved cheese into each bowl and garnish with chives. Serve at once.

Starters

With so many fresh ingredients readily available, it is very easy to create some deliciously different starters to make the perfect introduction to a vegetarian meal. The ideas in this chapter are an inspiration to cook and a treat to eat, and they give an edge to the appetite that makes the main course even more enjoyable. When choosing a starter,

make sure that you provide a good balance of flavors, colors, and textures that offer variety and contrast. Balance the nature of the recipes too — a rich main course is best preceded by a light starter, which is just enough to interest the palate and stimulate the tastebuds.

Heavenly Garlic Dip

Anyone who loves garlic will adore this dip — it is very potent! Serve it at a barbecue and dip raw vegetables or chunks of French bread into it.

NUTRITIONAL INFORMATION

Calories ...... .344 Sugars 2g
Protein .... .6g Fat .... .34g
Carbohydrate ....3g Saturates 5g

 15 MINS 🕐 20 MINS

SERVES 4

I N G R E D I E N T S

2 bulbs garlic

6 tbsp olive oil

1 small onion, finely chopped

2 tbsp lemon juice

3 tbsp sesame seed paste

2 tbsp chopped parsley

salt and pepper

TO SERVE

fresh vegetable crudités

French bread or warmed pocket breads

1 Separate the bulbs of garlic into individual cloves. Place them on a baking sheet and roast in a preheated oven, 400°F, for 8–10 minutes. Set aside to cool for a few minutes.

VARIATION

If you come across smoked garlic, use it in this recipe — it tastes wonderful. There is no need to roast the smoked garlic, so omit the first step. This dip can also be used to baste kabobs and vegetarian burgers.

2 When they are cool enough to handle, peel the garlic cloves and then chop them finely.

3 Heat the olive oil in a saucepan or skillet and add the garlic and onion. Fry over a low heat, stirring occasionally, for 8–10 minutes, until softened. Remove the pan from the heat.

4 Mix in the lemon juice, sesame seed paste, and parsley. Season to taste with salt and pepper. Transfer to a small heatproof bowl and keep warm at one side of the barbecue.

5 Serve with fresh vegetable crudités, chunks of French bread, or warm pocket breads.

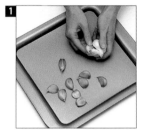

Mint & Cannellini Bean Dip

This dip is ideal for pre-dinner drinks or for handing around at a party. The cannellini beans require soaking overnight, so prepare in advance.

NUTRITIONAL INFORMATION

Calories 208	Sugars 1g
Protein 10g	Fat 12g
Carbohydrate ...16g	Saturates 2g

 40 MINS   30 MINS

SERVES 6

INGREDIENTS

1 cup dried cannellini beans

1 small garlic clove, crushed

1 bunch scallions, roughly chopped

handful of mint leaves

2 tbsp sesame seed paste

2 tbsp olive oil

1 tsp ground cumin

1 tsp ground coriander

lemon juice

salt and pepper

sprigs of mint, to garnish

TO SERVE

fresh vegetable crudités, such as cauliflower florets, carrots, cucumber, radishes, and bell peppers

1 Soak the cannellini beans overnight in plenty of cold water.

2 Rinse and drain the beans, put them into a large saucepan and cover them with cold water. Bring to a boil and boil rapidly for 10 minutes. Reduce the heat, cover and simmer until tender.

3 Drain the beans and transfer them to a bowl or food processor. Add the garlic, scallions, mint, sesame seed paste, and olive oil.

4 Process the mixture for about 15 seconds or mash well by hand, until smooth.

5 Transfer the mixture to a bowl, stir in the cumin, coriander, and lemon juice and season to taste with salt and pepper. Mix thoroughly, cover and leave in a cool place for 30 minutes to allow the flavors to develop fully.

6 Spoon the dip into serving bowls, garnish with sprigs of fresh mint, and surround with vegetable crudités. Serve at room temperature.

Buttered Nut & Lentil Dip

This tasty dip is very easy to make. It is perfect to have at barbecues, as it gives your guests something to nibble while they are waiting.

NUTRITIONAL INFORMATION

Calories ....395 Sugars 4g
Protein ....12g Fat 31g
Carbohydrate ...18g Saturates 10g

 5-10 MINS　 40 MINS

SERVES 4

I N G R E D I E N T S

¼ cup butter

1 small onion, chopped

⅓ cup red lentils

1¼ cups vegetable stock

½ cup blanched almonds

½ cup pine nuts

½ tsp ground coriander

½ tsp ground cumin

½ tsp grated gingerroot

1 tsp chopped fresh cilantro

salt and pepper

sprigs of fresh cilantro to garnish

TO SERVE

fresh vegetable crudités

bread sticks

VARIATION

Green or brown lentils can
be used, but they will take
longer to cook than red lentils.
If you wish, substitute peanuts for
the almonds. Ground ginger can be
used instead of fresh — substitute
½ teaspoon and add it with the
other spices.

1 Melt half the butter in a saucepan and fry the onion over a medium heat, stirring frequently, until golden brown.

2 Add the lentils and vegetable stock. Bring to a boil, then reduce the heat and simmer gently, uncovered, for about 25–30 minutes, until the lentils are tender. Drain well.

3 Melt the remaining butter in a small skillet. Add the almonds and pine nuts and fry them over a low heat, stirring frequently, until golden brown. Remove from the heat.

4 Put the lentils, almonds, and pine nuts, with any remaining butter, into a food processor. Add the ground coriander, cumin, ginger, and fresh cilantro. Process for about 15–20 seconds, until the mixture is smooth. Alternatively, press the lentils through a strainer to purée them and then mix with the finely chopped nuts, spices, and herbs.

5 Season the dip with salt and pepper and garnish with sprigs of fresh cilantro. Serve with fresh vegetable crudités and bread sticks.

Cheese, Garlic, & Herb Pâté

This wonderful soft cheese pâté is fragrant with the aroma of fresh herbs and garlic. Serve with triangles of Melba toast for a perfect starter.

NUTRITIONAL INFORMATION

Calories 392	Sugars 1g
Protein 17g	Fat 28g
Carbohydrate ...18g	Saturates 18g

 20 MINS   10 MINS

SERVES 4

I N G R E D I E N T S

1 tbsp butter

1 garlic clove, crushed

3 scallions, finely chopped

½ cup full-fat soft cheese

2 tbsp chopped mixed herbs,
   such as parsley, chives, marjoram,
   oregano, and basil

1½ cups finely grated sharp hard cheese

pepper

4–6 slices of white bread from a
   medium-cut sliced loaf

mixed salad greens and cherry
   tomatoes, to serve

TO GARNISH

ground paprika

herb sprigs

1 Melt the butter in a small skillet and gently fry the garlic and scallions together for 3–4 minutes, until softened. Allow to cool.

2 Beat the soft cheese in a large mixing bowl until smooth, then add the garlic and scallions. Stir in the herbs, mixing well.

3 Add the hard cheese and work the mixture together to form a stiff paste. Cover and chill until ready to serve.

4 To make the Melba toast, toast the slices of bread on both sides, and then cut off the crusts. Using a sharp bread knife, cut through the slices horizontally to make very thin slices. Cut into triangles and then lightly broil the untoasted sides until golden.

5 Arrange the mixed greens, on 4 serving plates with the cherry tomatoes. Pile the cheese pâté on top and sprinkle with a little paprika. Garnish with sprigs of fresh herbs and serve with the Melba toast.

Walnut, Egg, & Cheese Pâté

This unusual pâté, flavored with parsley and dill, can be served with crackers, crusty bread, or toast. The pâté requires chilling until set.

NUTRITIONAL INFORMATION

Calories	438	Sugars	.........2g
Protein	........21g	Fat	..........38g
Carbohydrate	....2g	Saturates	......18g

 20 MINS   2 MINS

SERVES 2

INGREDIENTS

1 celery stalk

1–2 scallions, trimmed

¼ cup shelled walnuts

1 tbsp chopped fresh parsley

1 tsp chopped fresh dill or ½ tsp dried dill

1 garlic clove, crushed

dash of vegetarian Worcestershire sauce

½ cup cottage cheese

½ cup blue cheese, such as
    Stilton or Danish Blue

1 hard-cooked egg

2 tbsp butter

salt and pepper

herbs, to garnish

crackers, toast, or crusty bread and
    crudités, to serve

COOK'S TIP

You can also use this as a stuffing for vegetables. Cut the tops off extra-large tomatoes, scoop out the seeds, and fill with the pâté, piling it well up, or spoon into the hollows of celery stalks cut into 2 inch pieces.

1 Finely chop the celery, slice the scallions very finely, and chop the walnuts evenly. Place in a bowl.

2 Add the chopped herbs, garlic and Worcestershire sauce to taste and mix well, then stir the cottage cheese evenly through the mixture.

3 Grate the blue cheese and hard-cooked egg finely into the pâté mixture, and season with salt and pepper.

4 Melt the butter and stir through the pâté, then spoon into one serving dish or two individual dishes, but do not press down firmly. Chill until set.

5 Garnish with fresh herbs and serve with crackers, toast, or fresh, crusty bread, and a few crudités, if liked.

Lentil Pâté

Red lentils are used in this spicy recipe for speed as they do not require pre-soaking. You can substitute other types of lentils, if preferred.

NUTRITIONAL INFORMATION

Calories ....267 Sugars 12g
Protein ....14g Fat 8g
Carbohydrate ...37g Saturates 1g

 30 MINS   1¼ HOURS

SERVES 4

I N G R E D I E N T S

1 tbsp vegetable oil, plus extra for greasing

1 onion, chopped

2 garlic cloves, crushed

1 tsp garam masala

½ tsp ground coriander

3¾ cups vegetable stock

¾ cup red lentils

1 small egg

2 tbsp milk

2 tbsp mango chutney

2 tbsp chopped parsley

fresh parsley sprigs, to garnish

salad greens and toast, to serve

1 Heat the oil in a large saucepan and sauté the onion and garlic, stirring constantly, for 2–3 minutes. Add the spices and cook for a further 30 seconds.

2 Stir in the stock and lentils and bring the mixture to a boil. Reduce the heat and simmer for 20 minutes, until the lentils are cooked, and softened. Remove the pan from the heat and drain off any excess moisture.

3 Put the mixture in a food processor and add the egg, milk, mango chutney, and parsley. Process until smooth.

4 Grease and line the base of a 1 lb loaf pan and spoon in the mixture, leveling the surface. Cover and cook in a preheated oven, 400°F, for 40–45 minutes, or until firm to the touch.

5 Cool in the pan for 20 minutes, then transfer to the refrigerator.

6 Turn out the pâté on to a serving plate, slice, and garnish with fresh parsley. Serve with salad greens and toast.

COOK'S TIP

It is always better to make your own stock, if you have time, rather than use bouillon cubes, as the flavor of homemade stock is far superior.

Mixed Bean Pâté

This is a really quick starter to prepare if canned beans are used. Choose a wide variety of beans for color and flavor.

NUTRITIONAL INFORMATION

Calories ....126 Sugars 3g
Protein ....5g Fat 6g
Carbohydrate ...13g Saturates 1g

 45 MINS 🕐 0 MINS

SERVES 4

INGREDIENTS

14 oz can mixed beans, drained

2 tbsp olive oil

juice of 1 lemon

2 garlic cloves, crushed

1 tbsp chopped cilantro

2 scallions, chopped

salt and pepper

shredded scallions, to garnish

1 Rinse the beans thoroughly under cold running water and drain well.

2 Transfer the beans to a food processor and process until smooth. Alternatively, place the beans in a bowl and mash thoroughly with a fork or potato masher.

3 Add the olive oil, lemon juice, garlic, cilantro, and scallions and blend until fairly smooth. Season with salt and pepper to taste.

4 Transfer the pâté to a serving bowl and chill in the refrigerator for at least 30 minutes.

5 Garnish with shredded scallions and serve.

Avocado Cream Terrine

The smooth, rich taste of ripe avocados combines well with thick, creamy yogurt and light cream to make this impressive terrine.

NUTRITIONAL INFORMATION

Calories 327	Sugars 3g	
Protein 6g	Fat 32g	
Carbohydrate 4g	Saturates 8g	

2¼ HOURS   0 MINS

SERVES 6

INGREDIENTS

2 ripe avocados

4 tbsp cold water

2 tsp vegetarian gelozone

1 tbsp lemon juice

4 tbsp mayonnaise

⅔ cup thick unsweetened yogurt

⅔ cup light cream

salt and pepper

mixed salad greens, to serve

TO GARNISH

cucumber slices

nasturtium flowers

1 Peel the avocados and remove and discard the pits. Put the flesh in a food processor or a large bowl, together with the water, vegetarian gelozone, lemon juice, mayonnaise, yogurt, and cream. Season to taste with salt and pepper.

2 Process for about 10–15 seconds, or beat by hand, using a fork or whisk, until smooth.

3 Transfer the mixture to a small saucepan and heat gently, stirring constantly, until just boiling.

4 Pour the mixture into a 3½ cup plastic food storage box or terrine, and smooth the top. Allow the mixture to cool and set, and then leave to chill in the refrigerator for about 1½–2 hours.

5 Turn the mixture out of its container and cut into neat slices. Arrange a bed of salad greens on 6 serving plates. Place a slice of avocado terrine on top and garnish with cucumber slices and nasturtium flowers.

Toasted Nibbles

These tiny cheese balls are rolled in fresh herbs, toasted nuts, or paprika to make tasty nibbles for parties, buffets, or pre-dinner drinks.

NUTRITIONAL INFORMATION

Calories 310	Sugars 1g
Protein 15g	Fat 27g
Carbohydrate 1g	Saturates 12g

40 MINS   5 MINS

SERVES 4

INGREDIENTS

½ cup ricotta cheese

1 cup finely grated brick cheese

2 tsp chopped parsley

½ cup chopped mixed nuts

3 tbsp chopped herbs, such as parsley, chives, marjoram, lovage, and chervil

2 tbsp mild paprika

pepper

herb sprigs, to garnish

1 Mix together the ricotta and brick cheeses. Add the parsley and pepper and work together until thoroughly combined.

2 Form the mixture into small balls and place on a plate. Cover and chill in the refrigerator for about 20 minutes, until they are firm.

3 Scatter the chopped nuts on to a baking sheet, and place them under a preheated broiler until lightly browned. Take care as they can easily burn. Leave them to cool.

4 Sprinkle the nuts, herbs, and paprika into 3 separate small bowls. Remove the cheese balls from the refrigerator and

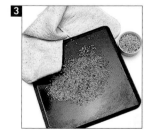

divide into 3 equal piles. Roll 1 quantity of the cheese balls in the nuts, 1 quantity in the herbs and 1 quantity in the paprika until they are all well coated.

5 Arrange the coated cheese balls alternately on a large serving platter. Chill in the refrigerator until ready to serve and then garnish with sprigs of fresh herbs.

Spinach Phyllo Baskets

If you use frozen spinach, it only needs to be thawed and drained before being mixed with the cheeses and seasonings.

NUTRITIONAL INFORMATION

Calories	533	Sugars	.........3g
Protein	........24g	Fat	..........38g
Carbohydrate	...26g	Saturates	......22g

  55 MINS   30 MINS

MAKES 2

INGREDIENTS

3 cups fresh leaf spinach,
   washed and chopped roughly, or
   ½ cup thawed frozen spinach

2–4 scallions, trimmed and chopped,
   or 1 tbsp finely chopped onion

1 garlic clove, crushed

2 tbsp grated Parmesan cheese

¾ cup grated sharp cheese

pinch of ground allspice

1 egg yolk

4 sheets phyllo pastry

2 tbsp butter, melted

salt and pepper

2 scallions, to garnish

1 If using fresh spinach, cook it in the minimum of boiling salted water for 3–4 minutes, until tender. Drain very thoroughly, using a potato masher to remove excess liquid, then chop and put into a bowl. If using frozen spinach, simply drain and chop.

2 Add the scallions or onion, garlic, cheeses, allspice, egg yolk, and seasoning, and mix well.

3 Grease 2 individual muffin pans, or ovenproof dishes or pans about 5 inches in diameter, and 1½ inches deep. Cut the phyllo pastry sheets in half to make 8 pieces and brush each lightly with melted butter.

4 Place one piece of phyllo pastry in a pan or dish and then cover with a second piece at right angles to the first. Add two more pieces at right angles, so that all the corners are in different places. Line the other pan in the same way.

5 Spoon the spinach mixture into the 'baskets' and cook in a preheated oven, 350°F, for about 20 minutes, or until the pastry is golden brown. Garnish with a scallion tassel and serve hot or cold.

6 Make scallion tassels about 30 minutes before required. Trim off the root end and cut to a length of 2–3 inches. Make a series of cuts from the green end to within ¾ inch of the other end. Place in a bowl of iced water to open out. Drain well before use.

Feta Cheese Tartlets

These crisp-baked bread cases, filled with sliced tomatoes, feta cheese, black olives, and quail's eggs, are quick to make and taste delicious.

NUTRITIONAL INFORMATION

Calories	570	Sugars	.........3g
Protein	........14g	Fat	..........42g
Carbohydrate	...36g	Saturates	......23g

 30 MINS 10 MINS

SERVES 4

INGREDIENTS

8 slices bread from a medium-cut large loaf

½ cup butter, melted

4½ oz feta cheese, cut into small cubes

4 cherry tomatoes, cut into wedges

8 pitted black or green olives, halved

8 quail's eggs, hard-cooked

2 tbsp olive oil

1 tbsp wine vinegar

1 tsp wholegrain mustard

pinch of superfine sugar

salt and pepper

parsley sprigs, to garnish

1 Remove the crusts from the bread. Trim the bread into squares and flatten each piece with a rolling pin.

2 Brush the bread with melted butter, and then arrange them in bun or muffin pans. Press a piece of crumpled foil into each bread case to secure in place. Bake in a preheated oven, 375°F, for about 10 minutes, or until crisp and browned.

3 Meanwhile, mix together the feta cheese, tomatoes, and olives. Shell the eggs and quarter them. Mix together the

olive oil, vinegar, mustard, and sugar. Season to taste with salt and pepper.

4 Remove the bread cases from the oven and discard the foil. Leave to cool.

5 Just before serving, fill the bread cases with the cheese and tomato mixture. Arrange the eggs on top and spoon over the dressing. Garnish with parsley sprigs.

Tzatziki & Black Olive Dip

Tzatziki is a Greek dish, made with yogurt, mint, and cucumber.
It tastes superb with warm pocket bread.

NUTRITIONAL INFORMATION

Calories 381	Sugars 8g
Protein 11g	Fat 15g
Carbohydrate . . .52g	Saturates 2g

 1 HOUR   3 MINS

SERVES 4

I N G R E D I E N T S

½ cucumber

225 g/8 oz/1 cup thick unsweetened yogurt

1 tbsp chopped mint

salt and pepper

4 pocket breads

D I P

2 garlic cloves, crushed

1 cup pitted black olives

4 tbsp olive oil

2 tbsp lemon juice

1 tbsp chopped parsley

T O   G A R N I S H

mint sprigs

parsley sprigs

COOK'S TIP

Sprinkling the cucumber
with salt draws out some of its
moisture, making it crisper. If
you are in a hurry, you can omit
this procedure. Use green olives
instead of black ones if you prefer.

1 To make the tzatziki, peel the cucumber and chop roughly. Sprinkle it with salt and leave to stand for 15–20 minutes. Rinse with cold water and drain well.

2 Mix the cucumber, yogurt, and mint together. Season to taste with salt and pepper and transfer to a serving bowl. Cover and chill for 20–30 minutes.

3 To make the black olive dip, put the crushed garlic and olives into a food processor and process for 15–20 seconds. Alternatively, chop them very finely.

4 Add the olive oil, lemon juice, and parsley to the food processor and process for a few more seconds. Alternatively, mix with the chopped garlic and olives, and mash together. Season with salt and pepper.

5 Wrap the pocket breads in foil and place over a barbecue for 2–3 minutes, turning once to warm through. Alternatively, heat in the oven or under the broiler. Cut into pieces and serve with the tzatziki and black olive dip, garnished with sprigs of fresh mint and parsley.

Hummus & Garlic Toasts

Hummus is a real favorite spread on these flavorsome garlic toasts for a delicious starter or snack.

NUTRITIONAL INFORMATION

Calories 731   Sugars 2g
Protein . . . . .22g   Fat 55g
Carbohydrate . . .39g   Saturates 8g

  20 MINS   3 MINS

SERVES 4

I N G R E D I E N T S

H U M M U S

14 oz can garbanzo beans

juice of 1 large lemon

6 tbsp sesame seed paste

2 tbsp olive oil

2 garlic cloves, crushed

salt and pepper

chopped cilantro and
   black olives, to garnish

T O A S T S

1 ciabatta loaf, sliced

2 garlic cloves, crushed

1 tbsp chopped cilantro

4 tbsp olive oil

COOK'S TIP

Make the hummus 1 day in advance, and chill, covered, in the refrigerator until required. Garnish and serve.

1 To make the hummus, firstly drain the garbanzo beans, reserving a little of the liquid. Put the garbanzo beans and liquid in a food processor and process, gradually adding the reserved liquid and lemon juice. Blend well after each addition until smooth.

2 Stir in the sesame seed paste and all but 1 teaspoon of the olive oil. Add the garlic, season to taste, and blend again until smooth.

3 Spoon the hummus into a serving dish and smooth the top. Drizzle the

remaining olive oil over the top, garnish with chopped cilantro and olives. Set aside in the refrigerator to chill while you are preparing the toasts.

4 Place the slices of ciabatta on a broiler rack in a single layer.

5 Mix the garlic, cilantro, and olive oil together and drizzle over the bread slices. Cook under a hot broiler, turning once, for about 2–3 minutes, until golden brown. Serve the toasts immediately with the hummus.

Onions à la Grecque

This is a well-known method of cooking vegetables
and is perfect with shallots or onions, served with a crisp salad.

NUTRITIONAL INFORMATION

Calories	...200	Sugars	...26g
Protein	...2g	Fat	...9g
Carbohydrate	...28g	Saturates	...1g

 10 MINS 15 MINS

SERVES 4

I N G R E D I E N T S

1 lb shallots

3 tbsp olive oil

3 tbsp clear honey

2 tbsp garlic wine vinegar

3 tbsp dry white wine

1 tbsp tomato paste

2 celery stalks, sliced

2 tomatoes, seeded and chopped

salt and pepper

chopped celery leaves, to garnish

1 Peel the shallots. Heat the oil in a large saucepan, add the shallots and cook, stirring, for 3–5 minutes, or until they begin to brown.

2 Add the honey and cook over a high heat for a further 30 seconds, then add the garlic wine vinegar and dry white wine, stirring well.

3 Stir in the tomato paste, celery, and tomatoes and bring the mixture to a boil. Cook over a high heat for 5–6 minutes. Season to taste and leave to cool slightly.

4 Garnish with chopped celery leaves and serve warm. Alternatively chill in the refrigerator before serving.

Spanish Tortilla

This classic Spanish dish is often served as part of an appetizer selection. A variety of cooked vegetables can be added to this recipe.

NUTRITIONAL INFORMATION

Calories	430	Sugars	.........6g
Protein	........16g	Fat	..........20g
Carbohydrate	...50g	Saturates	.......4g

10 MINS   35 MINS

SERVES 4

INGREDIENTS

2 lb 4 oz waxy potatoes, thinly sliced

4 tbsp vegetable oil

1 onion, sliced

2 garlic cloves, crushed

1 green bell pepper, seeded, and diced

2 tomatoes, seeded, and chopped

25 g/1 oz canned corn, drained

6 large eggs, beaten

2 tbsp chopped parsley

salt and pepper

1 Parboil the potatoes in a saucepan of lightly salted boiling water for 5 minutes. Drain well.

2 Heat the oil in a large skillet, add the potato and onions, and sauté over a low heat, stirring constantly, for

5 minutes, until the potatoes have browned.

3 Add the garlic, diced bell pepper, chopped tomatoes, and corn, mixing well.

4 Pour in the eggs and add the chopped parsley. Season well with salt and pepper. Cook for 10-12 minutes, until the underside is cooked through.

5 Remove the skillet from the heat and continue to cook the tortilla under a preheated medium broiler for 5-7 minutes, or until the tortilla is set and the top is golden brown.

6 Cut the tortilla into wedges or cubes, depending on your preference, and transfer to serving dishes. Serve with salad. In Spain tortillas are served hot, cold, or warm.

COOK'S TIP

Ensure that the handle of your pan is heatproof before placing it under the broiler and be sure to use an oven glove when removing it as it will be very hot.

Fiery Salsa

Make this Mexican-style salsa to perk up jaded palates. Its lively flavors really get the tastebuds going. Serve with hot tortilla chips.

NUTRITIONAL INFORMATION

Calories	328	Sugars	.........2g
Protein	.........4g	Fat	..........26g
Carbohydrate	...21g	Saturates	.......5g

 30 MINS   0 MINS

SERVES 4

I N G R E D I E N T S

2 small fresh red chilies

1 tbsp lime or lemon juice

2 large ripe avocados

2 inch piece of cucumber

2 tomatoes, peeled

1 small garlic clove, crushed

few drops of Tabasco sauce

salt and pepper

lime or lemon slices, to garnish

tortilla chips, to serve

1 Remove and discard the stem and seeds from 1 fresh red chili. Chop the flesh very finely and place in a large mixing bowl.

2 To make a chili 'flower' for garnish, using a small, sharp knife, slice the remaining chili from the stem to the tip several times without removing the stem. Place in a bowl of iced water, so that the 'petals' open out.

3 Add the lime or lemon juice to the mixing bowl. Halve, pit, and peel the avocados. Add the flesh to the mixing bowl and mash thoroughly with a fork. The salsa should be slightly chunky. (The lime or lemon juice prevents the avocado from turning brown.)

4 Chop the cucumber and tomatoes finely and add to the avocado mixture with the crushed garlic.

5 Stir in the Tabasco sauce and season with salt and pepper. Transfer the dip to a serving bowl. Garnish with slices of lime or lemon and the chili flower.

6 Put the bowl on a large plate, surround with tortilla chips and serve. Do not keep this dip standing for long or it will discolor.

Spring Rolls

Thin slices of vegetables are wrapped in pastry and deep-fried until crisp. Spring roll wrappers are available fresh or frozen.

NUTRITIONAL INFORMATION

Calories 186	Sugars 2g	
Protein 4g	Fat 11g	
Carbohydrate ...18g	Saturates 1g	

45 MINS   25-30 MINS

MAKES 12

INGREDIENTS

5 Chinese dried mushrooms (if unavailable, use open-cup mushrooms)

1 large carrot

1 cup canned bamboo shoots

2 scallions

2 oz Chinese cabbage

2 tbsp vegetable oil

4 cups beansprouts

1 tbsp soy sauce

12 spring roll wrappers

1 egg, beaten

vegetable oil, for deep-frying

salt

1 Place the dried mushrooms in a small bowl and cover with warm water. Leave to soak for 20–25 minutes.

2 Drain the mushrooms and squeeze out the excess water. Remove the tough centers and slice the mushroom caps thinly. Cut the carrot and bamboo shoots into very thin julienne strips. Chop the scallions and shred the Chinese cabbage.

3 Heat the 2 tablespoons of oil in a wok. Add the mushrooms, carrot, and bamboo shoots and stir-fry for 2 minutes. Add the scallions, Chinese cabbage, beansprouts, and soy sauce. Season with salt and stir-fry for 2 minutes. Leave to cool.

4 Divide the mixture into 12 equal portions and place one portion on the edge of each spring roll wrapper. Fold in the sides and roll each one up, brushing the join with a little beaten egg to seal.

5 Deep-fry the spring rolls in batches in hot oil in a wok or large saucepan for 4–5 minutes, or until golden and crispy. Take care that the oil is not too hot or the spring rolls will brown on the outside before cooking on the inside. Remove and drain on paper towels. Keep each batch warm while the others are being cooked. Serve at once.

COOK'S TIP

If spring roll wrappers are unavailable, use sheets of phyllo pastry instead.

Tofu Tempura

Crispy coated vegetables and tofu accompanied by a sweet, spicy dip give a real taste of the Orient in this Japanese-style dish.

NUTRITIONAL INFORMATION

Calories 582   Sugars 10g
Protein . . . . .16g   Fat 27g
Carbohydrate . . .65g   Saturates 4g

15 MINS   20 MINS

SERVES 4

I N G R E D I E N T S

4½ oz baby zucchini

4½ oz baby carrots

4½ oz baby corn-on-the-cobs

4½ oz baby leeks

2 baby eggplants

8 oz tofu

vegetable oil, for deep-frying

julienne strips of carrot, gingerroot, and
   baby leek to garnish

noodles, to serve

B A T T E R

2 egg yolks

1¼ cups water

2 cups all-purpose flour

D I P P I N G   S A U C E

5 tbsp mirin or dry sherry

5 tbsp Japanese soy sauce

2 tsp clear honey

1 garlic clove, crushed

1 tsp grated gingerroot

1 Slice the zucchini and carrots in half lengthways. Trim the corn. Trim the leeks at both ends. Quarter the eggplants. Cut the tofu into 1 inch cubes.

2 To make the batter, mix the egg yolks with the water. Sift in 1½ cups of the flour and beat with a balloon whisk to form a thick batter. Don't worry if there are any lumps. Heat the oil for deep-frying to 350°F or until a cube of bread browns in 30 seconds.

3 Place the remaining flour on a large plate and toss the vegetables and tofu until lightly coated.

4 Dip the tofu in the batter and deep-fry for 2–3 minutes, until lightly golden. Drain on paper towels and keep warm.

5 Dip the vegetables in the batter and deep-fry, a few at a time, for 3–4 minutes, until golden. Drain and place on a warmed serving plate.

6 To make the dipping sauce, mix all the ingredients together. Serve with the vegetables and tofu, accompanied with noodles and garnished with julienne strips of vegetables.

Mixed Bhajis

These small bhajis are often served as accompaniments to a main meal, but they are delicious as a starter with a small salad and yogurt sauce.

NUTRITIONAL INFORMATION

Calories . . . . .414 Sugars 7g
Protein . . . . .9g Fat 26g
Carbohydrate . . .38g Saturates 3g

25 MINS   30 MINS

SERVES 4

INGREDIENTS

BHAJIS

1¼ cups besan

1 tsp baking soda

2 tsp ground coriander

1 tsp garam masala

1½ tsp turmeric

1½ tsp cayenne pepper

2 tbsp chopped cilantro

1 small onion, halved, and sliced

1 small leek, sliced

3½ oz cooked cauliflower

9-12 tbsp cold water

salt and pepper

vegetable oil, for deep-frying

SAUCE

⅔ cup unsweetened yogurt

2 tbsp chopped mint

½ tsp turmeric

1 garlic clove, crushed

mint sprigs, to garnish

1 Sift the besan, baking soda, and salt to taste into a mixing bowl and add the spices and fresh cilantro. Mix thoroughly.

2 Divide the mixture into 3 and place in separate bowls. Stir the onion into one bowl, the leek into another and the cauliflower into the third bowl. Add 3–4 tbsp of water to each bowl and mix each to form a smooth paste.

3 Heat the oil for deep-frying in a deep fryer to 350°F or until a cube of bread browns in 30 seconds. Using 2 dessert spoons, form the mixture into rounds and cook each in the oil for 3–4 minutes, until browned. Remove with a draining spoon and drain well on paper towels. Keep the bhajis warm in the oven while cooking the remainder.

4 Mix all of the sauce ingredients together and pour into a small serving bowl. Garnish with mint sprigs and serve with the warm bhajis.

Hyderabad Pickles

This is a very versatile dish that will go with almost anything and can be served warm or cold. It is perfect as a starter for a dinner party.

NUTRITIONAL INFORMATION

Calories ....732 Sugars 6g
Protein ....6g Fat 75g
Carbohydrate ....8g Saturates 10g

30 MINS   30 MINS

SERVES 6

INGREDIENTS

2 tsp ground coriander

2 tsp ground cumin

2 tsp shredded coconut

2 tsp sesame seeds

1 tsp mixed mustard and onion seeds

1¼ cups vegetable oil

3 medium onions, sliced

1 tsp finely chopped gingerroot

1 tsp crushed garlic

½ tsp turmeric

1½ tsp cayenne pepper

1½ tsp salt

3 medium eggplants, halved lengthways

1 tbsp tamarind paste

1¼ cups water

3 hard-cooked eggs, halved,
    to garnish

BAGHAAR

1 tsp mixed onion and mustard seeds

1 tsp cumin seeds

4 dried red chilies

⅔ cup vegetable oil

cilantro leaves

1 green chili, finely chopped

1 Dry-fry the ground coriander, cumin, coconut, sesame seeds, and mustard and onion seeds in a pan. Grind in a mortar and pestle or food processor and set aside.

2 Heat the oil in a skillet and fry the onions until golden. Reduce the heat and add the ginger, garlic, turmeric, cayenne pepper, and salt, stirring. Leave to cool, then grind this mixture to form a paste.

3 Make 4 cuts across each eggplant half. Blend the spices with the onion paste. Spoon this mixture into the slits in the eggplants.

4 In a bowl, mix the tamarind paste and 3 tbsp water to make a fine paste and set aside.

5 For the baghaar, fry the onion and mustard seeds, cumin seeds, and chilies in the oil. Reduce the heat, place the eggplants in the baghaar and stir gently. Stir in the tamarind paste and remaining water and cook over a medium heat for 15–20 minutes. Add the cilantro and chilies.

6 When cool, transfer to a serving dish and serve garnished with the hard-cooked eggs.

Garlicky Mushroom Pakoras

Whole mushrooms are dunked in a spiced garlicky batter and deep-fried until golden. They are at their most delicious served very hot.

NUTRITIONAL INFORMATION

Calories 297	Sugars 3g
Protein 5g	Fat 21g
Carbohydrate ...24g	Saturates 2g

   20 MINS   10-15 MINS

SERVES 6

I N G R E D I E N T S

1½ cups besan

½ tsp salt

¼ tsp baking powder

1 tsp cumin seeds

½–1 tsp cayenne pepper

scant 1 cup water

2 garlic cloves, crushed

1 small onion, finely chopped

vegetable oil, for deep-frying

1 lb 2 oz button mushrooms,
    trimmed and wiped

lemon wedges and cilantro
    sprigs, to garnish

COOK'S TIP

Besan flour is a pale yellow flour made from garbanzo beans. It is now readily available from larger supermarkets, as well as oriental food shops and some ethnic delicatessens. Besan is also used to make onion bhajis.

  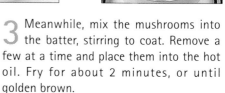

1 Put the besan, salt, baking powder, cumin, and cayenne pepper into a bowl and mix well together. Make a well in the center of the mixture and gradually stir in the water, mixing thoroughly to form a batter.

2 Stir the crushed garlic and the chopped onion into the batter and leave the mixture to infuse for 10 minutes. One-third fill a deep-fat fryer or pan with vegetable oil and heat to 350°F or until a cube of bread browns in 30 seconds. Lower the basket into the hot oil.

3 Meanwhile, mix the mushrooms into the batter, stirring to coat. Remove a few at a time and place them into the hot oil. Fry for about 2 minutes, or until golden brown.

4 Remove the mushrooms from the pan with a draining spoon and drain on paper towels while you are cooking the remainder in the same way.

5 Serve hot, sprinkled with coarse salt and garnished with lemon wedges and cilantro sprigs.

Dumplings in Yogurt Sauce

Adding a baghaar (seasoned oil dressing) just before serving makes this a mouthwatering accompaniment to any meal.

NUTRITIONAL INFORMATION

Calories 719   Sugars 9g
Protein . . . . .9g   Fat 60g
Carbohydrate . . .38g   Saturates 7g

35 MINS   35 MINS

SERVES 4

INGREDIENTS

DUMPLINGS

¾ cup besan

1 tsp cayenne pepper

½ tsp baking soda

1 medium onion, finely chopped

2 green chilies

cilantro leaves, chopped

⅔ cup water

1¼ cups vegetable oil

salt

YOGURT SAUCE

1¼ cups unsweetened yogurt

3 tbsp besan

⅔ cup water

1 tsp chopped gingerroot

1 tsp crushed garlic

1½ tsp cayenne pepper

½ tsp turmeric

1 tsp ground coriander

1 tsp ground cumin

SEASONED DRESSING

⅔ cup vegetable oil

1 tsp white cumin seeds

6 dried red chilies

1 To make the dumplings, sift the besan into a large bowl. Add the cayenne pepper, ½ teaspoon salt, baking soda, onion, green chilies, and cilantro and mix. Add the water and mix to form a thick paste. Heat the oil in a skillet. Place teaspoonfuls of the paste in the oil and fry over a medium heat, turning once, until a crisp golden brown. Set aside.

2 To make the sauce, place the yogurt in a bowl and whisk with the besan and the water. Add all of the spices and 1½ teaspoons salt and mix well.

3 Press this mixture through a large strainer into a saucepan. Bring to a boil over a low heat, stirring constantly. If the yogurt sauce becomes too thick, add a little extra water.

4 Pour the sauce into a deep serving dish and arrange all the dumplings on top. Set aside and keep warm.

5 To make the dressing, heat the oil in a skillet. Add the white cumin seeds and the dried red chilies and fry until darker in color and giving off their aroma. Pour the dressing over the dumplings and serve hot.

Samosas

Samosas, which are a sort of oriental savory turnover, make excellent snacks. In India, they are popular snacks at roadside stalls.

NUTRITIONAL INFORMATION

Calories 261   Sugars 0.4g
Protein . . . . .2g   Fat 23g
Carbohydrate . . .13g   Saturates 4g

  40 MINS   40 MINS

MAKES 12

INGREDIENTS

PASTRY

¾ cup self-rising flour

½ tsp salt

3 tbsp butter, cut into small pieces

4 tbsp water

FILLING

3 medium potatoes, boiled

1 tsp finely chopped gingerroot

1 tsp crushed garlic

½ tsp white cumin seeds

½ tsp mixed onion and mustard seeds

1 tsp salt

½ tsp crushed red chilies

2 tbsp lemon juice

2 small green chilies, finely chopped

ghee or oil, for deep-frying

1 Sift the flour and salt into a bowl. Add the butter and rub into the flour until the mixture resembles fine breadcrumbs.

2 Pour in the water and mix with a fork to form a dough. Pat it into a ball and knead for 5 minutes, or until smooth. Cover and leave to rise.

3 To make the filling, mash the boiled potatoes gently, and mix with the ginger, garlic, white cumin seeds, onion and mustard seeds, salt, crushed red chilies, lemon juice and green chilies.

4 Break small balls off the dough and roll each out very thinly to form a round. Cut in half, dampen the edges and shape into cones. Fill the cones with a little of the filling, dampen the top and bottom edges of the cones and pinch together to seal. Set aside.

5 Fill a deep pan one-third full with oil and heat to 350°F or until a small cube of bread browns in 30 seconds. Carefully lower the samosas into the oil, a few at a time, and fry for 2-3 minutes, or until golden brown. Remove from the oil and drain thoroughly on paper towels. Serve hot or cold.

Vegetable Timbales

This is a great way to serve pasta as a starter, wrapped in an eggplant mold. It looks really impressive, yet it is very easy.

NUTRITIONAL INFORMATION

Calories 291   Sugars 11g
Protein . . . . .8g   Fat 18g
Carbohydrate . . .25g   Saturates 4g

 30 MINS   ⏱ 45 MINS

SERVES 4

I N G R E D I E N T S

1 large eggplant

½ cup macaroni

1 tbsp vegetable oil

1 onion, chopped

2 garlic cloves, crushed

2 tbsp drained canned corn

2 tbsp frozen peas, thawed

3½ oz spinach

¼ cup grated hard cheese

1 egg, beaten

3 cups canned, chopped tomatoes

1 tbsp chopped basil

salt and pepper

S A U C E

4 tbsp olive oil

2 tbsp white wine vinegar

2 garlic cloves, crushed

3 tbsp chopped basil

1 tbsp superfine sugar

1 Cut the eggplant lengthways into thin strips, using a potato peeler. Place in a bowl of salted boiling water and leave to stand for 3–4 minutes. Drain well.

2 Lightly grease four ⅔ cup individual ramekin dishes and use the eggplant slices to line the dishes, leaving 1 inch of eggplant overlapping.

3 Cook the pasta in a pan of boiling water for 8–10 minutes until al dente. Drain. Heat the oil in a pan and sauté the onion and garlic for 2–3 minutes. Stir in the corn and peas and remove from the heat.

4 Blanch the spinach, drain well, chop, and reserve. Add the pasta to the onion mixture with the cheese, egg, tomatoes, and basil. Season and mix.

5 Half-fill each ramekin with some of the pasta. Place the spinach on top and then the remaining pasta mixture. Fold the eggplant over the pasta filling to cover. Put the ramekins in a roasting pan half-filled with boiling water, cover and cook in a preheated oven, 350°F, for 20–25 minutes, or until set. Meanwhile, heat the sauce ingredients in a pan. Turn out the ramekins and serve immediately with the sauce.

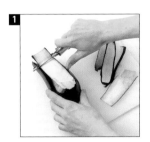

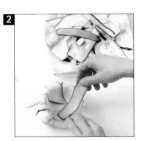

Vegetable Fritters

These mixed vegetable fritters are coated in a light batter and deep-fried until golden. They are ideal with the sweet and sour dipping sauce.

NUTRITIONAL INFORMATION

Calories . . . . . . .479 Sugars 18g
Protein . . . . .8g Fat 32g
Carbohydrate . . .42g Saturates 5g

20 MINS 20 MINS

SERVES 4

INGREDIENTS

¾ cup whole wheat flour

pinch of cayenne pepper

4 tsp olive oil

12 tbsp cold water

3½ oz broccoli florets

3½ oz cauliflower florets

1¾ oz snow peas

1 large carrot, cut into batons

1 red bell pepper, seeded, and sliced

2 egg whites, beaten

oil, for deep-frying

salt

SAUCE

⅔ cup pineapple juice

⅔ cup vegetable stock

2 tbsp white wine vinegar

2 tbsp light brown sugar

2 tsp cornstarch

2 scallions, chopped

1 Sift the flour and a pinch of salt into a mixing bowl and add the cayenne pepper. Make a well in the center and gradually beat in the oil and cold water to make a smooth batter.

2 Cook the vegetables in boiling water for 5 minutes and drain well.

3 Whisk the egg whites until they form peaks and gently fold them into the flour batter.

4 Dip the vegetables into the batter, turning to coat well. Drain off any excess batter. Heat the oil for deep-frying in a deep-fryer to 350°F or until a cube of bread browns in 30 seconds. Fry the coated vegetables, in batches, for 1–2 minutes, until golden. Remove from the oil with a draining spoon and drain on paper towels.

5 Place all of the sauce ingredients in a pan and bring to the boil, stirring, until thickened and clear. Serve with the fritters.

Cauliflower Roulade

A light-as-air mixture of eggs and vegetables produces a stylish vegetarian dish that can be enjoyed hot or cold.

NUTRITIONAL INFORMATION

Calories 271   Sugars 4g
Protein . . . . .15g   Fat 20g
Carbohydrate . . . .7g   Saturates 11g

30 MINS   40 MINS

SERVES 6

I N G R E D I E N T S

1 small cauliflower, divided into florets

4 eggs, separated

¾ cup grated hard cheese

¼ cup cottage cheese

pinch of grated nutmeg

½ tsp mustard powder

salt and pepper

F I L L I N G

1 bunch watercress, trimmed

¼ cup butter

¼ cup flour

¾ cup unsweetened yogurt

¼ cup grated hard cheese

¼ cup cottage cheese

1 Line a jelly roll pan with baking parchment.

2 Steam the cauliflower until just tender, then drain under cold water. Process the cauliflower in a food processor or chop and press through a strainer.

3 Beat the egg yolks, then stir in the cauliflower, ½ cup of the hard cheese and the cottage cheese. Season with nutmeg, mustard, and salt and pepper.

Whisk the egg whites until stiff but not dry, then fold them in.

4 Spread the mixture evenly in the pan. Bake in a preheated oven, 375°F, for about 20-25 minutes, until risen and golden.

5 Chop the watercress, reserving a few sprigs for garnish. Melt the butter in a small pan. Cook the watercress, stirring, for 3 minutes, until wilted. Blend in the flour, then stir in the yogurt and simmer for 2 minutes. Stir in the cheeses.

6 Turn out the roulade on to a damp dish cloth covered with baking parchment. Peel off the paper and leave for a minute to allow the steam to escape. Roll up the roulade, including a new sheet of paper, starting from one narrow end.

7 Unroll the roulade, spread the filling to within 1 inch of the edges, and roll up. Transfer to a baking sheet, sprinkle with the remaining cheese and return to the oven for 5 minutes. Serve immediately if serving hot or allow to cool completely.

Mini Vegetable Puffs

These are ideal with a more formal meal, as they take a little time to prepare and look really impressive.

NUTRITIONAL INFORMATION

Calories	649	Sugars	.........3g
Protein	.........9g	Fat	..........45g
Carbohydrate	...57g	Saturates	......18g

15 MINS 35 MINS

SERVES 4

I N G R E D I E N T S

1 lb puff pastry, thawed if frozen

1 egg, beaten

FILLING

8 oz sweet potato, cubed

3½ oz baby asparagus spears

2 tbsp butter or margarine

1 leek, sliced

2 small open-cap mushrooms, sliced

1 tsp lime juice

1 tsp chopped thyme

pinch of dried mustard

salt and pepper

1 Cut the pastry into 4 equal pieces. Roll each piece out on a lightly floured surface to form a 5 inch square. Place on a dampened baking sheet and score a smaller 2.5 inch square inside each one.

2 Brush with beaten egg and cook in a preheated oven, 400°F, for 20 minutes, or until risen and golden brown.

3 Meanwhile, make the filling, cook the sweet potato in a saucepan of boiling water for 15 minutes, until tender. Drain well and set aside. Blanch the asparagus in a saucepan of boiling water for about 10 minutes, or until tender. Drain and reserve.

4 Remove the pastry squares from the oven, then carefully cut out the central square of pastry with a sharp knife, lift out and reserve.

5 Melt the butter or margarine in a saucepan and sauté the leek and mushrooms for 2–3 minutes. Add the lime juice, thyme, and mustard, season well and stir in the sweet potatoes and asparagus. Spoon the mixture into the pastry cases, top with the reserved pastry squares and serve immediately.

Mushroom & Garlic Soufflés

These individual soufflés are very impressive starters, but must be cooked just before serving to prevent them from sinking.

NUTRITIONAL INFORMATION

Calories 179	Sugars 3g	
Protein 6g	Fat 14g	
Carbohydrate 8g	Saturates 8g	

10 MINS   20 MINS

SERVES 4

INGREDIENTS

4 tbsp butter

1 cup chopped flat mushrooms,

2 tsp lime juice

2 garlic cloves, crushed

2 tbsp chopped marjoram

¼ cup all-purpose flour

1 cup milk

salt and pepper

2 eggs, separated

1 Lightly grease the inside of four ²/₃ cup individual soufflé dishes with a little butter.

2 Melt 2 tbsp of the butter in a skillet. Add the mushrooms, lime juice, and garlic and sauté for 2–3 minutes. Remove the mushroom mixture from the skillet

with a slotted spoon and transfer to a mixing bowl. Stir in the marjoram.

3 Melt the remaining butter in a pan. Add the flour and cook for 1 minute, then remove from the heat. Stir in the milk and return to the heat. Bring to the boil, stirring until thickened.

4 Mix the sauce into the mushroom mixture and beat in the egg yolks.

5 Whisk the egg whites until they form peaks and fold into the mushroom mixture until fully incorporated.

6 Divide the mixture between the soufflé dishes. Place the dishes on a baking sheet and cook in a preheated oven, 400°F, for about 8–10 minutes, or until the soufflés have risen and are cooked through. Serve immediately.

COOK'S TIP

Insert a skewer into the center of the soufflés to test if they are cooked through — it should come out clean. If not, cook for a few minutes longer, but do not overcook otherwise they will become rubbery.

Snacks & Light Meals

The ability to rustle up a simple snack or a quickly-prepared light meal can be very important in our busy lives. Sometimes we may not feel like eating a full-scale

meal but nevertheless want something appetizing and satisfying. Or if lunch or dinner is going to be served very late, then we may want something to tide us over and stave off those hunger pangs! Whether it is for a sustaining snack to break the day, or hearty nibbles to serve with pre-dinner drinks, or an informal lunch or supper party, you'll find a mouthwatering collection of recipes in this chapter.

Roasted Vegetables

Roasted vegetables are delicious and attractive. Served on warm muffins with a herb sauce, they are unbeatable.

NUTRITIONAL INFORMATION

Calories 509   Sugars 12g
Protein . . . . .15g   Fat 28g
Carbohydrate . . .50g   Saturates 12g

1¼ HOURS   30 MINS

SERVES 4

I N G R E D I E N T S

1 red onion, cut into 8 pieces

1 eggplant, halved and sliced

1 yellow bell pepper, seeded, and sliced

1 zucchini, sliced

4 tbsp olive oil

1 tbsp garlic vinegar

2 tbsp vermouth

2 garlic cloves, crushed

1 tbsp chopped thyme

2 tsp light brown sugar

4 muffins, halved

salt and pepper

S A U C E

2 tbsp butter

1 tbsp flour

⅔ cup milk

3 fl oz vegetable stock

¾ cup grated hard cheese

1 tsp wholegrain mustard

3 tbsp chopped mixed herbs

1 Arrange the vegetables in a shallow ovenproof dish. Mix together the oil, vinegar, vermouth, garlic, thyme, and sugar and pour over the vegetables. Set aside to marinate for 1 hour.

2 Transfer the vegetables to a baking sheet. Cook in a preheated oven, 400°F, for 20–25 minutes, or until the vegetables have softened and become tender.

3 Meanwhile, make the sauce. Melt the butter in a small pan and add the flour. Cook for 1 minute, stirring constantly, and then remove from the heat. Gradually, stir in the milk and stock and return the pan to the heat. Bring to a boil, stirring constantly, until thickened. Stir in the cheese, mustard, and mixed herbs and season to taste with salt and pepper.

4 Preheat the broiler to high. Cut the muffins in half and broil for 2–3 minutes, until golden brown, then remove and arrange on a serving plate.

5 Spoon the roasted vegetables on to the muffins and pour the sauce over the top. Serve immediately.

Lentils & Mixed Vegetables

The green lentils used in this recipe require soaking but are worth it for the flavor. If time is short, you could use red split peas instead.

NUTRITIONAL INFORMATION

Calories	386	Sugars	........16g
Protein	........12g	Fat	..........23g
Carbohydrate	...35g	Saturates	......12g

45 MINS   40-45 MINS

SERVES 4

I N G R E D I E N T S

¾ cups green lentils

4 tbsp butter or margarine

2 garlic cloves, crushed

2 tbsp olive oil

1 tbsp cider vinegar

1 red onion, cut into 8

1¾ oz baby-corn-on-the-cobs, halved lengthways

1 yellow bell pepper, seeded, and cut into strips

1 red bell pepper, seeded, and cut into strips

1¾ oz green beans, halved

6 tbsp vegetable stock

2 tbsp clear honey

salt and pepper

crusty bread, to serve

VARIATION

This pan-fry is very versatile: you can use a mixture of your favorite vegetables, if you prefer. Try zucchini, carrots or snow peas.

1 Soak the lentils in a large saucepan of cold water for 25 minutes. Bring to the boil, reduce the heat and simmer for 20 minutes. Drain thoroughly.

2 Add 1 tablespoon of the butter or margarine, 1 garlic clove, 1 tablespoon of oil, and the vinegar to the lentils and mix well.

3 Melt the remaining butter, garlic, and oil in a skillet and stir-fry the onion,

corn cobs, bell peppers and beans for 3–4 minutes.

4 Add the vegetable stock and bring to a boil. Boil for about 10 minutes, or until the liquid has evaporated.

5 Add the honey and season with salt and pepper to taste. Stir in the lentil mixture and cook for 1 minute to heat through. Spoon on to warmed serving plates and serve with crusty bread.

Vegetable Enchiladas

This Mexican dish uses prepared tortillas which are readily available in supermarkets, which are then filled with a spicy vegetable mixture.

NUTRITIONAL INFORMATION

Calories	309	Sugars	14g
Protein	12g	Fat	19g
Carbohydrate	23g	Saturates	8g

 20 MINS 55 MINS

SERVES 4

INGREDIENTS

4 flour tortillas

¾ cup grated hard cheese

FILLING

2¾ oz spinach

2 tbsp olive oil

8 baby-corn-on-the-cobs, sliced

1 tbsp frozen peas, thawed

1 red bell pepper, seeded, and diced

1 carrot, diced

1 leek, sliced

2 garlic cloves, crushed

1 red chili, chopped

salt and pepper

SAUCE

1¼ cups sieved tomatoes

2 shallots, chopped

1 garlic clove, crushed

1¼ cups vegetable stock

1 tsp superfine sugar

1 tsp cayenne pepper

1 To make the filling, blanch the spinach in a pan of boiling water for 2 minutes. Drain well, pressing out as much excess moisture as possible, and chop.

2 Heat the oil in a skillet over a medium heat. Add the baby corn-on-the-cobs, peas, bell pepper, carrot, leek, garlic, and chili and sauté, stirring briskly, for 3–4 minutes. Stir in the spinach and season well with salt and pepper to taste.

3 Put all the sauce ingredients in a heavy-bottomed saucepan and bring to a boil, stirring constantly. Cook over a high heat, stirring constantly, for 20 minutes, until thickened and reduced by a third.

4 Spoon a quarter of the filling along the center of each tortilla. Roll the tortillas around the filling and place, seam side down, in a single layer in an ovenproof dish.

5 Pour the sauce over the tortillas and sprinkle the cheese on top. Cook in a preheated oven, 350°F, for 20 minutes, or until the cheese has melted and browned. Serve immediately.

Vegetable Crêpes

Crêpes or pancakes are ideal for filling with your favorite ingredients. In this recipe they are packed with a spicy vegetable filling.

NUTRITIONAL INFORMATION	
Calories 509	Sugars 10g
Protein 17g	Fat 34g
Carbohydrate ...36g	Saturates 9g

 15 MINS   45 MINS

SERVES 4

INGREDIENTS

CREPES

¾ cup all-purpose flour

pinch of salt

1 egg, beaten

1¼ cups milk

vegetable oil, for frying

FILLING

2 tbsp vegetable oil

1 leek, shredded

½ tsp cayenne pepper

½ tsp ground cumin

1¾ oz snow peas

3½ oz button mushrooms,

1 red bell pepper, sliced

¼ cup cashew nuts, chopped

SAUCE

2 tbsp margarine

3 tbsp all-purpose flour

⅔ cup vegetable stock

⅔ cup milk

1 tsp Dijon mustard

¾ cup grated hard cheese

2 tbsp chopped cilantro

1 For the crêpes, sift the flour and salt into a bowl. Beat in the egg and milk to make a batter.

2 For the filling, heat the oil and sauté the leek for 2–3 minutes. Add the remaining ingredients and cook, stirring, for 5 minutes.

3 For the sauce, melt the margarine in a pan and add the flour. Cook, stirring, for 1 minute. Remove from the heat, stir in the stock and milk and return to the heat. Bring to the boil, stirring until thick.

Add the mustard, half the cheese and the cilantro; cook for 1 minute.

4 Heat 1 tbsp of oil in a small skillet. Pour off the oil and add an eighth of the batter. Tilt to cover the base. Cook for 2 minutes, turn and cook the other side for 1 minute. Repeat with the remaining batter. Spoon a little of the filling along the center of each crêpe and roll up. Place in a flameproof dish and pour the sauce on top. Top with cheese and heat under a hot broiler for 3–5 minutes or until the cheese melts.

Vegetable Jambalaya

This dish traditionally contains spicy sausage, but it is equally delicious filled with vegetables in this spicy vegetarian version.

NUTRITIONAL INFORMATION

Calories	181	Sugars	.........8g
Protein	.........6g	Fat	...........7g
Carbohydrate	...25g	Saturates	.......1g

10 MINS   55 MINS

SERVES 4

I N G R E D I E N T S

½ cup brown rice

2 tbsp olive oil

2 garlic cloves, crushed

1 red onion, cut into eight

1 eggplant, diced

1 green bell pepper, diced

1¾ oz baby-corn-on-the-cobs,
   halved lengthways

½ cup frozen peas

3½ oz small broccoli florets

⅔ cup vegetable stock

8 oz can chopped tomatoes

1 tbsp tomato paste

1 tsp creole seasoning

½ tsp chili flakes

salt and pepper

COOK'S TIP

Use a mixture of different kinds of rice, such as wild or red rice, for color and texture. Cook the rice in advance for a speedier recipe.

1 Cook the rice in a large saucepan of salted boiling water for 20 minutes, or until cooked through. Drain, rinse with boiling water, drain again and set aside.

2 Heat the oil in a heavy-bottomed skillet and cook the garlic and onion, stirring constantly, for 2–3 minutes.

3 Add the eggplant, bell pepper, corn, peas, and broccoli to the pan and cook, stirring occasionally, for 2–3 minutes.

4 Stir in the vegetable stock and canned tomatoes, tomato paste, creole seasoning and chili flakes.

5 Season to taste and cook over a low heat for 15–20 minutes, or until the vegetables are tender.

6 Stir the brown rice into the vegetable mixture and cook, mixing well, for 3–4 minutes, or until hot. Transfer the vegetable jambalaya to a warm serving dish and serve immediately.

Vegetable Burgers & Fries

These spicy vegetable burgers are delicious, especially when served with the light oven fries and in a warm bun or roll.

NUTRITIONAL INFORMATION

Calories 461	Sugars 4g
Protein 18g	Fat 17g
Carbohydrate . . .64g	Saturates 2g

 45 MINS 1 HOUR

SERVES 4

I N G R E D I E N T S

VEGETABLE BURGERS

3½ oz spinach

1 tbsp olive oil

1 leek, chopped

2 garlic cloves, crushed

1½ cups chopped mushrooms

10½ oz firm tofu, chopped

1 tsp cayenne pepper

1 tsp curry powder

1 tbsp chopped cilantro

1½ cups fresh whole wheat breadcrumbs

1 tbsp olive oil

burger bap or roll and salad, to serve

FRIES

2 large potatoes

2 tbsp flour

1 tsp cayenne pepper

2 tbsp olive oil

1 To make the burgers, cook the spinach in a little boiling water for 2 minutes. Drain thoroughly and pat dry with paper towels.

2 Heat the oil in a skillet and sauté the leek and garlic for 2–3 minutes. Add the remaining ingredients, except the breadcrumbs, and cook for 5–7 minutes, until the vegetables have softened. Toss in the spinach and cook for 1 minute.

3 Transfer the mixture to a food processor and process for 30 seconds, until almost smooth. Transfer to a bowl, stir in the breadcrumbs, mixing well, and leave until cool enough to handle. Using floured hands, form the mixture into four equal-size burgers. Leave to chill for 30 minutes.

4 To make the fries, cut the potatoes into thin wedges and cook in a pan of boiling water for 10 minutes. Drain and toss in the flour and cayenne pepper. Lay the fries on a baking sheet and sprinkle with the oil. Cook in a preheated oven, 400°F, for 30 minutes, or until golden.

5 Meanwhile, heat 1 tbsp oil in a skillet and cook the burgers for 8–10 minutes, turning once. Serve with salad in a bap with the fries.

Falafel

These are a very tasty, well-known Middle Eastern dish of small garbanzo bean based balls, spiced, and deep-fried.

NUTRITIONAL INFORMATION

Calories	.491	Sugars	.3g
Protein	.15g	Fat	.30g
Carbohydrate	.43g	Saturates	.3g

 25 MINS   10-15 MINS

SERVES 4

I N G R E D I E N T S

675 g/1½ lb/6 cups canned
    garbanzo beans, drained

1 red onion, chopped

3 garlic cloves, crushed

3½ oz whole wheat bread

2 small fresh red chilies

1 tsp ground cumin

1 tsp ground coriander

½ tsp turmeric

1 tbsp chopped cilantro, plus
    extra to garnish

1 egg, beaten

1 cup whole wheat breadcrumbs

vegetable oil, for
    deep-frying

salt and pepper

tomato and cucumber salad
    and lemon wedges, to serve

1 Put the garbanzo beans, onion, garlic, bread, chilies, spices, and cilantro in a food processor and process for 30 seconds. Stir and season to taste with salt and pepper.

2 Remove the mixture from the food processor and shape into walnut-sized balls.

3 Place the beaten egg in a shallow bowl and place the whole wheat breadcrumbs on a plate. Dip the balls first into the egg to coat and then roll them in the breadcrumbs, shaking off any excess.

4 Heat the oil for deep-frying to 350°F or until a cube of bread browns in 30 seconds. Fry the falafel, in batches if necessary, for 2–3 minutes, until crisp and browned. Remove from the oil with a draining spoon and dry on absorbent paper towels. Garnish with cilantro and serve with a tomato and cucumber salad and lemon wedges.

Potato Fritters with Relish

These are incredibly simple to make and sure to be popular served as a tempting snack or as an accompaniment to almost any Indian meal.

NUTRITIONAL INFORMATION

Calories 294	Sugars 4g
Protein 4g	Fat 24g
Carbohydrate . . .18g	Saturates 3g

🥔 40 MINS   🕐 15 MINS

SERVES 8

I N G R E D I E N T S

½ cup plain whole wheat flour

½ tsp ground coriander

½ tsp cumin seeds

¼ tsp cayenne pepper

½ tsp ground turmeric

¼ tsp salt

1 egg

3 tbsp milk

12 oz potatoes, peeled

1-2 garlic cloves, crushed

4 scallions, chopped

2 oz corn kernels

vegetable oil, for shallow frying

O N I O N & T O M A T O R E L I S H

1 onion, peeled

8 oz tomatoes

2 tbsp chopped cilantro

2 tbsp chopped mint

2 tbsp lemon juice

½ tsp roasted cumin seeds

¼ tsp salt

pinch of cayenne pepper

1 First make the relish. Cut the onion and tomatoes into small dice and place in a bowl with the remaining ingredients. Mix together well and leave to stand for at least 15 minutes before serving to allow time for the flavors to blend.

2 Place the flour in a bowl, stir in the spices and salt and make a well in the center. Add the egg and milk and mix to form a fairly thick batter.

3 Coarsely grate the potatoes, place in a sieve, and rinse well under cold running water. Drain and squeeze dry, then stir into the batter with the garlic, scallions, and corn.

4 Heat about ¼ inch vegetable oil in a large frying pan and add a few tablespoonfuls of the mixture at a time, flattening each one to form a thin cake. Fry over a low heat, turning frequently, for 2-3 minutes, or until golden brown and cooked through.

5 Drain on paper towels and keep hot while frying the remaining mixture in the same way. Serve hot with onion and tomato relish.

Potato & Mushroom Bake

Use any mixture of mushrooms to hand for this creamy layered bake. It can be served straight from the dish in which it is cooked.

NUTRITIONAL INFORMATION

Calories 304	Sugars 2g	
Protein 4g	Fat 24g	
Carbohydrate ...20g	Saturates 15g	

15 MINS   1 HOUR

SERVES 4

INGREDIENTS

2 tbsp butter

1 lb 2 oz waxy potatoes, thinly sliced

2 cups sliced mixed mushrooms

1 tbsp chopped rosemary

4 tbsp chopped chives

2 garlic cloves, crushed

⅔ cup heavy cream

salt and pepper

snipped chives, to garnish

1 Grease a shallow round ovenproof dish with butter.

2 Parboil the sliced potatoes in a saucepan of boiling water for 10 minutes. Drain well. Layer a quarter of the potatoes in the base of the dish.

COOK'S TIP

For a special occasion, the bake may be made in a lined cake pan and then turned out to serve.

3 Arrange one-quarter of the mushrooms on top of the potatoes and sprinkle with one-quarter of the rosemary, chives, and garlic. Continue making layers in the same order, finishing with a layer of potatoes on top.

4 Pour the cream over the top of the potatoes. Season to taste with salt and pepper.

5 Cook in a preheated oven, 375°F, for about 45 minutes, or until the bake is golden brown and very hot.

6 Garnish with snipped chives and serve at once straight from the dish.

Broiled Potatoes

This dish is ideal with broiled or barbecued foods, as the potatoes themselves may be cooked by either method.

NUTRITIONAL INFORMATION

Calories 417	Sugars 1g
Protein 3g	Fat 37g
Carbohydrate . . .20g	Saturates 10g

15 MINS   20 MINS

SERVES 4

I N G R E D I E N T S

1 lb potatoes, unpeeled and scrubbed

3 tbsp butter, melted

2 tbsp chopped thyme

paprika, for dusting

LIME MAYONNAISE

⅔ cup mayonnaise

2 tsp lime juice

finely grated rind of 1 lime

1 garlic clove, crushed

pinch of paprika

salt and pepper

1 Cut the potatoes into ½ inch thick slices.

2 Cook the potatoes in a saucepan of boiling water for 5–7 minutes — they should still be quite firm. Remove the potatoes with a draining spoon and drain thoroughly.

3 Line a broiler pan with kitchen foil. Place the potato slices on top of the foil.

4 Brush the potatoes with the melted butter and sprinkle the chopped thyme on top. Season to taste with salt and pepper.

5 Cook the potatoes under a preheated broiler at medium heat for 10 minutes, turning once.

6 Meanwhile, make the lime mayonnaise. Thoroughly combine the mayonnaise, lime juice, lime rind, garlic, paprika, and salt and pepper to taste in a small bowl.

7 Dust the hot potato slices with a little paprika and serve immediately with the lime mayonnaise.

COOK'S TIP

The lime mayonnaise may be spooned over the broiled potatoes to coat them just before serving, if you prefer.

Paprika Chips

These wafer-thin potato chips are great cooked over a barbecue and served with spicy vegetable kabobs.

NUTRITIONAL INFORMATION

Calories . . . . . . .149 Sugars 0.6g
Protein . . . . .2g Fat 8g
Carbohydrate . . .17g Saturates 1g

 5 MINS   7 MINS

SERVES 4

INGREDIENTS

2 large potatoes

3 tbsp olive oil

½ tsp paprika

salt

1 Using a sharp knife, slice the potatoes very thinly so that they are almost transparent. Drain the potato slices thoroughly and pat dry with paper towels.

2 Heat the oil in a large skillet and add the paprika, stirring constantly to ensure that the paprika doesn't catch and burn.

3 Add the potato slices to the skillet and cook them in a single layer for about 5 minutes or until the potato slices just begin to curl slightly at the edges.

VARIATION

You could use curry powder or any other spice to flavor the chips instead of the paprika, if you prefer.

4 Remove the potato slices from the pan using a draining spoon and transfer them to paper towels to drain thoroughly.

5 Thread the potato slices on to several wooden kabob skewers.

6 Sprinkle the potato slices with a little salt and cook over a medium hot barbecue or under a medium broiler, turning frequently, for 10 minutes, until the potato slices begin to crispen. Sprinkle with a little more salt, if preferred, and serve immediately.

Mixed Bean Pan-Fry

Fresh green beans have a wonderful flavor that is hard to beat.
If you cannot find fresh beans, use thawed, frozen beans instead.

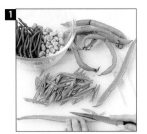

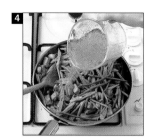

NUTRITIONAL INFORMATION

Calories 179	Sugars 4g	
Protein 10g	Fat 11g	
Carbohydrate ...10g	Saturates 1g	

 10 MINS   15 MINS

SERVES 4

I N G R E D I E N T S

4 cups mixed green beans,
    such as green and
    fava beans, podded

2 tbsp vegetable oil

2 garlic cloves, crushed

1 red onion, halved and sliced

8 oz firm marinated tofu, diced

1 tbsp lemon juice

½ tsp turmeric

1 tsp ground mixed spice

⅔ cup vegetable stock

2 tsp sesame seeds

1 Trim and chop the green beans and set aside until required.

2 Heat the oil in a medium skillet. Add the garlic and onion and sauté, stirring frequently, over a low heat for 2 minutes.

3 Add the tofu and cook for 2–3 minutes, until just beginning to turn golden brown.

4 Add the green beans and fava beans. Stir in the lemon juice, turmeric, ground mixed spice, and vegetable stock and bring to the boil over a medium heat.

5 Reduce the heat and simmer for 5–7 minutes, or until the beans are tender. Sprinkle with sesame seeds and serve immediately.

VARIATION

Use smoked tofu instead of marinated tofu for an alternative and quite distinctive flavor.

Stuffed Mushrooms

Use large open-cap mushrooms for this recipe for their flavor and suitability for filling.

NUTRITIONAL INFORMATION

Calories	273	Sugars	.........5g
Protein	........13g	Fat	..........18g
Carbohydrate	...15g	Saturates	.......5g

 15 MINS   25 MINS

SERVES 4

INGREDIENTS

8 open-cap mushrooms

1 tbsp olive oil

1 small leek, chopped

1 celery stalk, chopped

3½ oz firm tofu, diced

1 zucchini, chopped

1 carrot, chopped

1 cup whole wheat breadcrumbs

2 tbsp chopped basil

1 tbsp tomato paste

2 tbsp pine nuts

¾ cup grated hard cheese

⅔ cup vegetable stock

salt and pepper

salad, to serve

1 Remove the stalks from the mushrooms and chop finely. Reserve the caps.

2 Heat the olive oil in a large, heavy-bottomed skillet over a medium heat. Add the chopped mushroom stalks, leek, celery, tofu, zucchini, and carrot and cook, stirring constantly, for 3–4 minutes.

3 Stir in the breadcrumbs, chopped basil, tomato paste and pine nuts. Season with salt and pepper to taste and mix thoroughly.

4 Spoon the mixture into the mushroom caps and top with the grated cheese.

5 Place the mushrooms in a shallow ovenproof dish and pour the vegetable stock around them.

6 Cook in a preheated oven, 425°F, for 20 minutes, or until cooked through and the cheese has melted. Remove the mushrooms from the dish and serve immediately with a salad.

Stuffed Globe Artichokes

This imaginative and attractive recipe for artichokes stuffed with nuts, tomatoes, olives, and mushrooms, has been adapted for the microwave.

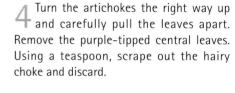

NUTRITIONAL INFORMATION

Calories	.248	Sugars	.8g
Protein	.5g	Fat	.19g
Carbohydrate	.16g	Saturates	.2g

  30 MINS 25 MINS

SERVES 4

I N G R E D I E N T S

4 globe artichokes

8 tbsp water

4 tbsp lemon juice

1 onion, chopped

1 garlic clove, crushed

2 tbsp olive oil

2 cups button mushrooms, chopped

½ cup pitted black olives, sliced

¼ cup sun-dried tomatoes in oil, drained, and chopped

1 tbsp chopped fresh basil

1 cup fresh white breadcrumbs

¼ cup pine nuts, toasted

oil from the jar of sun-dried tomatoes for drizzling

salt and pepper

1 Cut the stalks and lower leaves off the artichokes. Snip off the leaf tips with scissors. Place 2 artichokes in a large bowl with half the water and half the lemon juice. Cover and cook on HIGH power for 10 minutes, turning the artichokes over halfway through, until a leaf pulls away

easily from the base. Leave to stand, covered, for 3 minutes before draining. Turn the artichokes upside down and leave to cool. Repeat to cook the remaining artichokes.

2 Place the onion, garlic, and oil in a bowl. Cover and cook on HIGH power for 2 minutes, stirring once. Add the mushrooms, olives, and sun-dried tomatoes. Cover and cook on HIGH power for 2 minutes.

3 Stir in the basil, breadcrumbs, and pine nuts. Season to taste with salt and pepper.

4 Turn the artichokes the right way up and carefully pull the leaves apart. Remove the purple-tipped central leaves. Using a teaspoon, scrape out the hairy choke and discard.

5 Divide the stuffing into 4 equal portions and spoon into the center of each artichoke. Push the leaves back around the stuffing.

6 Arrange in a shallow dish and drizzle over a little oil from the jar of sun-dried tomatoes. Cook on HIGH power for 7–8 minutes to reheat, turning the artichokes around halfway through.

Spinach Pancakes

Serve these pancakes as a light lunch or supper dish, with a tomato and basil salad for a dramatic color contrast.

NUTRITIONAL INFORMATION

Calories	663	Sugars	.........9g
Protein	........32g	Fat	..........48g
Carbohydrate	...28g	Saturates	......18g

🥔 25 MINS 🕐 1¼ HOURS

SERVES 4

INGREDIENTS

¾ cup whole wheat flour

1 egg

⅔ cup unsweetened yogurt

3 tbsp water

1 tbsp vegetable oil, plus extra for brushing

7 oz frozen leaf spinach, thawed,
   and puréed

pinch of grated nutmeg

salt and pepper

TO GARNISH

lemon wedges

fresh cilantro sprigs

FILLING

1 tbsp vegetable oil

3 scallions, thinly sliced

1 cup ricotta cheese

4 tbsp unsweetened yogurt

¾ cup grated Gruyère cheese

1 egg, lightly beaten

1 cup unsalted cashew nuts

2 tbsp chopped parsley

pinch of cayenne pepper

1 Sift the flour and salt into a bowl and tip in any bran in the strainer. Beat together the egg, yogurt, water, and oil. Gradually pour it on to the flour, beating constantly. Stir in the spinach and season with pepper and nutmeg.

2 To make the filling, heat the oil in a pan and fry the scallions until translucent. Remove with a draining spoon and drain on paper towels. Beat together the ricotta, yogurt, and half the Gruyère. Beat in the egg and stir in the cashew nuts and parsley. Season with salt and cayenne.

3 Lightly brush a small, heavy skillet with oil and heat. Pour in 3–4 tablespoons of the pancake batter and tilt the pan so that it covers the base. Cook for about 3 minutes, until bubbles appear in the center. Turn and cook the other side for about 2 minutes, until lightly browned. Slide the pancake on to a warmed plate, cover with foil and keep warm while you cook the remainder. The batter should make 8–12 pancakes.

4 Spread a little filling over each pancake and fold in half and then half again, envelope style. Spoon the remaining filling into the opening.

5 Grease a shallow, ovenproof dish, and arrange the pancakes in a single layer. Sprinkle on the remaining cheese and cook in a preheated oven, 350°F, for about 15 minutes. Serve hot, garnished with lemon wedges and cilantro sprigs.

Marinated Fennel

Fennel has a wonderful aniseed flavor which is ideal for broiling or barbecuing. This marinated recipe is really delicious.

NUTRITIONAL INFORMATION

Calories	117	Sugars	.........3g
Protein	.........1g	Fat	...........11g
Carbohydrate	....3g	Saturates	.......2g

🍲 1¼ HOURS 🕐 10 MINS

SERVES 4

I N G R E D I E N T S

2 fennel bulbs

1 red bell pepper, seeded and cut into
    large cubes

1 lime, cut into 8 wedges

M A R I N A D E

2 tbsp lime juice

4 tbsp olive oil

2 garlic cloves, crushed

1 tsp wholegrain mustard

1 tbsp chopped thyme

fennel fronds, to garnish

crisp salad, to serve

1 Cut each of the fennel bulbs into 8 pieces and place in a shallow dish. Mix in the bell peppers.

2 To make the marinade, combine the lime juice, oil, garlic, mustard, and thyme. Pour the marinade over the fennel and bell peppers, toss to coat thoroughly and set aside to marinate for 1 hour.

3 Thread the fennel and bell peppers on to wooden skewers with the lime wedges. Preheat a broiler to medium and broil the kabobs, turning and basting frequently with the marinade, for about 10 minutes.

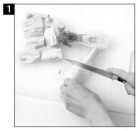

4 Transfer to serving plates, garnish with fennel fronds, and serve immediately with a crisp salad.

COOK'S TIP

Soak the skewers in cold water for 20 minutes before using to prevent them from burning during broiling. You could substitute 2 tablespoons orange juice for the lime juice and add 1 tbsp honey, if you prefer.

Garlic Mushrooms on Toast

This is so simple to prepare and looks great if you use a variety of mushrooms for shape and texture.

NUTRITIONAL INFORMATION

Calories . . . . . . .366 Sugars 2g
Protein . . . . .9g Fat 18g
Carbohydrate . . .45g Saturates 4g

 10 MINS 10 MINS

SERVES 4

I N G R E D I E N T S

6 tbsp margarine

2 garlic cloves, crushed

4 cups mixed mushrooms, such as
open-cap, button, oyster, and
shiitake, sliced

8 slices French bread

1 tbsp chopped parsley

salt and pepper

1 Melt the margarine in a skillet. Add the crushed garlic and cook, stirring constantly, for 30 seconds.

2 Add the mushrooms and cook, turning occasionally, for 5 minutes.

3 Toast the French bread slices under a preheated medium broiler for 2–3 minutes, turning once. Transfer the toasts to a serving plate.

COOK'S TIP

Always store mushrooms for a maximum of 24–36 hours in the refrigerator, in paper bags, as they sweat in plastic. Wild mushrooms should be washed but other varieties can simply be wiped with paper towels.

4 Toss the parsley into the mushrooms, mixing well, and season well with salt and pepper to taste.

5 Spoon the mushroom mixture over the bread and serve immediately.

Creamy Mushroom & Potato

These oven-baked mushrooms are covered with a creamy potato and mushroom filling topped with melted cheese.

NUTRITIONAL INFORMATION

Calories 214	Sugars 1g
Protein 5g	Fat 17g
Carbohydrate 11g	Saturates 11g

40 MINS   40 MINS

SERVES 4

INGREDIENTS

1 oz dried porcini

8 oz mealy potatoes, diced

2 tbsp butter, melted

4 tbsp heavy cream

2 tbsp chopped fresh chives

¼ cup grated Emmenthal cheese

8 large open-capped mushrooms

⅔ cup vegetable stock

salt and pepper

fresh chives, to garnish

1 Place the dried porcini in a small bowl. Add sufficient boiling water to cover and set aside to soak for 20 minutes.

2 Meanwhile, cook the potatoes in a medium saucepan of lightly salted boiling water for 10 minutes, until cooked through and tender. Drain well and mash until smooth.

3 Drain the soaked porcini and then chop them finely. Mix them into the mashed potato.

4 Thoroughly blend the butter, cream, and chives together and pour the mixture into the porcini and potato mixture, mixing well. Season to taste with salt and pepper.

5 Remove the stalks from the open-capped mushrooms. Chop the stalks and stir them into the potato mixture. Spoon the mixture into the open-capped mushrooms and sprinkle the cheese over the top.

6 Arrange the filled mushrooms in a shallow ovenproof dish and pour in the vegetable stock.

7 Cover the dish and cook in a preheated oven, 425°F, for 20 minutes. Remove the lid and cook for 5 minutes until golden.

8 Garnish the mushrooms with fresh chives and serve at once.

VARIATION

Use fresh mushrooms instead of the dried porcini, if preferred, and stir a mixture of chopped nuts into the mushroom stuffing mixture for extra crunch.

Indian-Style Omelet

Omelets are very versatile: they go with almost anything and you can also serve them at any time of the day.

NUTRITIONAL INFORMATION

Calories	132	Sugars	.........1g
Protein	.........7g	Fat	...........11g
Carbohydrate	....2g	Saturates	.......2g

 10 MINS 20 MINS

SERVES 4

INGREDIENTS

1 small onion, very finely chopped

2 green chilies, finely chopped

cilantro leaves, finely chopped

4 medium eggs

1 tsp salt

2 tbsp oil

toasted bread or crisp
   green salad, to serve

1 Place the onion, chilies and cilantro in a large mixing bowl. Mix together until well combined.

2 Place the eggs in a separate bowl and whisk together.

3 Add the onion mixture to the eggs and mix together.

4 Add the salt to the egg and onion mixture and whisk together well.

5 Heat 1 tbsp of the oil in a large skillet. Place a ladleful of the omelet batter into the pan.

6 Fry the omelet, turning once and pressing down with a flat spoon to make sure that the egg is cooked right through, until the omelet is a golden brown color.

7 Repeat the same process for the remaining batter. Set the omelets aside and keep warm while you make the remaining batches of omelets.

8 Serve the omelets immediately with toasted bread. Alternatively, simply serve the omelets with a crisp green salad for a light lunch.

COOK'S TIP

Indian cooks use a variety of vegetable oils, and groundnut or sunflower oils make good alternatives for most dishes, although sometimes more specialist ones, such as coconut oil, mustard oil, and sesame oil, are called for.

Cabbage & Walnut Stir-Fry

This is a really quick, one-pan dish using white and red cabbage for both color and flavor.

NUTRITIONAL INFORMATION

Calories 422   Sugars 9g
Protein . . . . .13g   Fat 37g
Carbohydrate . . .10g   Saturates 5g

10 MINS   10 MINS

SERVES 4

INGREDIENTS

12 oz white cabbage

12 oz red cabbage

4 tbsp peanut oil

1 tbsp walnut oil

2 garlic cloves, crushed

8 scallions

225 g/8 oz firm tofu, cubed

2 tbsp lemon juice

3½ oz walnut halves

2 tsp Dijon mustard

2 tsp poppy seeds

salt and pepper

1 Using a sharp knife, shred the white and red cabbages thinly and set aside until required.

2 Heat the peanut and walnut oils in a preheated wok or heavy-bottomed skillet. Add the garlic, cabbage, scallions, and tofu and cook, stirring constantly, for 5 minutes.

3 Add the lemon juice, walnuts, and Dijon mustard, season to taste with salt and pepper and cook for a further 5 minutes, or until the cabbage is tender.

4 Transfer the stir-fry to a warm serving bowl, sprinkle with poppy seeds and serve immediately.

COOK'S TIP

As well as adding protein, vitamins and useful fats to the diet, nuts and seeds add flavor and texture to vegetarian meals. Keep a good supply of them in your store-cupboard as they can be used in a great variety of dishes — salads, bakes, stir-fries to name but a few.

Cress & Cheese Tartlets

These individual tartlets are great for lunchtime or for picnic food.
Watercress is a good source of folic acid, important in early pregnancy.

NUTRITIONAL INFORMATION

Calories	410	Sugars	.....4g
Protein	.....15g	Fat	.....29g
Carbohydrate	...24g	Saturates	.....19g

 20 MINS   25 MINS

SERVES 4

I N G R E D I E N T S

¾ cup all-purpose flour

pinch of salt

½ cup butter or margarine

2–3 tbsp cold water

2 bunches watercress

2 garlic cloves, crushed

1 shallot, chopped

scant 1½ cups grated hard cheese

4 tbsp unsweetened yogurt

½ tsp paprika

1 Sift the flour into a mixing bowl and add the salt. Rub ⅓ cup of the butter or margarine into the flour until the mixture resembles breadcrumbs.

2 Stir in enough of the cold water to make a smooth dough.

3 Roll the dough out on a lightly floured surface and use to line four 4 inch tartlet pans. Prick the bases with a fork and leave to chill.

4 Heat the remaining butter or margarine in a skillet. Discard the stems from the watercress and add to the pan with the garlic and shallot, cooking for 1–2 minutes, until the watercress has wilted.

5 Remove the pan from the heat and stir in the grated cheese, yogurt, and paprika.

6 Spoon the mixture into the pastry cases and cook in a preheated oven, 350°F, for 20 minutes, or until the filling is firm. Turn out the tartlets and serve immediately.

VARIATION

Use spinach instead of the watercress, making sure it is well drained before mixing with the remaining filling ingredients.

Hash Browns

Hash Browns are a popular recipe of fried potato squares, often served as brunch. This recipe includes extra vegetables.

NUTRITIONAL INFORMATION

Calories 339   Sugars 9g
Protein . . . . .10g   Fat 21g
Carbohydrate . . .29g   Saturates 7g

 20 MINS   45 MINS

SERVES 4

I N G R E D I E N T S

1 lb 2 oz waxy potatoes

1 carrot, diced

1 celery stalk, diced

2 oz button mushrooms, diced

1 onion, diced

2 garlic cloves, crushed

¼ cup frozen peas, thawed

⅔ cup grated Parmesan cheese

4 tbsp vegetable oil

2 tbsp butter

salt and pepper

S A U C E

1¼ cups sieved tomatoes

2 tbsp chopped fresh cilantro

1 tbsp vegetarian Worcestershire sauce

½ tsp chili powder

2 tsp brown sugar

2 tsp American mustard

⅓ cup vegetable stock

1 Cook the potatoes in a saucepan of lightly salted boiling water for 10 minutes. Drain and leave to cool. Meanwhile, cook the carrot in lightly salted boiling water for 5 minutes.

2 Set the potato aside to cool. When cool enough to handle, grate it with a coarse grater.

3 Drain the carrot and add it to the grated potato, together with the celery, mushrooms, onion, garlic, peas, and cheese. Season to taste with salt and pepper.

4 Put all of the sauce ingredients in a small saucepan and bring to a boil. Reduce the heat to low and simmer for 15 minutes.

5 Divide the potato mixture into 8 portions of equal size and shape into flattened rectangles with your hands.

6 Heat the oil and butter in a skillet and cook the hash browns over a low heat for 4–5 minutes on each side, until crisp and golden brown.

7 Transfer the hash browns to a serving plate and serve immediately with the tomato sauce.

Corn Patties

These are a delicious addition to any party buffet, and very simple to prepare. Serve with a sweet chili sauce.

NUTRITIONAL INFORMATION

Calories 90	Sugars 3g
Protein 2g	Fat 5g
Carbohydrate 11g	Saturates 0.6g

10 MINS   10 MINS

SERVES 6

I N G R E D I E N T S

11½ oz can corn, drained

1 onion, finely chopped

1 tsp curry powder

1 garlic clove, crushed

1 tsp ground coriander

2 scallions, chopped

3 tbsp all-purpose flour

½ tsp baking powder

1 large egg

4 tbsp sunflower oil

salt

1 Mash the drained corn lightly in a medium-sized bowl. Add the onion, curry powder, garlic, ground coriander, scallions, flour, baking powder, and egg, one at a time, stirring after each addition. Season to taste with salt.

2 Heat the sunflower oil in a skillet. Drop tablespoonfuls of the mixture carefully on to the hot oil, far enough apart for them not to run into each other as they cook.

3 Cook for about 4–5 minutes, turning each patty once, until they are golden brown and firm to the touch. Take care not to turn them too soon, or they will break up in the pan.

4 Remove the patties from the pan with a slice and drain on paper towels. Serve immediately while still warm.

COOK'S TIP

To make this dish more attractive, you can serve the patties on large leaves, like those shown in the photograph. Be sure to cut the scallions on the diagonal, as shown, for a more elegant appearance.

Buck Rarebit

This substantial version of cheese on toast — a creamy cheese sauce topped with a poached egg — makes a tasty, filling snack.

NUTRITIONAL INFORMATION

Calories 478	Sugars 2g
Protein 29g	Fat 34g
Carbohydrate . . .14g	Saturates 20g

10 MINS   15-20 MINS

SERVES 4

INGREDIENTS

12 oz sharp hard cheese

4½ oz Gouda, Gruyère, or Emmenthal cheese

1 tsp mustard powder

1 tsp wholegrain mustard

2-4 tbsp brown ale, cider, or milk

½ tsp vegetarian Worcestershire sauce

4 thick slices white or brown bread

4 eggs

salt and pepper

TO GARNISH

tomato wedges

watercress sprigs

1 Grate the cheeses and place in a non-stick saucepan.

2 Add the mustards, seasoning, brown ale, cider, or milk and vegetarian Worcestershire sauce and mix well.

VARIATION

For a change, you can use part or all Stilton or other blue cheese; the appearance is not so attractive but the flavor is very good.

 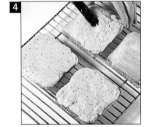 

3 Heat the cheese mixture gently, stirring until it has melted and is completely thick and creamy. Remove from the heat and leave to cool a little.

4 Toast the slices of bread on each side under a preheated broiler then spread the rarebit mixture evenly over each piece. Put under a moderate broiler until golden brown and bubbling.

5 Meanwhile, poach the eggs. If using a poacher, grease the cups, heat the water in the pan, and, when just boiling, break the eggs into the cups. Cover and simmer for 4-5 minutes until just set. Alternatively, bring about 1½ inches of water to a boil in a skillet or large saucepan and for each egg quickly swirl the water with a knife and drop the egg into the "hole" created. Cook for about 4 minutes until just set.

6 Top the rarebits with a poached egg and serve garnished with tomato wedges and sprigs of watercress.

Carrot & Potato Soufflé

Hot soufflés have a reputation for being difficult to make, but this one is both simple and impressive. Make sure you serve it as soon as it is ready.

NUTRITIONAL INFORMATION

Calories 294	Sugars 6g
Protein 10g	Fat 9g
Carbohydrate ...46g	Saturates 4g

  1¼ HOURS   40 MINS

SERVES 4

INGREDIENTS

2 tbsp butter, melted

4 tbsp fresh whole wheat breadcrumbs

1½ lb mealy potatoes, baked
   in their skins

2 carrots, grated

2 eggs, separated

2 tbsp orange juice

¼ tsp grated nutmeg

salt and pepper

carrot curls, to garnish

1 Brush the inside of a 3¾ cup soufflé dish with butter. Sprinkle three-quarters of the breadcrumbs over the base and sides.

2 Cut the baked potatoes in half and scoop the flesh into a mixing bowl.

3 Add the carrot, egg yolks, orange juice, and nutmeg to the potato flesh. Season to taste with salt and pepper.

4 In a separate bowl, whisk the egg whites until soft peaks form, then gently fold into the potato mixture with a metal spoon until well incorporated.

5 Gently spoon the potato and carrot mixture into the prepared soufflé dish. Sprinkle the remaining breadcrumbs over the top of the mixture.

6 Cook in a preheated oven, 400°F, for 40 minutes, until risen and golden. Do not open the oven door during the cooking time, otherwise the soufflé will sink. Serve at once, garnished with carrot curls.

COOK'S TIP

To bake the potatoes, prick the skins and cook in a preheated oven, 375°F, for about 1 hour.

Lentil Croquettes

These croquettes are an ideal light lunch served with a crisp salad and a sesame seed paste dip.

NUTRITIONAL INFORMATION

Calories 409	Sugars 5g
Protein 19g	Fat 17g
Carbohydrate . . .48g	Saturates 2g

 10 MINS   55 MINS

SERVES 4

I N G R E D I E N T S

1¼ cups split red lentils

1 green bell pepper, seeded, and
    finely chopped

1 red onion, finely chopped

2 garlic cloves, crushed

1 tsp garam masala

½ tsp cayenne pepper

1 tsp ground cumin

2 tsp lemon juice

2 tbsp chopped unsalted peanuts

2½ cups water

1 egg, beaten

3 tbsp all-purpose flour

1 tsp turmeric

1 tsp cayenne pepper

4 tbsp vegetable oil

salt and pepper

salad greens and herbs, to serve

1 Put the lentils in a large saucepan with the bell pepper, onion, garlic, garam masala, cayenne pepper, ground cumin, lemon juice, and peanuts. Add the water and bring to a boil. Reduce the heat and simmer, stirring occasionally, for about 30 minutes, or until the liquid has been absorbed.

2 Remove the mixture from the heat and leave to cool slightly. Beat in the egg and season to taste with salt and pepper. Leave to cool completely.

3 With floured hands, form the mixture into 8 rectangles

4 Mix the flour, turmeric, and cayenne pepper together on a small plate. Roll the croquettes in the spiced flour mixture to coat thoroughly.

5 Heat the oil in a large skillet. Add the croquettes, in batches, and fry, turning once, for about 10 minutes, until crisp on both sides. Transfer to warm serving plates and serve the croquettes with crisp salad greens and fresh herbs.

Potato Mushroom Cakes

These cakes will be loved by vegetarians and meat-eaters alike. Packed with creamy potato and as wide a variety of mushrooms as possible.

NUTRITIONAL INFORMATION

Calories 298   Sugars 0.8g
Protein . . . . .5g   Fat 22g
Carbohydrate . . .22g   Saturates 5g

20 MINS   25 MINS

SERVES 4

I N G R E D I E N T S

1 lb 2 oz mealy potatoes, diced

2 tbsp butter

6 oz mixed mushrooms, chopped

2 garlic cloves, crushed

1 small egg, beaten

1 tbsp chopped fresh chives, plus extra
   to garnish

flour, for dusting

oil, for frying

salt and pepper

1 Cook the potatoes in a pan of lightly salted boiling water for 10 minutes, or until cooked through

2 Drain the potatoes well, mash with a potato masher or fork and set aside.

3 Meanwhile, melt the butter in a skillet. Add the mushrooms and garlic and cook, stirring constantly, for 5 minutes. Drain well.

4 Stir the mushrooms and garlic into the potato, together with the beaten egg and chives.

5 Divide the mixture equally into 4 portions and shape them into round cakes. Toss them in the flour until the outsides of the cakes are completely coated.

6 Heat the oil in a skillet. Add the potato cakes and fry over a medium heat for 10 minutes until they are golden brown, turning them over halfway through. Serve the cakes at once, with a simple crisp salad.

COOK'S TIP

Prepare the cakes in advance, cover and leave to chill in the refrigerator for up to 24 hours, if you wish.

Stuffed Vegetable Snacks

In this recipe, eggplants are filled with a spicy bulghur wheat and vegetable stuffing for a delicious light meal.

NUTRITIONAL INFORMATION

Calories 360	Sugars 17g
Protein 9g	Fat 16g
Carbohydrate ...50g	Saturates 2g

40 MINS   30 MINS

SERVES 4

INGREDIENTS

4 medium eggplants

salt

¾ cup bulghur wheat

1¼ cups boiling water

3 tbsp olive oil

2 garlic cloves, crushed

2 tbsp pine nuts

½ tsp turmeric

1 tsp cayenne pepper

2 celery sticks, chopped

4 scallions, chopped

1 carrot, grated

¾ cup button mushrooms, chopped

2 tbsp raisins

2 tbsp chopped cilantro

green salad, to serve

 1 Cut the eggplants in half lengthways and scoop out the flesh with a teaspoon. Chop the flesh and set aside. Rub the insides of the eggplants with a little salt and leave to stand for 20 minutes.

2 Meanwhile, put the bulghur wheat in a mixing bowl and pour the boiling water over the top. Leave to stand for 20 minutes, or until the water has been completely absorbed.

3 Heat the oil in a skillet. Add the garlic, pine nuts, turmeric, cayenne pepper, celery, scallions, carrot, mushrooms, and raisins and cook for 2–3 minutes.

4 Stir in the reserved eggplant flesh and cook for a further 2–3 minutes. Add the chopped cilantro, mixing well.

5 Remove the pan from the heat and stir in the bulghur wheat. Rinse the eggplant shells under cold water and pat dry with paper towels.

6 Spoon the bulghur filling into the eggplants and place in a roasting pan. Pour in a little boiling water and cook in a preheated oven, 350°F, for about 15–20 minutes, until very hot. Remove from the oven and serve hot with a green salad.

Vegetable Samosas

These Indian snacks are perfect for a quick or light meal. Served with a salad they can be made in advance and frozen for ease.

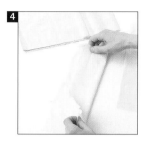

NUTRITIONAL INFORMATION

Calories 291	Sugars 2g
Protein 4g	Fat 23g
Carbohydrate . . .18g	Saturates 3g

 20 MINS   30 MINS

MAKES 12

I N G R E D I E N T S

FILLING

2 tbsp vegetable oil

1 onion, chopped

½ tsp ground coriander

½ tsp ground cumin

pinch of turmeric

½ tsp ground ginger

½ tsp garam masala

1 garlic clove, crushed

1½ cups potatoes, diced

1 cup frozen peas, thawed

2 cups spinach, chopped

PASTRY

12 sheets phyllo pastry

oil, for deep-frying

1 To make the filling, heat the oil in a skillet. Add the onion and sauté, stirring frequently, for 1–2 minutes, until soft. Stir in all of the spices and garlic and cook for 1 minute.

2 Add the potatoes and cook over a low heat, stirring frequently, for 5 minutes, until they begin to soften.

3 Stir in the peas and spinach and cook for a further 3–4 minutes.

4 Lay the phyllo pastry sheets out on a clean counter and fold each sheet in half lengthways.

5 Place 2 tablespoons of the vegetable filling at one end of each folded pastry sheet. Fold over one corner to make a triangle. Continue folding in this way to make a triangular package and seal the edges with water.

6 Repeat with the remaining pastry and the remaining filling.

7 Heat the oil for deep-frying to 350°F or until a cube of bread browns in 30 seconds. Fry the samosas in batches, for 1–2 minutes until golden. Drain on paper towels and keep warm while cooking the remainder. Serve immediately.

Stuffed Parathas

This bread can be quite rich and is usually made for special occasions. It can be eaten on its own or with a vegetable curry.

NUTRITIONAL INFORMATION

Calories . . . . .391 Sugars 2g
Protein . . . . .6g Fat 24g
Carbohydrate . . .40g Saturates 2.5g

 25 MINS   30-35 MINS

SERVES 6

I N G R E D I E N T S

D O U G H

1¾ cups wholewheat flour

½ tsp salt

scant 1 cup water

8 tbsp vegetable ghee

2 tbsp ghee, for frying

F I L L I N G

3 medium potatoes

½ tsp turmeric

1 tsp garam masala

1 tsp finely chopped gingerroot

fresh cilantro leaves

3 green chilies, finely chopped

1 tsp salt

1 To make the parathas, mix the flour, salt, water, and ghee in a bowl to form a dough.

2 Divide the dough into 6-8 equal portions. Roll each portion out on to a floured work surface. Brush the middle of the dough portions with ½ tsp ghee. Fold the dough portions in half, roll into a pipe-like shape, flatten with the palms of your hand, then roll around your finger to form a coil. Roll out again, using flour to dust as and when necessary, to form a round about 7 inches in diameter.

3 Place the potatoes in a saucepan of boiling water and cook until soft enough to be mashed.

4 Blend the turmeric, garam masala, ginger, cilantro, chilies, and salt together in a bowl.

5 Add the spice mixture to the mashed potato and mix well. Spread about 1 tablespoon of the spicy potato mixture on each dough portion and cover with another rolled-out piece of dough. Seal the edges well.

6 Heat 2 teaspoons ghee in a heavy-bottomed skillet. Place the parathas gently in the pan, in batches, and fry, turning and moving them about gently with a flat spoon, until golden.

7 Remove the parathas from the skillet and serve immediately.

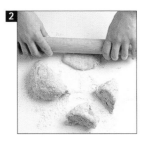

Bombay Bowl

You can use dried garbanzo beans for this popular snack, but the canned sort are quick and easy without sacrificing much flavor.

NUTRITIONAL INFORMATION

Calories 183	Sugars 6g
Protein 9g	Fat 3g
Carbohydrate ...33g	Saturates 0.3g

 15 MINS   🕐 15 MINS

SERVES 4

I N G R E D I E N T S

14 oz can garbanzo beans, drained

2 medium potatoes

1 medium onion

2 tbsp tamarind paste

6 tbsp water

1 tsp cayenne pepper

2 tsp sugar

1 tsp salt

T O   G A R N I S H

1 tomato, sliced

2 fresh green chilies, chopped

fresh cilantro leaves

COOK'S TIP

Cream-colored and resembling a hazelnut in appearance, garbanzo beans have a nutty flavor and slightly crunchy texture. Indian cooks grind these to make a flour called gram or besan, which is used to make breads and thicken sauces.

1 Place the drained garbanzo beans in a bowl.

2 Using a sharp knife, cut the potatoes into even-size dice.

3 Place the diced potatoes in a saucepan of water and boil until cooked through. Test by inserting the tip of a knife into the potatoes — they should feel soft and tender. Drain and set the potatoes aside until required.

4 Using a sharp knife, finely chop the onion. Set aside until required.

5 Mix together the tamarind paste and water in a small mixing bowl.

6 Add the cayenne pepper, sugar, and salt to the tamarind paste mixture and mix together. Pour the mixture over the garbanzo beans.

7 Add the onion and the diced potatoes, and stir to mix. Season to taste with a little salt.

8 Transfer to a serving bowl and garnish with the tomatoes, chilies, and cilantro leaves.

Brown Rice Gratin

This dish is extremely versatile and could be made with any vegetables that you have to hand.

NUTRITIONAL INFORMATION

Calories 321	Sugars 6g	
Protein 10g	Fat 18g	
Carbohydrate . . .32g	Saturates 9g	

15 MINS   1 HOUR

SERVES 4

INGREDIENTS

⅓ cup brown rice

2 tbsp butter or margarine, plus extra
    for greasing

1 red onion, chopped

2 garlic cloves, crushed

1 carrot, cut into matchsticks

1 zucchini, sliced

2¾ oz baby-corn-on-the-cobs,
    halved lengthways

2 tbsp sunflower seeds

3 tbsp chopped mixed herbs

1 cup grated mozzarella cheese

2 tbsp whole wheat breadcrumbs

salt and pepper

VARIATION

Use an alternative rice, such as basmati, and flavor the dish with curry spices, if you prefer.

1 Cook the rice in a saucepan of boiling, lightly salted water for 20 minutes. Drain well.

2 Lightly grease a 3¾ cup ovenproof dish with butter.

3 Heat the butter in a skillet. Add the onion and cook, stirring constantly, for 2 minutes, or until soft and translucent.

4 Add the garlic, carrot, zucchini, and corn-on-the-cobs and cook, stirring constantly, for a further 5 minutes.

5 Mix the rice with the sunflower seeds and mixed herbs and stir into the pan.

6 Stir in half of the mozzarella cheese and season with salt and pepper to taste.

7 Spoon the mixture into the prepared dish and top with the breadcrumbs and remaining cheese. Cook in a preheated oven, 350°F, for about 25–30 minutes, or until the cheese has begun to turn golden. Serve immediately.

Cheese & Onion Rösti

These grated potato cakes are also known as straw cakes, as they resemble a straw mat! Serve them with a tomato sauce or salad.

NUTRITIONAL INFORMATION

Calories 307   Sugars 4g
Protein . . . . .8g   Fat 13g
Carbohydrate . . .42g   Saturates 6g

10 MINS   40 MINS

SERVES 4

INGREDIENTS

2 lb potatoes

1 onion, grated

½ cup grated Gruyère cheese

2 tbsp chopped parsley

1 tbsp olive oil

2 tbsp butter

salt and pepper

TO GARNISH

shredded scallion

1 small tomato, quartered

1 Parboil the potatoes in a pan of lightly salted boiling water for 10 minutes and leave to cool. Peel the potatoes and grate with a coarse grater. Place the grated potatoes in a large mixing bowl.

COOK'S TIP

The potato cakes should be flattened as much as possible during cooking, otherwise the outside will be cooked before the center.

2 Stir in the onion, cheese, and parsley. Season well with salt and pepper. Divide the potato mixture into 4 portions of equal size and form them into cakes.

3 Heat half of the olive oil and butter in a skillet and cook 2 of the potato cakes over a high heat for 1 minute, then reduce the heat and cook for 5 minutes, until they are golden underneath. Turn them over and cook for a further 5 minutes.

4 Repeat with the other half of the oil and the remaining butter to cook the remaining 2 cakes. Transfer to warm individual serving plates, garnish and serve immediately.

Spiced Corn & Nut Mix

A tasty mixture of buttery-spiced nuts, raisins, and popcorn to enjoy as a snack or with pre-dinner drinks.

NUTRITIONAL INFORMATION

Calories	372	Sugars	.........9g
Protein	.........8g	Fat	..........31g
Carbohydrate	...16g	Saturates	.......9g

  5 MINS   10 MINS

SERVES 6

INGREDIENTS

2 tbsp vegetable oil

¼ cup popping corn

¼ cup butter

1 garlic clove, crushed

⅓ cup unblanched almonds

½ cup unsalted cashew nuts

½ cup unsalted peanuts

1 tsp vegetarian Worcestershire sauce

1 tsp curry powder or paste

¼ tsp cayenne pepper

⅓ cup seedless raisins

salt

1 Heat the oil in a saucepan. Add the popping corn, stir well, then cover and cook over a fairly high heat for 3-5 minutes, holding the saucepan lid firmly and shaking the pan frequently until the popping stops.

2 Turn the popped corn into a dish, discarding any unpopped corn kernels.

3 Melt the butter in a frying pan, add the garlic, almonds, cashew nuts and peanuts, then stir in the Worcestershire sauce, curry powder or paste, and cayenne pepper and cook over a medium heat, stirring frequently, for 2–3 minutes.

4 Remove the pan from the heat and stir in the raisins and popped corn. Season with salt to taste and mix thoroughly. Transfer to a serving bowl and serve warm or cold.

VARIATION

Use a mixture of any unsalted nuts of your choice — walnuts, pecans, hazelnuts, Brazils, macadamia, and pine nuts. For a less fiery flavor, omit the curry powder and cayenne pepper and add 1 tsp cumin seeds, 1 tsp ground coriander and ½ tsp paprika.

Three-Cheese Fondue

A hot cheese dip made from three different cheeses can be prepared easily and with guaranteed success in the microwave oven.

NUTRITIONAL INFORMATION

Calories	565	Sugars	.........1g
Protein	........29g	Fat	..........38g
Carbohydrate	...15g	Saturates	......24g

 15 MINS   10 MINS

SERVES 4

I N G R E D I E N T S

1 garlic clove

1¼ cups dry white wine

2 cups grated mild hard cheese

1 cup grated Gruyère cheese

1 cup grated mozzarella cheese

2 tbsp cornstarch

pepper

T O   S E R V E

French bread

vegetables, such as zucchini,
    mushrooms, baby-corn-on-the-cobs
    and cauliflower

1 Bruise the garlic by placing the flat side of a knife on top and pressing down with the heel of your hand.

2 Rub the garlic around the inside of a large bowl. Discard the garlic.

3 Pour the wine into the bowl and heat, uncovered, on HIGH power for 3–4 minutes, until hot but not boiling.

4 Gradually add the hard and Gruyère cheeses, stirring well after each addition, then add the mozzarella. Stir until completely melted.

5 Mix the cornstarch with a little water to a smooth paste and stir into the cheese mixture. Season to taste with pepper.

6 Cover and cook on MEDIUM power for 6 minutes, stirring twice during cooking, until the sauce is smooth.

7 Cut the French bread into cubes and the vegetables into batons, slices, or florets. To serve, keep the fondue warm over a spirit lamp or reheat as necessary in the microwave oven. Dip in cubes of French bread and batons, slices, or florets of vegetables.

COOK'S TIP

Make sure you add the cheese to the wine gradually, mixing well in between each addition, otherwise the mixture might curdle.

Cheese & Potato Slices

This recipe takes a while to prepare but it is well worth the effort. The golden potato slices coated in breadcrumbs and cheese are delicious.

NUTRITIONAL INFORMATION

Calories 560	Sugars 3g
Protein 19g	Fat 31g
Carbohydrate ...55g	Saturates 7g

10 MINS   40 MINS

SERVES 4

INGREDIENTS

3 large waxy potatoes, unpeeled and
 thickly sliced

1 cup fresh white breadcrumbs

½ cup grated Parmesan cheese

1½ tsp cayenne pepper

2 eggs, beaten

oil, for deep frying

cayenne pepper, for dusting (optional)

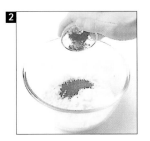

1 Cook the sliced potatoes in a saucepan of boiling water for about 10-15 minutes, or until the potatoes are just tender. Drain thoroughly.

2 Mix the breadcrumbs, cheese, and cayenne pepper together in a bowl, then transfer to a shallow dish. Pour the beaten eggs into a separate shallow dish.

3 Dip the potato slices first in egg and then roll them in the breadcrumbs to coat completely.

4 Heat the oil in a large saucepan or deep-fryer to 350°F or until a cube of bread browns in 30 seconds. Cook the cheese and potato slices, in several batches, for 4–5 minutes, or until a golden brown color.

5 Remove the cheese and potato slices from the oil with a draining spoon and drain thoroughly on paper towels. Keep the cheese and potato slices warm while you cook the remaining batches.

6 Transfer the cheese and potato slices to warm individual serving plates. Dust lightly with cayenne pepper, if using, and serve immediately.

COOK'S TIP

The cheese and potato slices may be coated in the breadcrumb mixture in advance and then stored in the refrigerator until ready to use.

Pasta, Legumes, & Pulses

Grains and legumes are universally important staple foods. They are highly nutritious as they are an excellent source of protein, iron, calcium, and B vitamins, and are virtually  fat-free. Grains include wheat, corn, barley, rye, oats, buckwheat, and many different varieties of rice, as well as associated flours. Legumes include garbanzo beans, yellow and green split peas, a fascinating variety of beans, together with many types of lentil. Grains and legumes form a substantial base to which other ingredients can be added. Each has its own flavor and texture, so it is worth experimenting for a variety of dishes.

Baked Pasta

This pasta dish is baked in a pudding bowl and served cut into slices. It looks and tastes terrific and is great when you want to impress.

NUTRITIONAL INFORMATION

Calories	179	Sugars	.........6g
Protein	.........8g	Fat	..........10g
Carbohydrate	...16g	Saturates	.......3g

 10 MINS 1 HR 5 MINS

SERVES 8

INGREDIENTS

1 cup dried pasta shapes, such as
   penne or casareccia

1 tbsp olive oil

1 leek, chopped

3 garlic cloves, crushed

1 green bell pepper, seeded and chopped

14 oz can chopped tomatoes

2 tbsp chopped, pitted black olives

2 eggs, beaten

1 tbsp chopped basil

TOMATO SAUCE

1 tbsp olive oil

1 onion, chopped

8 oz can chopped tomatoes

1 tsp superfine sugar

2 tbsp tomato paste

¾ cup vegetable stock

salt and pepper

1 Cook the pasta in a saucepan of boiling lightly salted water for 8 minutes. Drain thoroughly.

2 Meanwhile, heat the oil in a saucepan. Add the leek and garlic and stir-fry, stirring constantly, for 2 minutes. Add the bell pepper, tomatoes, and olives and cook for a further 5 minutes.

3 Remove the pan from the heat and stir in the pasta, beaten eggs and basil. Season well, and spoon into a lightly greased 4 cup ovenproof ovenproof bowl.

4 Place the pudding bowl in a roasting pan and half-fill the pan with boiling water. Cover and cook in a preheated oven 350°F for 40 minutes, until set.

5 To make the sauce, heat the oil in a pan and sauté the onion for 2 minutes. Add the remaining ingredients and cook for 10 minutes. Put the sauce in a food processor and process until smooth. Return to a clean saucepan and heat through.

6 Turn the pasta out of the pudding bowl on to a warm plate. Slice and serve with the tomato sauce.

Vegetable Cannelloni

This dish is made with prepared cannelloni tubes, but may also be made by rolling ready-bought lasagne sheets.

NUTRITIONAL INFORMATION

Calories	594	Sugars	........12g
Protein	........13g	Fat	..........38g
Carbohydrate	...52g	Saturates	.......7g

10 MINS   45 MINS

SERVES 4

INGREDIENTS

1 eggplant

½ cup olive oil

8 oz spinach

2 garlic cloves, crushed

1 tsp ground cumin

1 cup mushrooms, chopped

12 cannelloni tubes

salt and pepper

TOMATO SAUCE

1 tbsp olive oil

1 onion, chopped

2 garlic cloves, crushed

2 x 14 oz cans chopped tomatoes

1 tsp superfine sugar

2 tbsp chopped basil

½ cup sliced mozzarella

COOK'S TIP

You can prepare the tomato sauce in advance and store it in the refrigerator for up to 24 hours.

1 Cut the eggplant into small dice.

2 Heat the oil in a skillet. Add the eggplant and cook over a medium heat, stirring frequently, for 2–3 minutes.

3 Add the spinach, garlic, cumin, and mushrooms. Season and cook, stirring, for 2–3 minutes. Spoon the mixture into the cannelloni tubes and place in an ovenproof dish in a single layer.

4 To make the sauce, heat the olive oil in a saucepan and stir-fry the onion and garlic for 1 minute. Add the tomatoes, superfine sugar, and chopped basil and bring to a boil. Reduce the heat and simmer for about 5 minutes. Pour the sauce over the cannelloni tubes.

5 Arrange the sliced mozzarella on top of the sauce and cook in a preheated oven at 375°F for 30 minutes, or until the cheese is bubbling and golden brown. Serve immediately.

Vegetable Lasagne

This colorful and tasty lasagne has layers of vegetables in tomato sauce and eggplants, all topped with a rich cheese sauce.

NUTRITIONAL INFORMATION

Calories 544	Sugars 18g
Protein 20g	Fat 26g
Carbohydrate ...61g	Saturates 12g

  35 MINS   55 MINS

SERVES 4

INGREDIENTS

1 eggplant, sliced

3 tbsp olive oil

2 garlic cloves, crushed

1 red onion, halved and sliced

3 mixed bell peppers, seeded and diced

8 oz mixed mushrooms, sliced

2 celery stalks, sliced

1 zucchini, diced

½ tsp chili powder

½ tsp ground cumin

2 tomatoes, chopped

1¼ cups sieved tomatoes

2 tbsp chopped basil

8 no pre-cook lasagne verdi sheets

salt and pepper

CHEESE SAUCE

2 tbsp butter or margarine

1 tbsp flour

⅔ cup vegetable stock

1¼ cups milk

¾ cup grated hard cheese

1 tsp Dijon mustard

1 tbsp chopped basil

1 egg, beaten

1 Place the eggplant slices in a colander, sprinkle with salt, and leave for 20 minutes. Rinse under cold water, drain, and reserve.

2 Heat the oil in a pan and stir-fry the garlic and onion for 1–2 minutes. Add the bell peppers, mushrooms, celery, and zucchini and cook, stirring constantly, for 3–4 minutes.

3 Stir in the spices and cook for 1 minute. Mix in the tomatoes, sieved tomatoes, and basil and season to taste with salt and pepper.

4 For the sauce, melt the butter in a pan, stir in the flour, and cook for 1 minute. Remove from the heat, stir in the stock and milk, return to the heat, and add half the cheese and the mustard. Boil, stirring, until thickened. Stir in the basil. Remove from the heat and stir in the egg.

5 Place half the lasagne in an ovenproof dish. Top with half the vegetable mixture then half the eggplants. Repeat and spoon the cheese sauce on top. Sprinkle with cheese and cook in a preheated oven at 350°F for 40 minutes.

Penne & Vegetables

The sweet cherry tomatoes in this recipe add color and flavor and are complemented by the black olives and bell peppers.

NUTRITIONAL INFORMATION

Calories 380	Sugars 6g
Protein 8g	Fat 16g
Carbohydrate . . .48g	Saturates 7g

 10 MINS   25 MINS

SERVES 4

INGREDIENTS

2 cups dried penne

2 tbsp olive oil

2 tbsp butter

2 garlic cloves, crushed

1 green bell pepper, seeded and
   thinly sliced

1 yellow bell pepper, seeded and
   thinly sliced

16 cherry tomatoes, halved

1 tbsp chopped oregano

½ cup dry white wine

2 tbsp quartered, pitted black olives

1 bunch arugula

salt and pepper

oregano sprigs, to garnish

VARIATION

If arugula is unavailable, spinach is a good substitute. Follow the same cooking instructions as for arugula.

1 Cook the pasta in a saucepan of boiling salted water for 8–10 minutes or until al dente. Drain thoroughly.

2 Heat the oil and butter in a pan until the butter melts. Sauté the garlic for 30 seconds. Add the bell peppers and cook, stirring, for 3–4 minutes.

3 Stir in the cherry tomatoes, oregano, wine, and olives and cook for 3–4 minutes. Season well with salt and pepper and stir in the arugula until just wilted.

4 Transfer the pasta to a serving dish, spoon over the sauce and garnish.

Pear & Walnut Pasta

This is quite an unusual combination of ingredients in a savory dish, but is absolutely wonderful tossed into a fine pasta, such as spaghetti.

NUTRITIONAL INFORMATION

Calories	508	Sugars	.........9g
Protein	........15g	Fat	..........27g
Carbohydrate	...50g	Saturates	......11g

  10 MINS   20 MINS

SERVES 4

I N G R E D I E N T S

8 oz dried spaghetti

2 small ripe pears, peeled and sliced

¾ cup vegetable stock

6 tbsp dry white wine

2 tbsp butter

1 tbsp olive oil

1 red onion, quartered and sliced

1 garlic clove, crushed

½ cup walnut halves

2 tbsp chopped oregano

1 tbsp lemon juice

2¾ oz dolcelatte cheese

salt and pepper

oregano sprigs, to garnish

1 Cook the pasta in a saucepan of boiling, lightly salted water for about 8–10 minutes, or until al dente. Drain thoroughly and keep warm until required.

2 Meanwhile, place the pears in a pan and pour over the stock and wine. Poach the pears over a low heat for 10 minutes. Drain, reserve the cooking liquid, and set the pears aside.

3 Heat the butter and oil in a saucepan until the butter melts. Add the onion and garlic and sauté over a low heat, stirring frequently for 2–3 minutes.

4 Stir in the walnut halves, oregano, and lemon juice.

5 Stir in the reserved pears with 4 tablespoons of the poaching liquid.

6 Crumble the dolcelatte cheese into the pan and cook over a low heat, stirring occasionally, for 1–2 minutes, or until the cheese is just beginning to melt. Season with salt and pepper to taste.

7 Add the pasta and toss in the sauce, using two forks. Garnish and serve.

Spinach & Nut Pasta

Use any pasta shapes that you have for this recipe. Multicolored tricolore pasta is visually the most attractive to use.

NUTRITIONAL INFORMATION

Calories	603	Sugars	.........5g
Protein	........12g	Fat	..........41g
Carbohydrate	...46g	Saturates	.......6g

🍲 5 MINS   🕐 15 MINS

SERVES 4

INGREDIENTS

2 cups dried pasta shapes

½ cup olive oil

2 garlic cloves, crushed

1 onion, quartered and sliced

3 large flat mushrooms, sliced

8 oz spinach

2 tbsp pine nuts

6 tbsp dry white wine

salt and pepper

Parmesan shavings, to garnish

1 Cook the pasta in a saucepan of boiling salted water for 8–10 minutes, or until al dente. Drain well.

2 Meanwhile, heat the oil in a large saucepan and stir-fry the garlic and onion for 1 minute.

COOK'S TIP

Grate a little nutmeg over the dish for extra flavor, as this spice has a particular affinity with spinach.

3 Add the sliced mushrooms to the pan and cook over a medium heat, stirring occasionally, for 2 minutes.

4 Lower the heat, add the spinach to the pan, and cook, stirring occasionally, for 4–5 minutes, or until the spinach has wilted.

5 Stir in the pine nuts and wine, season to taste with salt and pepper, and cook for 1 minute.

6 Transfer the pasta to a warm serving bowl and toss the sauce into it, mixing well. Garnish with shavings of Parmesan cheese and serve.

Thai-Style Stir-Fried Noodles

This dish is considered the Thai national dish, as it is made and eaten everywhere – a one-dish, fast food for eating on the move.

NUTRITIONAL INFORMATION

Calories 407	Sugars 11g
Protein 14g	Fat 16g
Carbohydrate . . .56g	Saturates 3g

  15 MINS   5 MINS

SERVES 4

I N G R E D I E N T S

8 oz dried rice noodles

2 red chilies, seeded and finely chopped

2 shallots, finely chopped

2 tbsp sugar

2 tbsp tamarind water

1 tbsp lime juice

2 tbsp light soy sauce

1 tbsp sunflower oil

1 tsp sesame oil

¾ cup diced smoked bean curd

pepper

2 tbsp chopped roasted peanuts,
    to garnish

1 Cook the rice noodles as directed on the pack, or soak them in boiling water for 5 minutes.

2 Grind together the chilies, shallots, sugar, tamarind water, lime juice, light soy sauce, and pepper to taste.

3 Heat both the oils together in a preheated wok or large, heavy skillet over a high heat. Add the bean curd and stir for 1 minute.

4 Add the chili mixture, bring to a boil, and cook, stirring constantly, for about 2 minutes, until thickened.

5 Drain the rice noodles and add them to the chili mixture. Use 2 spoons to lift and stir them until they are no longer steaming. Serve immediately, garnished with the peanuts.

COOK'S TIP

This is a quick one-dish meal that is very useful if you are catering for a single vegetarian in the family.

Stir-Fried Japanese Noodles

This quick dish is an ideal lunchtime meal, packed with whatever mixture of mushrooms you like in a sweet sauce.

NUTRITIONAL INFORMATION

Calories 379	Sugars 8g	
Protein 12g	Fat 13g	
Carbohydrate ...53g	Saturates 3g	

🍲 15 MINS   🕐 15 MINS

SERVES 4

INGREDIENTS

8 oz Japanese egg noodles

2 tbsp sunflower oil

1 red onion, sliced

1 garlic clove, crushed

1 lb 2 oz mixed mushrooms, such as
  shiitake, oyster, brown cap

12 oz pak choi

2 tbsp sweet sherry

6 tbsp soy sauce

4 scallions, sliced

1 tbsp toasted sesame seeds

1 Place the egg noodles in a large bowl. Pour over enough boiling water to cover and leave to soak for 10 minutes.

2 Heat the sunflower oil in a large preheated wok.

3 Add the red onion and garlic to the wok and stir-fry for 2–3 minutes, or until softened.

4 Add the mushrooms to the wok and stir-fry for about 5 minutes, or until the mushrooms have softened.

5 Drain the Japanese egg noodles thoroughly and set aside.

6 Add the the pak choi, noodles, sweet sherry, and soy sauce to the wok. Toss all of the ingredients together to mix well and stir-fry for 2–3 minutes, or until the liquid is just bubbling.

7 Transfer the mushroom noodles to warm serving bowls and scatter with sliced scallions and toasted sesame seeds. Serve immediately.

COOK'S TIP

The variety of mushrooms in supermarkets has greatly improved and a good mixture should be easily obtainable. If not, use the readily available button and flat mushrooms.

Spicy Fried Noodles

This is a simple idea to add an extra kick to noodles, which accompany many main course dishes in Thailand.

NUTRITIONAL INFORMATION

Calories	...... .568	Sugars	.... .3g
Protein	........16g	Fat	.... .19g
Carbohydrate	...90g	Saturates	...... .4g

 15 MINS   3-5 MINS

SERVES 4

I N G R E D I E N T S

1 lb 2 oz medium egg noodles

1 cup beansprouts

½ oz chives

3 tbsp sunflower oil

1 garlic clove, crushed

4 fresh green chilies, seeded, sliced, and
  soaked in 2 tbsp rice vinegar

salt

1 Place the noodles in a bowl, cover with boiling water, and soak for 10 minutes. Drain and set aside.

2 Pick over the beansprouts and soak in cold water while you cut the chives into 1 inch pieces. Set a few chives aside for the garnish. Drain the beansprouts thoroughly.

3 Heat the oil in a preheated wok or large, heavy-bottomed skillet. Add the crushed garlic and stir; add the chilies, and stir-fry for about 1 minute, until fragrant.

4 Add the beansprouts, stir, and then add the noodles. Stir in salt to taste and add the chives. Using 2 spoons or a wok scoop, lift and toss the noodles for 1 minute.

5 Transfer the noodles to a warm serving dish, garnish with the reserved chives, and serve immediately.

COOK'S TIP

Soaking a chili in rice vinegar has the effect of distributing the hot chili flavor throughout the dish. To reduce the heat, you can slice the chili more thickly before soaking.

Special Fried Rice

In this simple recipe, cooked rice is fried with vegetables and cashew nuts. It can either be eaten on its own or served as an accompaniment.

NUTRITIONAL INFORMATION

Calories 355	Sugars 6g
Protein 9g	Fat 15g
Carbohydrate . . .48g	Saturates 3g

10 MINS   30 MINS

SERVES 4

I N G R E D I E N T S

generous ¾ cup long grain rice

½ cup cashew nuts

1 carrot

½ cucumber

1 yellow bell pepper

2 scallions

2 tbsp vegetable oil

1 garlic clove, crushed

¾ cup frozen peas, thawed

1 tbsp soy sauce

1 tsp salt

cilantro leaves, to garnish

1 Bring a large pan of water to a boil. Add the rice and simmer for 15 minutes. Tip the rice into a strainer and rinse; drain thoroughly.

COOK'S TIP

Replace any of the vegetables in this recipe with others suitable for a stir-fry. Using leftover rice makes this a perfect last-minute dish.

2 Heat a wok or large, heavy-bottomed skillet, add the cashew nuts, and dry-fry until lightly browned. Remove and set aside.

3 Cut the carrot in half along the length, then slice thinly into semi-circles. Halve the cucumber and remove the seeds, using a teaspoon, then dice the flesh. Seed and slice the bell pepper and chop the scallions.

4 Heat the oil in a wok or large skillet. Add the prepared vegetables and the garlic. Stir-fry for 3 minutes. Add the rice, peas, soy sauce, and salt. Continue to stir-fry until well mixed and thoroughly heated.

5 Stir in the reserved cashew nuts. Transfer to a warmed serving dish, garnish with cilantro leaves and serve immediately.

Chow Mein

Egg noodles are cooked and then fried with a colorful variety of vegetables to make this well-known and everpopular dish.

NUTRITIONAL INFORMATION

Calories 669   Sugars 9g
Protein . . . . .19g   Fat 23g
Carbohydrate . .100g   Saturates 4g

 15 MINS   10 MINS

SERVES 4

INGREDIENTS

1 lb 2 oz egg noodles

4 tbsp vegetable oil

1 onion, thinly sliced

2 carrots, cut into thin sticks

1⅓cups button mushrooms, quartered

4½ oz snow peas

½ cucumber, cut into sticks

2 cups spinach, shredded

2 cups beansprouts

2 tbsp dark soy sauce

1 tbsp sherry

1 tsp salt

1 tsp sugar

1 tsp cornstarch

1 tsp sesame oil

COOK'S TIP

For a spicy hot chow mein, add 1 tablespoon chili sauce or substitute chili oil for the sesame oil.

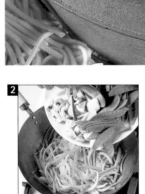  

1 Cook the noodles according to the directions on the package. Drain and rinse under cold running water until cool. Set aside.

2 Heat 3 tablespoons of the vegetable oil in a preheated wok or skillet. Add the onion and carrots, and stir-fry for 1 minute. Add the mushrooms, snow peas, and cucumber and stir-fry for 1 minute.

3 Stir in the remaining vegetable oil and add the drained noodles, together with the spinach and beansprouts.

4 Blend together all the remaining ingredients and pour over the noodles and vegetables.

5 Stir-fry until the noodle mixture is thoroughly heated through, transfer to a warm serving dish, and serve.

Risotto Verde

Risotto is an Italian dish which is easy to make and uses risotto rice, onion, and garlic as a base for a range of savory recipes.

NUTRITIONAL INFORMATION

Calories	374	Sugars	.........5g
Protein	........10g	Fat	...........9g
Carbohydrate	...55g	Saturates	.......2g

 5 MINS · 35 MINS

SERVES 4

I N G R E D I E N T S

7½ cups vegetable stock

2 tbsp olive oil

2 garlic cloves, crushed

2 leeks, shredded

1¼ cups risotto rice

1¼ cups dry white wine

4 tbsp chopped mixed herbs

8 oz baby spinach

3 tbsp unsweetened yogurt

salt and pepper

shredded leek, to garnish

1 Pour the stock into a large saucepan and bring to a boil. Reduce the heat to a simmer.

2 Meanwhile, heat the oil in a separate pan. Add the garlic and leeks and stir-fry over a low heat, stirring occasionally, for 2–3 minutes, until soft.

3 Stir in the rice and cook for 2 minutes, stirring until each grain is coated with oil.

4 Pour in half of the wine and a little of the hot stock. Cook over a low heat until all of the liquid has been absorbed. Add the remaining stock and the wine, a little at a time, and cook over a low heat for 25 minutes, or until the rice is creamy.

5 Stir in the chopped mixed herbs and baby spinach, season to taste with salt and pepper and cook for 2 minutes.

6 Stir in the unsweetened yogurt. Transfer to a warm serving dish, garnish with the shredded leek and serve immediately.

COOK'S TIP

Do not try to hurry the process of cooking the risotto as the rice must absorb the liquid slowly in order for it to reach the correct consistency.

Risotto in Shells

An eggplant is halved and filled with a risotto mixture, topped with cheese, and baked to make a snack or quick meal for two.

NUTRITIONAL INFORMATION

Calories 444   Sugars 20g
Protein . . . . .13g   Fat 23g
Carbohydrate . . .50g   Saturates 8g

 🍽 20 MINS   🕐 55 MINS

SERVES 2

I N G R E D I E N T S

¼ cup mixed long grain and wild rice

1 eggplant, about 12 oz

1 tbsp olive oil

1 small onion, finely chopped

1 garlic clove, crushed

½ small red bell pepper, seeded
    and chopped

2 tbsp water

3 tbsp raisins

¼ cup cashew nuts, roughly chopped

½ tsp dried oregano

⅓ cup grated sharp Cheddar or Parmesan
    cheese

salt and pepper

oregano or parsley to garnish

1 Cook the rice in boiling salted water for about 15 minutes, until just tender. Drain, rinse, and drain again.

2 Bring a large saucepan of water to a boil. Cut the stem off the eggplant and cut in half lengthways. Cut out the flesh from the center carefully, leaving about a ½ inch shell. Blanch the shells in a boiling water for 3–4 minutes. Drain thoroughly. Chop the eggplant flesh finely.

3 Heat the oil in a saucepan or skillet. Add the onion and garlic and fry over a low heat until beginning to soften, then add the bell pepper and eggplant flesh and continue cooking for a 2–3 minutes before adding the water and cooking for a further 2–3 minutes.

4 Stir the raisins, cashew nuts, dried oregano, and rice into the eggplant mixture and season to taste with salt and pepper.

5 Place the eggplant shells in an ovenproof dish and spoon in the rice mixture, piling it up well. Cover and cook in a preheated oven at 375°F for 20 minutes.

6 Remove the lid and sprinkle the cheese over the rice. Place under a preheated medium broiler and cook for 3–4 minutes, until golden brown and bubbling. Serve hot garnished with oregano or parsley.

Rice with Fruit & Nuts

Here is a tasty and filling rice dish that is nice and spicy and includes fruits for a refreshing flavor and toasted nuts for a crunchy texture.

NUTRITIONAL INFORMATION

Calories 423	Sugars 19g	
Protein 10g	Fat 17g	
Carbohydrate . . .62g	Saturates 2g	

 20 MINS · 1 HOUR

SERVES 6

INGREDIENTS

4 tbsp vegetable ghee or oil

1 large onion, chopped

2 garlic cloves, crushed

1 inch piece gingerroot, chopped

1 tsp chili powder

1 tsp cumin seeds

1 tbsp mild or medium curry powder
 or paste

1½ cups brown rice

3½ cups boiling vegetable stock

14 oz can chopped tomatoes

salt and pepper

6 oz ready-to-eat dried apricots or
 peaches, cut into slivers

1 red bell pepper, seeded and diced

¾ cup frozen peas

1-2 small, slightly green bananas

⅓-½ cup toasted nuts, such as almonds,
 cashews, and hazelnuts or pine kernels

cilantro sprigs, to garnish

1 Heat the ghee or oil in a large saucepan. Add the onion and fry over a low heat for 3 minutes. Stir in the garlic, ginger, spices and rice and cook gently, stirring constantly, for 2 minutes, until the rice is coated in the spiced oil.

2 Pour in the boiling stock, add the chopped tomatoes and season with salt and pepper to taste. Bring to the boil, then reduce the heat, cover and simmer gently for 40 minutes, or until the rice is almost cooked and most of the liquid has been absorbed.

3 Add the slivered apricots or peaches, diced red (bell) pepper and peas. Cover and continue cooking for 10 minutes. Remove from the heat and allow to stand for 5 minutes without uncovering.

4 Peel and slice the bananas. Uncover the rice mixture and fork through to mix the ingredients together. Add the toasted nuts and sliced banana and toss lightly. Transfer to a warm serving platter and garnish with coriander (cilantro) sprigs. Serve hot.

Deep South Rice & Beans

Cajun spices add a flavor of the Deep South to this colorful rice and red kidney bean salad.

NUTRITIONAL INFORMATION

Calories	336	Sugars	.........8g
Protein	.........7g	Fat	..........13g
Carbohydrate	...51g	Saturates	.......2g

 10 MINS   15 MINS

SERVES 4

I N G R E D I E N T S

scant 1 cup long grain rice

4 tbsp olive oil

1 small green bell pepper, seeded
   and chopped

1 small red bell pepper, seeded
   and chopped

1 onion, finely chopped

1 small red or green chili, seeded and
   finely chopped

2 tomatoes, chopped

½ cup canned red kidney beans,
   rinsed and drained

1 tbsp chopped fresh basil

2 tsp chopped fresh thyme

1 tsp Cajun spice

salt and pepper

fresh basil leaves, to garnish

1 Cook the rice in plenty of boiling, lightly salted water for about 12 minutes, until just tender. Rinse with cold water and drain well.

2 Meanwhile, heat the olive oil in a skillet and fry the green and red bell peppers and onion gently for about 5 minutes, until softened.

3 Add the chili and tomatoes, and cook for a further 2 minutes.

4 Add the vegetable mixture and red kidney beans to the rice. Stir well to combine thoroughly.

5 Stir the chopped herbs and Cajun spice into the rice mixture. Season to taste with salt and pepper, and serve, garnished with basil leaves.

Spiced Basmati Pilau

The whole spices are not meant to be eaten and may be removed before serving. Omit the broccoli and mushrooms for a plain, spiced pilau.

NUTRITIONAL INFORMATION

Calories	450	Sugars	........3g
Protein	.........9g	Fat	..........15g
Carbohydrate	...76g	Saturates	.......2g

 20 MINS   25 MINS

SERVES 6

I N G R E D I E N T S

2½ cups basmati rice

6 oz broccoli, trimmed

6 tbsp vegetable oil

2 large onions, chopped

3 cups sliced mushrooms

2 garlic cloves, crushed

6 cardamom pods, split

6 whole cloves

8 black peppercorns

1 cinnamon stick or piece of cassia bark

1 tsp ground turmeric

5 cups boiling vegetable stock or water

salt and pepper

⅓ cup seedless raisins

½ cup unsalted pistachios, coarsely
   chopped

VARIATION

For added richness, you could stir a spoonful of vegetable ghee through the rice mixture just before serving. A little diced red bell pepper and a few cooked peas forked through at step 4 add a colorful touch.

1 Place the rice in a strainer and wash well under cold running water. Drain. Trim off most of the broccoli stalk, cut into small florets, quarter the stalk lengthways, and cut diagonally into ½ inch pieces.

2 Heat the oil in a large saucepan. Add the onions and broccoli stalks and cook over a low heat, stirring frequently, for 3 minutes. Add the mushrooms, rice, garlic, and spices and cook for 1 minute, stirring, until the rice is coated in oil.

3 Add a boiling stock and season to taste with salt and pepper. Stir in the broccoli florets and return the mixture to a boil. Cover, reduce the heat, and cook over a low heat for 15 minutes without uncovering the pan.

4 Remove from the heat and leave to stand for 5 minutes without uncovering. Add the raisins and pistachios and gently fork through to fluff up the grains. Serve hot.

Thai Jasmine Rice

Every Thai meal has as its centerpiece a big bowl of steaming, fluffy Thai jasmine rice, to which salt should not be added.

NUTRITIONAL INFORMATION

Calories 239	Sugars 0g	
Protein 5g	Fat 2g	
Carbohydrate ...54g	Saturates 0.6g	

 5 MINS   10–15 MINS

SERVES 4

I N G R E D I E N T S

O P E N   P A N   M E T H O D

generous 1 cup Thai jasmine rice

4 cups water

A B S O R P T I O N   M E T H O D

generous 1 cup Thai jasmine rice

scant 2 cups water

COOK'S TIP

Thai jasmine rice can be frozen. Freeze in a plastic sealed container. Frozen rice is ideal for stir-fry dishes, as the process seems to separate the grains.

1 For the open pan method, rinse the rice in a strainer under cold running water and leave to drain.

2 Bring the water to a boil. Add the rice, stir once, and return to a medium boil. Cook, uncovered, for 8–10 minutes, until tender.

3 Drain thoroughly and fork through lightly before serving.

4 For the absorption method, rinse the rice under cold running water.

5 Put the rice and water into a saucepan and bring to a boil. Stir once and then cover the pan tightly. Lower the heat as much as possible. Cook for 10 minutes. Leave to rest for 5 minutes.

6 Fork through lightly and serve the rice immediately.

Vegetable Couscous

Couscous is a semolina grain which is very quick and easy to cook, and it makes a pleasant change from rice or pasta.

NUTRITIONAL INFORMATION

Calories ....280 Sugars 13g
Protein ....10g Fat 7g
Carbohydrate ...47g Saturates 1g

20 MINS   40 MINS

SERVES 4

I N G R E D I E N T S

2 tbsp vegetable oil

1 large onion, coarsely chopped

1 carrot, chopped

1 turnip, chopped

2½ cups vegetable stock

1 cup couscous

2 tomatoes, peeled and quartered

2 zucchini, chopped

1 red bell pepper, seeded and chopped

4½ oz green beans, chopped

grated rind of 1 lemon

pinch of ground turmeric (optional)

1 tbsp finely chopped fresh cilantro or
    parsley

salt and pepper

fresh flat leaf parsley sprigs,
    to garnish

1 Heat the oil in a large saucepan and fry the onion, carrot, and turnip for 3–4 minutes. Add the stock, bring to a boil, cover and simmer for 20 minutes.

2 Meanwhile, put the couscous in a bowl and moisten with a little boiling water, stirring, until the grains have swollen and separated.

3 Add the tomatoes, zucchini, bell pepper, and green beans to the saucepan.

4 Stir the lemon rind into the couscous and add the turmeric, if using, and mix thoroughly. Put the couscous in a steamer and position it over the saucepan of vegetables. Simmer the vegetables so that the couscous steams for about 8–10 minutes.

5 Pile the couscous on to warmed serving plates. Ladle the vegetables and some of the liquid over the top. Scatter with the cilantro or parsley and serve at once, garnished with parsley sprigs.

Couscous Royale

Serve this stunning dish as a centerpiece for a North African-style feast; it will prove to be a truly memorable meal.

NUTRITIONAL INFORMATION

Calories 329	Sugars 31g	
Protein 6g	Fat 13g	
Carbohydrate ...50g	Saturates 6g	

25 MINS   45 MINS

SERVES 6

I N G R E D I E N T S

3 carrots

3 zucchini

12 oz pumpkin or squash

5 cups vegetable stock

2 cinnamon sticks, broken in half

2 tsp ground cumin

1 tsp ground coriander

pinch of saffron strands

2 tbsp olive oil

pared rind and juice of 1 lemon

2 tbsp clear honey

2¾ cups pre-cooked couscous

¼ cup butter or, softened

1 cup large seedless raisins

salt and pepper

cilantro, to garnish

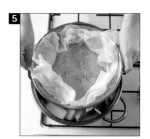

1 Cut the carrots and zucchini into 3 inch pieces and cut in half lengthways.

2 Trim the pumpkin or squash and discard the seeds. Peel and cut into pieces the same size as the carrots and zucchini.

3 Put the stock, spices, saffron, and carrots in a large saucepan. Bring to a boil, skim off any scum, and add the olive oil. Simmer for 15 minutes.

4 Add the lemon rind and juice to the pan, together with the honey, zucchini, and pumpkin or squash. Season well. Bring back to a boil and simmer for a further 10 minutes.

5 Meanwhile, soak the couscous according to the package directions. Transfer to a steamer or large strainer lined with cheesecloth and place over the vegetable pan. Cover and steam as directed. Stir in the butter.

6 Pile the couscous on to a warmed serving plate. Drain the vegetables, reserving the stock, lemon rind and cinnamon. Arrange the vegetables on top of the couscous. Put the raisins on top and spoon over 6 tablespoons of the reserved stock. Keep warm.

7 Return the remaining stock to the heat and boil for 5 minutes to reduce slightly. Discard the lemon rind and cinnamon. Garnish with sprigs of cilantro and serve immediately, handing the sauce separately.

Bulghur Pilaf

Bulghur wheat is very easy to use and, as well as being full of nutrients, it is a delicious alternative to rice, having a distinctive nutty flavor.

NUTRITIONAL INFORMATION

Calories	637	Sugars	........25g
Protein	........16g	Fat	..........26g
Carbohydrate	...90g	Saturates	......11g

15 MINS   35–40 MINS

SERVES 4

I N G R E D I E N T S

6 tbsp butter or margarine

1 red onion, halved, and sliced

2 garlic cloves, crushed

2 cups bulghur wheat

6 oz tomatoes, seeded, and chopped

1¾ oz baby-corn-on-the-cobs,
   halved lengthways

2¾ oz small broccoli florets

3¾ cups vegetable stock

2 tbsp clear honey

1¾ oz golden raisins

½ cup pine nuts

½ tsp ground cinnamon

½ tsp ground cumin

salt and pepper

sliced scallions, to garnish

COOK'S TIP

The dish is left to stand for 10 minutes so that the bulghur can finish cooking and the flavors will mingle.

1 Melt the butter or margarine in a large flameproof casserole.

2 Add the onion and garlic and sauté for 2–3 minutes, stirring occasionally.

3 Add the bulghur wheat, tomatoes, corn-on-the-cobs, broccoli, and stock and bring to a boil. Reduce the heat, cover and cook, stirring occasionally, for 15–20 minutes.

4 Stir in the honey, golden raisins, pine nuts, ground cinnamon, and cumin and season with salt and pepper to taste, mixing well. Remove the casserole from the heat, cover and set aside for 10 minutes.

5 Spoon the bulghur pilaf into a warmed serving dish.

6 Garnish the bulghur pilaf with thinly sliced scallions and serve immediately.

Tabbouleh Salad

This kind of salad is eaten widely throughout the Middle East. The flavor improves as it is kept, so it tastes even better on the second day.

NUTRITIONAL INFORMATION

Calories 637   Sugars 8g
Protein . . . . .20g   Fat 41g
Carbohydrate . . .50g   Saturates 11g

1½ HOURS   5–10 MINS

SERVES 2

I N G R E D I E N T S

1 cup bulghur wheat

2½ cups boiling water

1 red bell pepper, seeded, and halved

3 tbsp olive oil

1 garlic clove, crushed

grated rind of ½ lime

about 1 tbsp lime juice

1 tbsp chopped mint

1 tbsp chopped parsley

3–4 scallions, trimmed, and
   thinly sliced

8 pitted black olives, halved

½ cup large salted peanuts or
   cashew nuts

1–2 tsp lemon juice

2–3 oz Gruyère cheese

salt and pepper

mint sprigs, to garnish

warm pocket bread or crusty rolls,
   to serve

1 Put the bulghur wheat into a bowl and cover with a boiling water to reach about 1 inch above the bulghur. Set aside to soak for up to 1 hour, until most of the water is absorbed and is cold.

2 Meanwhile, put the halved red bell pepper, skin side upwards, on a broiler rack, and cook under a preheated moderate broiler until the skin is thoroughly charred and blistered. Leave to cool slightly.

3 When cool enough to handle, peel off the skin and discard the seeds. Cut the bell pepper flesh into narrow strips.

4 Whisk together the oil, garlic, lime rind and juice. Season to taste and whisk until thoroughly blended. Add 4½ teaspoons of the dressing to the bell peppers and mix lightly.

5 Drain the soaked bulghur wheat thoroughly, squeezing it in a dry cloth to make it even drier, then place in a bowl.

6 Add the chopped herbs, scallions, olives, and peanuts or cashew nuts to the bulghur and toss . Add the lemon juice to the remaining dressing, and stir through the salad. Spoon the salad on to 2 serving plates.

7 Cut the cheese into narrow strips and mix with the bell pepper strips. Spoon alongside the bulghur salad. Garnish with mint sprigs and serve with warm pocket bread or crusty rolls.

Rice & Nuts

Here is a tasty and filling rice dish that is nice and spicy and includes fruits for a refreshing flavor and toasted nuts for a crunchy texture.

NUTRITIONAL INFORMATION

Calories	.612	Sugars	.31g
Protein	.15g	Fat	.21g
Carbohydrate	.96g	Saturates	.3g

  20 MINS   55 MINS

SERVES 4

I N G R E D I E N T S

4 tbsp vegetable ghee or oil

1 large onion, chopped

2 garlic cloves, crushed

1 inch gingerroot, chopped finely

1 tsp cayenne pepper

1 tsp cumin seeds

1 tbsp mild or medium curry powder
or paste

1½ cups brown rice

3½ cups boiling vegetable stock

14 oz can chopped tomatoes

6 oz ready-soaked dried apricots or
peaches, cut into slivers

1 red bell pepper, cored, seeded, and diced

3 oz frozen peas

1-2 small, slightly green bananas

⅓-½ cup toasted mixed nuts

salt and pepper

1 Heat the ghee or oil in a large saucepan, add the onion and fry gently for 3 minutes.

2 Stir in the garlic, ginger, cayenne pepper, cumin seeds, curry powder or paste, and rice. Cook gently for 2 minutes, stirring all the time, until the rice is coated in the spiced oil.

3 Pour in a boiling stock, stirring to mix. Add the tomatoes and season with salt and pepper to taste. Bring the mixture to a boil, then reduce the heat, cover the pan and leave to simmer gently for 40 minutes or until the rice is almost cooked and most of the liquid is absorbed.

4 Add the apricots or peaches, red bell pepper, and peas to the rice mixture in the pan. Cover and cook for 10 minutes.

5 Remove the pan from the heat and leave to stand for 5 minutes without uncovering.

6 Peel and slice the bananas. Uncover the rice mixture and toss with a fork to mix. Add the toasted nuts and sliced banana and toss lightly.

7 Transfer the brown rice and fruit and nuts to a serving platter and serve very hot.

Stuffed Rice Pancakes

Dosas (pancakes) are widely eaten in southern India. The rice and urid dal need to soak and ferment, so prepare well in advance.

NUTRITIONAL INFORMATION

Calories ....748 Sugars 1g
Protein ....10g Fat 47g
Carbohydrate ...76g Saturates 5g

6¼ HOURS   40-45 MINS

SERVES 4

INGREDIENTS

1 cup rice and ¼ cup urid dhal, or
1¾ cups ground rice and 7 tbsp urid
dal flour (ata)

2–2½ cups water

1 tsp salt

4 tbsp vegetable oil

FILLING

4 medium potatoes, diced

3 fresh green chilies, chopped

½ tsp turmeric

1 tsp salt

⅔ cup oil

1 tsp mixed mustard and onion seeds

3 dried chilies

4 curry leaves

2 tbsp lemon juice

 To make the dosas (pancakes), soak the rice and urid dal for 3 hours. Grind the rice and urid dal to a smooth consistency, adding water if necessary. Set aside for a further 3 hours to ferment. Alternatively, if you are using ground rice and urid dal flour (ata), mix together in a bowl. Add the water and salt and stir until a batter is formed.

2 Heat about 1 tbsp of oil in a large, non-stick, skillet. Using a ladle, spoon the batter into the skillet. Tilt the skillet to spread the mixture over the base. Cover and cook over a medium heat for about 2 minutes. Remove the lid and turn the dosa over very carefully. Pour a little oil around the edge, cover and cook for a further 2 minutes. Repeat with the remaining batter.

3 To make the filling, cook the potatoes in a pan of boiling water. Add the chilies, turmeric, and salt and cook until the potatoes are just soft. Drain and mash lightly with a fork.

4 Heat the oil in a saucepan and fry the mustard and onion seeds, dried red chilies, and curry leaves, stirring constantly, for about 1 minute. Pour the spice mixture over the mashed potatoes, then sprinkle over the lemon juice and mix well. Spoon the potato filling on one half of each of the dosas (pancakes) and fold the other half over it. Transfer to a warmed serving dish and serve hot.

Pilau Rice

Plain boiled rice is eaten by most people in India every day, but for entertaining, a more interesting rice dish, such as this, is served.

NUTRITIONAL INFORMATION

Calories 265   Sugars 0g
Protein . . . . .4g   Fat 10g
Carbohydrate . . .43g   Saturates 6g

 5 MINS   25 MINS

SERVES 4

I N G R E D I E N T S

1 cup basmati rice

2 tbsp vegetable ghee

3 green cardamoms

2 cloves

3 peppercorns

½ tsp salt

½ tsp saffron

scant 2 cups water

1 Rinse the rice twice under running water and set aside until required.

2 Heat the ghee in a saucepan. Add the cardamoms, cloves, and peppercorns to the pan and fry, stirring constantly, for about 1 minute.

3 Add the rice and stir-fry over a medium heat for a further 2 minutes.

4 Add the salt, saffron, and water to the rice mixture and reduce the heat. Cover the pan and simmer over a low heat until the water has been absorbed.

5 Transfer the pilau rice to a serving dish and serve hot.

COOK'S TIP

The most expensive of all spices, saffron strands are the stamens of a type of crocus. They give dishes a rich, golden color, as well as adding a distinctive, slightly bitter taste. Saffron is sold as a powder or in the more expensive strands.

Tomato Rice

Rice cooked with tomatoes and onions will add color to your table, especially when garnished with green chilies and cilantro.

NUTRITIONAL INFORMATION

Calories	866	Sugars	.........7g
Protein	........15g	Fat	..........46g
Carbohydrate	..106g	Saturates	.......6g

10 MINS   35 MINS

SERVES 4

I N G R E D I E N T S

⅔ cup vegetable oil

2 medium onions, sliced

1 tsp onion seeds

1 tsp, finely chopped gingerroot

1 tsp crushed garlic

½ tsp turmeric

1 tsp cayenne pepper

1½ tsp salt

14 oz can tomatoes

2¼ cups basmati rice

2½ cups water

TO GARNISH

3 fresh green chilies, finely chopped

fresh cilantro leaves, chopped

3 hard-cooked eggs

1 Heat the oil in a saucepan. Add the onions and fry over a moderate heat, stirring frequently, for 5 minutes, until golden brown.

2 Add the onion seeds, ginger, garlic, turmeric, chili powder, and salt, stirring to combine.

3 Reduce the heat, add the tomatoes and stir-fry for 10 minutes, breaking them up.

4 Add the rice to the tomato mixture, stirring gently to coat the rice completely in the mixture. Stir in the water. Cover the pan and cook over a low heat until the water has been absorbed and the rice is cooked.

5 Transfer the tomato rice to a warmed serving dish. Garnish with the finely chopped green chilies, cilantro leaves and hard-cooked eggs. Serve the tomato rice immediately.

COOK'S TIP

Onion seeds are always used whole in Indian cooking. They are often used in pickles and often sprinkled over the top of naan breads. Onion seeds don't have anything to do with the vegetable, but they look similar to the plant's seed, hence the name.

Green Rice

Based on the Mexican dish *Arroz Verde*, this recipe is perfect for bell pepper and chili lovers. Serve with iced lemonade to quell the fire!

NUTRITIONAL INFORMATION

Calories 445   Sugars 6g
Protein . . . . .13g   Fat 12g
Carbohydrate . . .76g   Saturates 2g

25 MINS   30 MINS

SERVES 4

INGREDIENTS

2 large green bell peppers

2 fresh green chilies

2 tbsp, plus 1 tsp vegetable oil

1 large onion, finely chopped

1 garlic clove, crushed

1 tbsp ground coriander

1½ cups long grain rice

3 cups Vegetable stock

2 cups frozen peas

6 tbsp chopped cilantro

1 egg, beaten

salt and pepper

cilantro, to garnish

TO SERVE

tortilla chips

lime wedges

COOK'S TIP

There are hundreds of varieties of chilies, many of them very similar in appearance, so it is not always easy to tell how hot they are. As a general rule, small, pointed chilies are hotter than larger, more rounded ones, but this is not invariable.

1 Halve, core, and seed the bell peppers. Cut the flesh into small cubes. Seed and finely chop the chilies.

2 Heat 2 tablespoons of the oil in a saucepan and fry the onion, garlic, bell peppers, and chilies for 5–6 minutes, until softened, but not browned.

3 Stir in the ground coriander, rice, and stock. Bring to a boil, cover and simmer for 10 minutes. Add the peas, bring back to a boil, cover and simmer for a further 5 minutes, until the rice is tender. Remove from the heat and leave to stand, covered, for 10 minutes.

4 Season to taste with salt and pepper and mix in the fresh cilantro. Pile into a warmed serving dish and keep warm.

5 Heat the remaining oil in a small omelet pan. Pour in the egg and cook over a medium heat for 1–2 minutes on each side, until set. Slide the omelet on to a plate, roll up loosely and slice into thin rounds.

6 Arrange the omelet strips on top of the rice. Garnish with cilantro and serve immediately with tortilla chips and lime wedges.

Spinach & Nut Pilaf

Fragrant basmati rice is cooked with porcini mushrooms, spinach, and pistachio nuts in this easy microwave recipe.

NUTRITIONAL INFORMATION

Calories	403	Sugars	.........7g
Protein	........10g	Fat	..........15g
Carbohydrate	...62g	Saturates	.......2g

  55 MINS 15–20 MINS

SERVES 4

I N G R E D I E N T S

⅓ oz dried porcini mushrooms

1¼ cups hot water

1 onion, chopped

1 garlic clove, crushed

1 tsp grated gingerroot

½ fresh green chili, seeded, and chopped

2 tbsp oil

generous 1 cup basmati rice

1 large carrot, grated

¾ cup vegetable stock

½ tsp ground cinnamon

4 cloves

½ tsp saffron strands

6 cups fresh spinach, long stalks removed

½ cup pistachio nuts

1 tbsp chopped cilantro

salt and pepper

cilantro leaves to garnish

1 Place the porcini mushrooms in a small bowl. Pour over the hot water and leave to soak for 30 minutes.

2 Place the onion, garlic, ginger, chili, and oil in a large bowl. Cover and cook on HIGH power for 2 minutes. Rinse the rice, then stir it into the bowl, together with the carrot. Cover and cook on HIGH power for 1 minute.

3 Strain and coarsely chop the mushrooms. Add the mushroom soaking liquid to the stock to make scant 2 cups. Pour on to the rice. Stir in the mushrooms, cinnamon, cloves, saffron, and ½ teaspoon salt. Cover and cook on HIGH power for 10 minutes, stirring once. Leave to stand, covered, for 10 minutes.

4 Place the spinach in a large bowl. Cover and cook on HIGH power for 3½ minutes, stirring once. Drain well and chop coarsely.

5 Stir the spinach, pistachio nuts, and chopped cilantro into the rice. Season to taste with salt and pepper and garnish with cilantro leaves. Serve immediately.

Kitchouri

The traditional breakfast plate of kedgeree, reputedly has its roots in this Indian flavored rice dish, which English colonists adopted.

NUTRITIONAL INFORMATION

Calories 318   Sugars 5g
Protein . . . . .12g   Fat 10g
Carbohydrate . . .48g   Saturates 6g

10 MINS   30 MINS

SERVES 4

I N G R E D I E N T S

2 tbsp vegetable ghee or butter

1 red onion, finely chopped

1 garlic clove, crushed

½ celery stalk, finely chopped

1 tsp turmeric

½ tsp garam masala

1 green chili, seeded, and finely chopped

½ tsp cumin seeds

1 tbsp chopped cilantro

generous ½ cup basmati rice,
    rinsed under cold water

½ cup green lentils

1¼ cups vegetable juice

2½ cups vegetable stock

1 Heat the ghee or butter in a large heavy-bottomed saucepan. Add the onion, garlic, and celery and cook for about 5 minutes, until soft.

2 Add the turmeric, garam masala, green chili, cumin seeds, and cilantro. Cook over a moderate heat, stirring constantly, for about 1 minute, until fragrant.

3 Add the rice and lentils and cook for 1 minute, until the rice is translucent.

4 Pour the vegetable juice and stock into the saucepan and bring to a boil over a medium heat. Cover and simmer over a low heat, stirring occasionally, for about 20 minutes, or until the lentils are cooked. (They should be tender when pressed between two fingers.)

5 Transfer the kitchouri to a warmed serving dish and serve very hot.

COOK'S TIP

This is a versatile dish, and can be served as a great-tasting and satisfying one-pot meal. It can also be served as a winter lunch dish with tomatoes and yogurt.

Vegetable Biryani

The Biryani originated in the North of India, and was a dish reserved for festivals. The vegetables are marinated in a yogurt-bottomed marinade.

NUTRITIONAL INFORMATION

Calories	449	Sugars	........18g
Protein	........12g	Fat	..........12g
Carbohydrate	...79g	Saturates	.......6g

2¼ HOURS   1 HR 5 MINS

SERVES 4

I N G R E D I E N T S

1 large potato, cubed

3½ oz baby carrots

1¾ oz okra, thickly sliced

2 celery stalks, sliced

2¾ oz baby button mushrooms, halved

1 eggplant, halved, and sliced

1¼ cups unsweetened yogurt

1 tbsp grated gingerroot

2 large onions, grated

4 garlic cloves, crushed

1 tsp turmeric

1 tbsp curry powder

2 tbsp butter

2 onions, sliced

1¼ cups basmati rice

chopped cilantro, to garnish

1 Cook the potato cubes, carrots, and okra in a pan of boiling salted water for 7–8 minutes. Drain well and place in a large bowl. Mix with the celery, mushrooms, and eggplant.

2 Mix the unsweetened yogurt, ginger, grated onions, garlic, turmeric, and curry powder and spoon over the vegetables. Set aside in a cool place to marinate for at least 2 hours.

3 Heat the butter in a heavy-bottomed skillet. Add the sliced onions and cook over a medium heat for 5–6 minutes, until golden brown. Remove a few onions from the pan and reserve for the garnish.

4 Cook the rice in a large pan of boiling water for 7 minutes. Drain thoroughly and set aside.

5 Add the marinated vegetables to the onions and cook for 10 minutes.

6 Put half of the rice in a 8¾ cup casserole dish. Spoon the vegetables on top and cover with the remaining rice. Cover and cook in a preheated oven, 375°F, for 20–25 minutes, or until the rice is tender.

7 Spoon the biryani on to a serving plate, garnish with the reserved onions and cilantro and serve.

Daikon Curry

This is rather an unusual recipe for a vegetarian curry. The dish is good served hot with chapatis.

NUTRITIONAL INFORMATION

Calories	384	Sugars	.........4g
Protein	.........3g	Fat	..........38g
Carbohydrate	....9g	Saturates	.......4g

🥘 10 MINS   🕐 20 MINS

SERVES 4

I N G R E D I E N T S

1 lb 2 oz daikon, preferably
  with leaves

1 tbsp moong dal

2½ cups water

⅔ cup vegetable oil

1 medium onion, thinly sliced

1 tsp crushed garlic

1 tsp crushed dried red chilies

1 tsp salt

1 Rinse, peel, and roughly slice the daikon, together with its leaves, if using.

2 Place the daikon, the leaves, if using, and the moong dal in a large saucepan and pour over the water. Bring to a boil and cook over a medium heat until the daikon has softened enough to handle.

3 Drain the daikon thoroughly and squeeze out any excess water, using your hands.

4 Heat the vegetable oil in a heavy-bottomed saucepan. Add the onion, garlic, crushed red chilies, and salt and fry over a medium heat, stirring from time to time, for about 5–7 minutes, until the onions have softened and turned light golden brown in color.

5 Stir the daikon mixture into the spiced onion mixture and combine well. Reduce the heat and continue cooking, stirring frequently, for about 3–5 minutes.

6 Transfer the daikon curry to individual serving plates and serve hot with chapatis.

COOK'S TIP

The vegetable used in this recipe, daikon, looks a bit like a parsnip without the tapering end and is now sold in most supermarkets, as well as in oriental grocers.

Aloo Chat

Aloo Chat is one of a variety of Indian foods served at any time of the day. The garbanzo beans need to be soaked overnight.

NUTRITIONAL INFORMATION

Calories 262	Sugars 6g
Protein 13g	Fat 4g
Carbohydrate ... 46g	Saturates 0.5g

 35 MINS   1 HR 5 MINS

SERVES 4

INGREDIENTS

generous ½ cup garbanzo beans,
  soaked overnight in
  cold water and drained

1 dried red chili

1 lb 2 oz waxy potatoes, boiled in
  their skins, and peeled

1 tsp cumin seeds

2 tsp salt

1 tsp black peppercorns

½ tsp dried mint

½ tsp cayenne pepper

½ tsp ground ginger

2 tsp mango powder

½ cup unsweetened yogurt

oil, for deep frying

4 poppadoms

VARIATION

Instead of garbanzo beans, diced tropical fruits can be stirred into the potatoes and spice mix; add a little lemon juice to balance the sweetness.

1 Boil the garbanzo beans with the chili in plenty of water for about 1 hour, until tender. Drain.

2 Cut the potatoes into 1 inch dice and mix into the garbanzo beans while they are still warm. Set aside.

3 Grind together the cumin, salt, and peppercorns in a spice grinder or with a mortar and pestle. Stir in the mint, cayenne pepper, ginger, and mango powder.

4 Put a small saucepan or skillet over a low heat and add the spice mix. Stir until the spices give off their aroma and then immediately remove the pan from the heat.

5 Stir half of the spice mix into the garbanzo bean and potato mixture and stir the other half into the yogurt.

6 Cook the poppadoms according to the directions on the packet. Drain on plenty of paper towels. Break into bite-size pieces and stir into the potatoes and garbanzo beans, spoon over the spiced yogurt and serve immediately.

Tarka Dal

This is just one version of many dals that are served throughout India; as many people are vegetarian, they form a staple part of the diet.

NUTRITIONAL INFORMATION

Calories 183	Sugars 4g	
Protein 8g	Fat 8g	
Carbohydrate ...22g	Saturates 5g	

10 MINS   25 MINS

SERVES 4

INGREDIENTS

2 tbsp ghee

2 shallots, sliced

1 tsp yellow mustard seeds

2 garlic cloves, crushed

8 fenugreek seeds

½ inch piece of gingerroot, grated

½ tsp salt

½ cup red lentils

1 tbsp tomato paste

2½ cups water

2 tomatoes, peeled, and chopped

1 tbsp lemon juice

4 tbsp chopped cilantro

½ tsp cayenne pepper

½ tsp garam masala

1 Heat half of the ghee in a large saucepan and add the shallots. Cook for 2–3 minutes over a high heat, then add the mustard seeds. Cover the pan until the seeds begin to pop.

2 Immediately remove the lid from the pan and add the garlic, fenugreek, ginger, and salt.

3 Stir once and add the lentils, tomato paste, and water. Bring to a boil, then lower the heat and simmer for 10 minutes.

4 Stir in the tomatoes, lemon juice, and cilantro, and simmer for 4–5 minutes, until the lentils are tender.

5 Transfer to a serving dish. Heat the remaining ghee in a pan. Remove from the heat and stir in the garam masala and cayenne. Pour over the tarka dal; serve.

COOK'S TIP

The flavors in a dal can be altered to suit your taste; for extra heat, add more cayenne pepper or chilies, or add fennel seeds for an aniseed flavor.

Channa Dal

Dried legumes and lentils can be cooked in similar ways, but the soaking and cooking times do vary, so check the pack for directions.

NUTRITIONAL INFORMATION

Calories	195	Sugars 4g
Protein	. . . . .11g	Fat 5g
Carbohydrate	. . .28g	Saturates 3g

1 HR 10 MINS   50 MINS

SERVES 6

INGREDIENTS

2 tbsp vegetable ghee

1 large onion, finely chopped

1 garlic clove, crushed

1 tbsp grated gingerroot

1 tbsp cumin seeds, ground

2 tsp coriander seeds, ground

1 dried red chili

1 inch piece of cinnamon stick

1 tsp salt

½ tsp ground turmeric

1 cup split yellow peas, soaked
  in cold water for 1 hour, and drained

14 oz can plum tomatoes

1¼ cups water

2 tsp garam masala

1 Heat the ghee in a large saucepan, add the onion, garlic, and ginger and fry for 3–4 minutes, until the onion has softened slightly.

2 Add the cumin, coriander, chili, cinnamon, salt, and turmeric, then stir in the split peas until well mixed.

3 Add the tomatoes, together with their can juices, breaking the tomatoes up slightly with the back of a spoon.

4 Add the water and bring to a boil. Reduce the heat to very low and simmer, uncovered, stirring occasionally, for about 40 minutes, until most of the liquid has been absorbed and the split peas are tender. Skim the surface occasionally with a draining spoon to remove any scum.

5 Gradually stir in the garam masala, tasting after each addition, until it is of the required flavor. Serve hot.

COOK'S TIP

Use a nonstick saucepan if you have one, because the mixture is quite dense and does stick to the base of the pan occasionally. If the dal is overstirred the split peas will break up and the dish will not have much texture or bite.

Kofta Kabobs

Traditionally, koftas are made from a spicy meat mixture, but this bean and wheat version makes a tasty vegetarian alternative.

NUTRITIONAL INFORMATION

Calories 598	Sugars 7g	
Protein 26g	Fat 17g	
Carbohydrate ...90g	Saturates 3g	

🍲 1 HR 20 MINS ⏱ 1½ HOURS

SERVES 4

I N G R E D I E N T S

1 cup azuki beans

1 cup bulghur wheat

scant 2 cups vegetable stock

3 tbsp olive oil, plus extra for brushing

1 onion, finely chopped

2 garlic cloves, crushed

1 tsp ground coriander

1 tsp ground cumin

2 tbsp chopped fresh cilantro

3 eggs, beaten

¾ cup dried breadcrumbs

salt and pepper

T A B B O U L E H

1 cup bulghur wheat

2 tbsp lemon juice

1 tbsp olive oil

6 tbsp chopped parsley

4 scallions, finely chopped

2 oz cucumber, finely chopped

3 tbsp chopped mint

1 extra-large tomato, finely chopped

T O   S E R V E

black olives

pocket bread

1 Cook the azuki beans in boiling water for 40 minutes, until tender. Drain, rinse, and leave to cool. Cook the bulghur wheat in the stock for 10 minutes, until the stock is absorbed. Set aside.

2 Heat 1 tablespoon of the oil in a skillet and fry the onion, garlic, and spices for 4–5 minutes.

3 Transfer to a bowl, together with the beans, cilantro, seasoning, and eggs and mash with a potato masher or fork. Add the breadcrumbs and bulghur wheat and stir well. Cover and chill for 1 hour, until firm.

4 To make the tabbouleh, soak the bulghur wheat in scant 2 cups of boiling water for 15 minutes. Combine with the remaining ingredients. Cover and chill.

5 With wet hands, mold the kofta mixture into 32 oval shapes.

6 Press on to skewers, brush with oil and broil for 5–6 minutes until golden. Turn, brush with oil again, and cook for 5–6 minutes. Drain on paper towels. Garnish and serve with the tabbouleh, black olives, and pocket bread.

Black-Eyed Peas

This is very good served with chapatis and a vegetable curry. The peas need to be soaked overnight so prepare well in advance.

NUTRITIONAL INFORMATION

Calories 757   Sugars 5g
Protein . . . . .10g   Fat 69g
Carbohydrate . . .26g   Saturates 7g

 5 MINS   1 HOUR

SERVES 4

INGREDIENTS

1 cup black-eyed peas

1¼ cups vegetable oil

2 medium onions, sliced

1 tsp finely chopped gingerroot

1 tsp crushed garlic

1 tsp cayenne pepper

1½ tsp salt

1½ tsp ground coriander

1½ tsp ground cumin

⅔ cup water

2 green chilies

cilantro leaves

1 tbsp lemon juice

COOK'S TIP

Black-eyed peas are oval-shaped, grey, or beige peas with a dark dot in the center. They have a slightly smoky flavor. They are sold canned, as well as dried.

1 Rinse the black-eyed peas, place them in a bowl, cover with cold water and set aside to soak overnight.

2 Drain the black-eyed peas, place in a pan of water and bring to a boil over a low heat. Simmer for about 30 minutes. Drain the peas thoroughly and set aside.

3 Heat the oil in a heavy-bottomed pan. Add the onions and fry, stirring frequently, for 5–8 minutes, until golden brown. Add the ginger, garlic, cayenne pepper, salt, ground coriander, and ground cumin and stir-fry the mixture for 3–5 minutes.

4 Add the water to the pan, cover and simmer until all of the water has completely evaporated.

5 Add the black-eyed peas, green chilies and cilantro leaves to the onions and stir-fry for 3–5 minutes.

6 Transfer the black-eyed peas to a serving dish, sprinkle over the lemon juice and serve immediately. Alternatively, allow the peas to cool and serve cold.

White Lentils

This dal is dry when cooked, so give it a baghaar (seasoned oil dressing). It makes an excellent accompaniment to any meal of kormas.

NUTRITIONAL INFORMATION

Calories . . . . . . .129 Sugars 1g
Protein . . . . .6g Fat 6g
Carbohydrate . . .14g Saturates 1g

5 MINS   45 MINS

SERVES 4

I N G R E D I E N T S

½ cup urid dal

1 tsp finely chopped gingerroot

2½ cups water

1 tsp salt

1 tsp pepper

2 tbsp vegetable ghee

2 garlic cloves

2 fresh red chilies, finely chopped

mint leaves, to garnish

chapatis, to serve

1 Rinse the lentils thoroughly and put them in a large saucepan, together with the ginger.

2 Add the water and bring to a boil. Cover and simmer over a medium heat for about 30 minutes. Check to see whether the lentils are cooked by rubbing them between your finger and thumb. If they are still a little hard in the middle, cook for a further 5–7 minutes. If necessary, remove the lid and cook until any remaining water has evaporated.

3 Add the salt and pepper to the lentils, mix well and set aside.

4 To make the baghaar, heat the ghee in a separate saucepan. Add the cloves of garlic and chopped red chilies and stir well to mix thoroughly.

5 Pour the garlic and chili mixture over the lentils and then garnish with the fresh mint leaves.

6 Transfer the white lentils to warm individual serving dishes and serve hot with chapatis.

COOK'S TIP

Ghee was traditionally made from clarified butter, which can withstand higher temperatures than ordinary butter. Vegetable ghee has largely replaced it now because it is lower in saturated fats.

Stir-Fries & Sautés

Stir-frying is one of the most convenient and nutritious ways of cooking vegetarian food as ingredients are cooked quickly over a very high heat in very little oil. The high

heat seals in the natural juices and helps preserve nutrients. The short cooking time makes the vegetables more succulent and preserves texture as well as the natural flavor and color. A round-bottomed wok is ideal for stir-frying as it conducts and retains heat evenly and requires the use of less oil. You need a flat-bottomed pan for sautéing so that the food can be easily tossed and stirred. A brisk heat is essential so that the food turns golden brown and crisp.

Vegetable Curry

This colorful and interesting mixture of vegetables, cooked in a spicy sauce, is excellent served with pilauf rice and naan bread.

NUTRITIONAL INFORMATION

Calories . . . . .421 Sugars 20g
Protein . . . . .12g Fat 24g
Carbohydrate . . .42g Saturates 3g

 15 MINS   45 MINS

SERVES 4

I N G R E D I E N T S

8 oz turnips or rutabaga

1 eggplant

12 oz new potatoes

8 oz cauliflower

8 oz button mushrooms

1 large onion

8 oz carrots

6 tbsp vegetable ghee or oil

2 garlic cloves, crushed

2 inch piece of gingerroot,
   finely chopped

1-2 fresh green chilies,
   seeded and chopped

1 tbsp paprika

2 tsp ground coriander

1 tbsp mild or medium curry powder
   or paste

1¾ cups vegetable stock

14 oz can chopped tomatoes

1 green bell pepper, seeded and sliced

1 tbsp cornstarch

⅔ cup coconut milk

2-3 tbsp ground almonds

salt

cilantro sprigs, to garnish

1 Cut the turnips or rutabaga, eggplant, and potatoes into ½ inch cubes. Divide the cauliflower into small florets. Leave the mushrooms whole, or slice thickly if preferred. Slice the onion and carrots.

2 Heat the ghee or oil in a large saucepan. Add the onion, turnip, or rutabaga, potato, and cauliflower and cook over a low heat, stirring frequently, for 3 minutes.

3 Add the garlic, ginger, chilies, paprika, ground coriander, and curry powder or paste and cook, stirring, for 1 minute.

4 Add the stock, tomatoes, eggplant, and mushrooms and season with salt. Cover and simmer, stirring occasionally, for about 30 minutes, or until tender. Add the green bell pepper, and carrots, cover, and continue cooking for a further 5 minutes.

5 Blend the cornstarch with the coconut milk to a smooth paste and stir into the mixture. Add the ground almonds and simmer, stirring constantly, for 2 minutes. Season if necessary. Transfer the curry to serving plates and serve hot, garnished with sprigs of fresh cilantro.

Potato Curry

Very little meat is eaten in India, their diet being mainly vegetarian. This potato curry with added vegetables makes a very substantial main meal.

NUTRITIONAL INFORMATION

Calories . . . . .301 Sugars 10g
Protein . . . . .9g Fat 12g
Carbohydrate . . .41g Saturates 1g

15 MINS   45 MINS

SERVES 4

I N G R E D I E N T S

4 tbsp vegetable oil

1½ lb waxy potatoes,
    cut into large chunks

2 onions, quartered

3 garlic cloves, crushed

1 tsp garam masala

½ tsp turmeric

½ tsp ground cumin

½ tsp ground coriander

1 inch piece of gingerroot, grated

1 fresh red chili, chopped

8 oz cauliflower florets

4 tomatoes, peeled, and quartered

¾ cup frozen peas

2 tbsp chopped cilantro

1¼ cups vegetable stock

shredded cilantro, to garnish

COOK'S TIP

Use a large heavy-based saucepan or skillet for this recipe to ensure that the potatoes are cooked thoroughly.

1 Heat the vegetable oil in a large heavy-based saucepan or skillet. Add the potato chunks, onion, and garlic and fry over a low heat, stirring frequently, for 2–3 minutes.

2 Add the garam masala, turmeric, ground cumin, ground coriander, grated ginger, and chopped chili to the pan, mixing the spices into the vegetables. Fry over a low heat, stirring constantly, for 1 minute.

3 Add the cauliflower florets, tomatoes, peas, chopped cilantro, and vegetable stock to the curry mixture.

4 Cook the potato curry over a low heat for 30–40 minutes, or until the potatoes are tender and completely cooked through.

5 Garnish the potato curry with fresh cilantro and serve with plain boiled rice or warm Indian bread.

Potato & Cauliflower Curry

Potatoes and cauliflower go very well together. Served with a dal and rice, or bread, this dish makes a perfect vegetarian meal.

NUTRITIONAL INFORMATION

Calories 426	Sugars 6g	
Protein 4g	Fat 35g	
Carbohydrate . . .26g	Saturates 4g	

 10 MINS   25 MINS

SERVES 4

INGREDIENTS

⅔ cup vegetable oil

½ tsp white cumin seeds

4 dried red chilies

2 medium onions, sliced

1 tsp finely chopped gingerroot

1 tsp crushed garlic

1 tsp cayenne pepper

1 tsp salt

pinch of turmeric

3 medium potatoes, chopped

½ cauliflower, cut into small florets

2 green chilies (optional)

cilantro leaves

⅔ cup water

1 Heat the oil in a large heavy-bottomed saucepan. Add the white cumin seeds and dried red chilies to the pan, stirring to mix.

2 Add the onions to the pan and fry over a medium heat, stirring occasionally, for about 5–8 minutes, until golden brown.

3 Mix the ginger, garlic, cayenne pepper, salt, and turmeric together. Add the spice mixture to the onions and stir-fry for about 2 minutes.

4 Add the potatoes and cauliflower to the pan and stir to coat thoroughly with the spice mixture. Reduce the heat and add the green chilies (if using), cilantro leaves and water to the pan. Cover and simmer for about 10-15 minutes, until the vegetables are cooked through and tender.

5 Transfer the potato and cauliflower curry to warmed serving plates and serve immediately.

COOK'S TIP

Ground ginger is no substitute for the fresh root. It is less aromatic and flavorsome and cannot be used in fried or sautéed dishes, as it burns easily at the high temperatures required.

Muttar Panir

Panir is a delicious fresh, soft cheese frequently used in Indian cooking. It is easily made at home, but must be made the day before it's required.

NUTRITIONAL INFORMATION

Calories ....550 Sugars 25g
Protein ....19g Fat 39g
Carbohydrate ...33g Saturates 12g

15 MINS   25 MINS

SERVES 6

INGREDIENTS

⅔ cup vegetable oil

2 onions, chopped

2 garlic cloves, crushed

1 inch piece of gingerroot, chopped

1 tsp garam masala

1 tsp ground turmeric

1 tsp cayenne pepper

4 cups frozen peas

8 oz can chopped tomatoes

½ cup vegetable stock

salt and pepper

2 tbsp chopped cilantro

PANIR

10 cups pasteurized full-cream milk

5 tbsp lemon juice

1 garlic clove, crushed (optional)

1 tbsp chopped cilantro (optional)

1 To make the panir, bring the milk to a rolling boil in a pan. Remove from the heat and stir in the lemon juice. Return to the heat for about 1 minute until the curds and whey separate. Remove from the heat. Line a colander with double thickness muslin and pour the mixture through the muslin, adding the garlic and cilantro, if using. Squeeze all the liquid from the curds and leave to drain.

2 Transfer to a dish, cover with a plate and a heavy weight and leave overnight in the refrigerator.

3 Cut the pressed panir into small cubes. Heat the oil in a large skillet. Add the panir and fry until golden on all sides. Remove from the pan and drain on paper towels.

4 Pour off some of the oil, leaving about 4 tablespoons in the pan. Add the onions, garlic, and ginger and fry gently, stirring frequently, for 5 minutes. Stir in the spices and fry gently for 2 minutes. Add the peas, tomatoes, and stock and season with salt and pepper. Cover and simmer, stirring occasionally, for 10 minutes, until the onion is tender. Add the fried panir cubes and cook for a further 5 minutes. Taste and adjust the seasoning, if necessary. Sprinkle with the cilantro and serve at once.

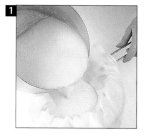

Tomato Curry

This vegetarian tomato curry is served topped with a few hard-cooked eggs. It is a lovely accompaniment to any Indian meal.

NUTRITIONAL INFORMATION

Calories 170   Sugars 3g
Protein . . . . .6g   Fat 15g
Carbohydrate . . . .3g   Saturates 2g

 25 MINS   15 MINS

SERVES 4

I N G R E D I E N T S

14 oz can tomatoes

1 tsp finely chopped gingerroot

1 tsp crushed garlic

1 tsp cayenne pepper

1 tsp salt

½ tsp ground coriander

½ tsp ground cumin

4 tbsp oil

½ tsp onion seeds

½ tsp mustard seeds

½ tsp fenugreek seeds

pinch of white cumin seeds

3 dried red chilies

2 tbsp lemon juice

3 eggs, hard-cooked

fresh cilantro leaves

1 Place the tomatoes in a large mixing bowl. Add the ginger, garlic, cayenne pepper, salt, ground coriander, and ground cumin and blend well.

2 Heat the oil in a saucepan. Add the onion, mustard, fenugreek, and white cumin seeds, and the dried red chilies, and stir-fry for about 1 minute, until they give off their aroma. Remove the pan from the heat.

3 Add the tomato mixture to the spicy oil mixture and return the pan to the heat. Stir-fry for about 3 minutes, then reduce the heat and cook, half covered with a lid, stirring frequently, for 7-10 minutes.

4 Sprinkle over 1 tablespoon of the lemon juice. Taste the curry and add the remaining lemon juice, if required.

5 Transfer the tomato curry to a warmed serving dish, set aside and keep warm until required.

6 Shell the hard-cooked eggs and cut them into quarters. Gently add them, yolk end downwards, to the tomato curry.

7 Garnish with fresh cilantro leaves and serve hot.

Green Pumpkin Curry

The Indian pumpkin used in this curry is long and green and sold by weight. It can easily be bought from any oriental grocers.

NUTRITIONAL INFORMATION

Calories	347	Sugars	.........6g
Protein	.........2g	Fat	..........34g
Carbohydrate	....8g	Saturates	.......4g

10 MINS   30 MINS

SERVES 4

I N G R E D I E N T S

⅔ cup vegetable oil

2 medium-sized onions, sliced

½ tsp white cumin seeds

1 lb 2 oz green pumpkin, cubed

1 tsp dried mango powder

1 tsp finely chopped gingerroot

1 tsp crushed garlic

1 tsp crushed red chili

½ tsp salt

1¼ cups water

chapatis or naan bread, to serve

1 Heat the oil in a large heavy-bottomed skillet. Add the onions and cumin seeds, and fry over a medium heat, stirring occasionally, for about 5 minutes, until the onions are a light golden brown color.

2 Add the cubed pumpkin to the pan and stir-fry over a low heat for 3–5 minutes.

3 Mix the dried mango powder, ginger, garlic, chili, and salt together. Add the spice mixture to the pan, stirring well to combine with the vegetables.

4 Add the water, cover and cook over a low heat, stirring occasionally, for 10–15 minutes.

5 Transfer to serving plates and serve with chapatis or naan bread.

COOK'S TIP

Cumin seeds are popular with Indian cooks because of their warm, pungent flavor, and aroma. The seeds are sold whole or ground, and are usually included as one of the flavorings in garam masala.

Okra Curry

This is a delicious dry bhujia (vegetarian curry) which should be served hot with chapatis. As okra is such a tasty vegetable it needs few spices.

NUTRITIONAL INFORMATION

Calories . . . . .371 Sugars 8g
Protein . . . . .4g Fat 35g
Carbohydrate . . .10g Saturates 4g

10 MINS   30 MINS

SERVES 4

I N G R E D I E N T S

1 lb okra

⅔ cup oil

2 medium onions, sliced

3 green chilies, finely chopped

2 curry leaves

1 tsp salt

1 tomato, sliced

2 tbsp lemon juice

cilantro leaves

1 Rinse the okra and drain thoroughly. Using a sharp knife, chop and discard the ends of the okra. Cut the okra into 1 inch long pieces.

2 Heat the oil in a large, heavy-bottomed skillet. Add the onions, green chilies, curry leaves, and salt and mix together. Stir-fry the vegetables for 5 minutes.

3 Gradually add the okra, mixing in gently with a draining spoon. Stir-fry the vegetable mixture over a medium heat for 12–15 minutes.

4 Add the sliced tomato to the pan and sprinkle over half the lemon juice. taste and add more if required.

5 Garnish with cilantro leaves, cover, and simmer for a further 3–5 minutes.

6 Transfer to warmed serving plates and serve hot.

COOK'S TIP

Okra has a remarkable glutinous quality which naturally thickens curries and casseroles.

Red Curry with Cashews

This is a wonderfully quick dish to prepare. If you don't have time to prepare the curry paste, it can be bought ready-made.

NUTRITIONAL INFORMATION

Calories . . . . . . .274 Sugars 5g
Protein . . . . .10g Fat 10g
Carbohydrate . . .38g Saturates 3g

25 MINS   15 MINS

SERVES 4

INGREDIENTS

1 cup coconut milk

1 kaffir lime leaf

¼ tsp light soy sauce

4 baby-corn-on-the-cobs,
   halved lengthways

1¼ cups broccoli florets

4½ oz green beans, cut into
   2 inch pieces

¼ cup cashew nuts

15 fresh basil leaves

1 tbsp chopped cilantro

1 tbsp chopped roast peanuts, to garnish

RED CURRY PASTE

7 fresh red chilies, halved, seeded,
   and blanched

2 tsp cumin seeds

2 tsp coriander seeds

1 inch piece galangal, chopped

½ stalk lemon grass, chopped

1 tsp salt

grated rind of 1 lime

4 garlic cloves, chopped

3 shallots, chopped

2 kaffir lime leaves, shredded

1 tbsp vegetable oil

1 To make the curry paste, grind all the ingredients together in a large mortar and pestle. Alternatively, process briefly in a food processor. The quantity of red curry paste is more than required for this recipe. However, it will keep for up to 3 weeks in a sealed container in the refrigerator.

2 Put a wok or large, heavy-bottomed skillet over a high heat, add 3 tablespoons of the red curry paste and stir until it gives off its aroma. Reduce the heat to medium.

3 Add the coconut milk, kaffir lime leaf, light soy sauce, baby-corn-on-the-cobs, broccoli florets, green beans, and cashew nuts. Bring to the boil and simmer for about 10 minutes, until the vegetables are cooked, but still firm and crunchy.

4 Remove and discard the lime leaf and stir in the basil leaves and cilantro. Transfer to a warmed serving dish, garnish with peanuts and serve immediately.

Egg Curry

This curry can be made very quickly. It can either be served as a side dish or, with parathas, as a light lunch.

NUTRITIONAL INFORMATION

Calories 189   Sugars 3g
Protein ....7g   Fat 16g
Carbohydrate ....4g   Saturates 3g

10 MINS   15 MINS

SERVES 4

INGREDIENTS

4 tbsp vegetable oil

1 medium onion, sliced

1 fresh red chili, finely chopped

½ tsp cayenne pepper

½ tsp fresh gingerroot, finely chopped

½ tsp fresh garlic, crushed

4 medium eggs

1 firm tomato, sliced

fresh cilantro leaves

parathas, to serve (optional)

1 Heat the oil in a large heavy-bottomed saucepan. Add the sliced onion to the pan and fry over a medium heat, stirring occasionally, for about 5 minutes, until it is just softened and a light golden color.

2 Lower the heat. Add the red chili, cayenne pepper, chopped ginger, and crushed garlic and fry over a low heat, stirring constantly, for about 1 minute.

3 Add the eggs and tomatoes to the pan and continue cooking, stirring to break up the eggs when they begin to cook, for 3–5 minutes.

4 Sprinkle over the fresh cilantro leaves.

5 Transfer the egg curry to warm serving plates and serve hot with parathas, if you wish.

COOK'S TIP

Both the leaves and finely chopped stems of cilantro are used in Indian cooking, to flavor dishes and as edible garnishes. It has a very distinctive and pronounced taste.

Spicy Mixed Vegetable Curry

You can vary the vegetables used in this recipe according to personal preferences — experiment!

NUTRITIONAL INFORMATION

Calories 408	Sugars 20
Protein 11g	Fat 24g
Carbohydrate . . .39g	Saturates 3g

30 MINS   45 MINS

SERVES 4

INGREDIENTS

8 oz turnips or rutabaga, peeled

1 eggplant, leaf end trimmed

12 oz new potatoes, scrubbed

8 oz cauliflower

8 oz button mushrooms, wiped

1 large onion, peeled

8 oz carrots, peeled

6 tbsp vegetable ghee or oil

2 garlic cloves, peeled and crushed

2 inch piece of gingerroot, peeled
   and chopped

1-2 fresh green chilies, seeded and
   chopped

1 tbsp paprika

2 tsp ground coriander

1 tbsp mild or medium curry powder or
   paste

1¾ cups vegetable stock

14 oz can chopped tomatoes

salt

1 green bell pepper, seeded and sliced

1 tbsp cornstarch

⅔ cup coconut milk

2-3 tbsp ground almonds

cilantro sprigs, to garnish

1 Using a sharp knife, cut the turnips or rutabaga, eggplant, and potatoes into ½ inch cubes.

2 Divide the cauliflower into small florets. Leave the mushrooms whole, or slice thickly. Slice the onion and carrots.

3 Heat the ghee or oil in a large saucepan, add the onion, turnip, potato, and cauliflower and cook gently for 3 minutes, stirring frequently.

4 Add the garlic, ginger, chili, and spices and cook for 1 minute, stirring.

5 Add the stock, tomatoes, eggplant, and mushrooms and season with salt. Cover and simmer gently for about 30 minutes or until tender, stirring occasionally. Add the green bell pepper, cover and continue cooking for a further 5 minutes.

6 Blend the cornstarch with the coconut milk and stir into the mixture. Add the ground almonds and simmer for 2 minutes, stirring all the time. Taste and adjust the seasoning, if necessary. Serve hot, garnished with cilantro sprigs.

Green Curry with Tempe

Green curry paste will keep for up to three weeks in the refrigerator. Serve the curry over rice or noodles.

NUTRITIONAL INFORMATION

Calories ....237 Sugars 4g
Protein ....16g Fat 17g
Carbohydrate ....5g Saturates 3g

🍲 20 MINS   🕐 15–20 MINS

SERVES 4

INGREDIENTS

1 tbsp sunflower oil

6 oz marinated or plain tempe, cut
　　into diamonds

6 scallions, cut into 1 inch pieces

⅔ cup coconut milk

grated rind of 1 lime

¼ cup fresh basil leaves

¼ tsp liquid seasoning, such as Maggi

GREEN CURRY PASTE

2 tsp coriander seeds

1 tsp cumin seeds

1 tsp black peppercorns

4 large green chilies, seeded

2 shallots, quartered

2 garlic cloves,

2 tbsp chopped cilantro

grated rind of 1 lime

1 tbsp roughly chopped galangal

1 tsp ground turmeric

salt

2 tbsp oil

TO GARNISH

cilantro leaves

2 green chilies, thinly sliced

1 To make the green curry paste, grind together the coriander and cumin seeds and the peppercorns in a food processor or in a mortar and pestle.

2 Blend the remaining ingredients together and add the ground spice mixture. Store in a clean, dry jar for up to 3 weeks in the refrigerator, or freeze in a suitable container.

3 Heat the oil in a wok or large, heavy skillet. Add the tempe and stir over a high heat for about 2 minutes until sealed on all sides. Add the scallions and stir-fry for 1 minute. Remove the tempe and scallions and reserve.

4 Put half the coconut milk into the wok or skillet and bring to a boil. Add 6 tablespoons of the curry paste and the lime rind, and cook for 1 minute, until fragrant. Add the reserved tempe and scallions.

5 Add the remaining coconut milk and simmer for 7–8 minutes. Stir in the basil leaves and liquid seasoning. Leave to simmer for 1 minute before serving, garnished with cilantro leaves, and chilies.

Green Bean & Potato Curry

You can use fresh or canned green beans for this semidry vegetable curry. Serve an oil-dressed dal for contrasting flavors and colors.

NUTRITIONAL INFORMATION

Calories	690	Sugars	.........4g
Protein	.........3g	Fat	..........69g
Carbohydrate	...16g	Saturates	.......7g

  15 MINS   30 MINS

SERVES 4

INGREDIENTS

1¼ cups oil

1 tsp white cumin seeds

1 tsp mustard and onion seeds

4 dried red chilies

3 fresh tomatoes, sliced

1 tsp salt

1 tsp finely chopped gingerroot

1 tsp crushed garlic

1 tsp cayenne pepper

7 oz green cut beans

2 medium potatoes, diced

1¼ cups water

cilantro leaves, chopped

2 green chilies, finely chopped

boiled rice, to serve

COOK'S TIP

Mustard seeds are often fried in oil or ghee to bring out their flavor before being combined with other ingredients.

1 Heat the oil in a large, heavy-bottomed saucepan. Lower the heat and add the white cumin seeds, mustard and onion seeds, and dried red chilies to the saucepan, stirring well.

2 Add the tomatoes to the pan and stir-fry the mixture for 3–5 minutes.

3 Mix together the salt, ginger, garlic, and cayenne pepper and spoon into the pan. Blend the mixture together.

4 Add the green beans and potatoes to the pan and stir-fry for about 5 minutes.

5 Add the water to the pan, reduce the heat to low and simmer for 10–15 minutes, stirring occasionally.

6 Garnish the green bean and potato curry with chopped cilantro leaves and green chilies and serve hot with boiled rice.

Fried Rice with Spicy Beans

This rice is really colorful and crunchy with the addition of corn and red kidney beans.

NUTRITIONAL INFORMATION

Calories	363	Sugars 3g
Protein	........10g	Fat 11g
Carbohydrate	...61g	Saturates 2g

 10 MINS   25 MINS

SERVES 4

INGREDIENTS

3 tbsp sunflower oil

1 onion, finely chopped

1 cup long-grain white rice

1 green bell pepper, seeded, and diced

1 tsp cayenne pepper

2½ cups boiling water

3½ oz canned corn

8 oz canned red kidney beans

2 tbsp chopped fresh cilantro

1 Heat the sunflower oil in a large preheated wok.

2 Add the finely chopped onion to the wok and stir-fry for about 2 minutes or until the onion has softened.

COOK'S TIP

For perfect fried rice, the raw rice should ideally be soaked in a bowl of water for a short time before cooking to remove excess starch. Short-grain Oriental rice can be substituted for the long-grain rice.

3 Add the long-grain rice, diced bell pepper, and cayenne pepper to the wok and stir-fry for 1 minute.

4 Pour 2½ cups of boiling water into the wok. Bring to a boil, then reduce the heat and leave the mixture to simmer for 15 minutes.

5 Add the corn, kidney beans, and cilantro to the wok and heat through, stirring occasionally.

6 Transfer to a serving bowl and serve hot, scattered with extra cilantro, if wished.

Pan Potato Cake

This tasty meal is made with sliced potatoes, tofu and vegetables cooked in the pan from which it is served.

NUTRITIONAL INFORMATION

Calories	452	Sugars	.........6g
Protein	........17g	Fat	..........28g
Carbohydrate	...35g	Saturates	......13g

15 MINS   30 MINS

SERVES 4

I N G R E D I E N T S

1½ lb waxy potatoes, unpeeled and sliced

1 carrot, diced

8 oz small broccoli florets

½ cup butter

2 tbsp vegetable oil

1 red onion, quartered

2 garlic cloves, crushed

6 oz tofu, diced

2 tbsp chopped sage

¾ cup grated sharp cheese

1 Cook the sliced potatoes in a large saucepan of boiling water for 10 minutes. Drain thoroughly.

2 Meanwhile, cook the carrot and broccoli florets in a separate pan of boiling water for 5 minutes. Drain with a draining spoon.

3 Heat the butter and oil in a 9 inch skillet. Add the onion and garlic and fry over a low heat for 2-3 minutes. Add half of the potato slices to the skillet, covering the base of the skillet.

4 Cover the potato slices with the carrot, broccoli, and the tofu. Sprinkle with half of the sage and cover with the remaining potato slices. Sprinkle the grated cheese over the top.

5 Cook over a moderate heat for 8-10 minutes. Place the pan under a preheated medium broiler for 2-3 minutes, or until the cheese melts and browns.

6 Garnish with the remaining sage and serve immediately, straight from the skillet.

COOK'S TIP

Make sure that the mixture fills the whole width of your skillet to enable the layers to remain intact.

Potato Hash

This is a variation of beef hash, which was made with salt beef and leftovers, and served to seagoing New Englanders.

NUTRITIONAL INFORMATION

Calories 302   Sugars 5g
Protein . . . . .15g   Fat 10g
Carbohydrate . . .40g   Saturates 4g

10 MINS   30 MINS

SERVES 4

INGREDIENTS

2 tbsp butter

1 red onion, halved, and sliced

1 carrot, diced

1 oz green beans, halved

3 large waxy potatoes, diced

2 tbsp all-purpose flour

1¼ cups vegetable stock

8 oz tofu, diced

salt and pepper

chopped parsley, to garnish

1 Melt the butter in a large, heavy-bottomed skillet. Add the onion, carrot, green beans, and potatoes and fry over a fairly low heat, stirring constantly, for about 5–7 minutes, or until the vegetables begin to turn golden brown.

2 Add the flour to the skillet and cook, stirring constantly, for 1 minute. Gradually pour in the stock, stirring constantly.

3 Reduce the heat to low and simmer for 15 minutes, or until the potatoes are tender.

4 Add the diced tofu to the pan and cook for a further 5 minutes. Season to taste with salt and pepper.

5 Sprinkle the chopped parsley over the top of the potato hash to garnish and then serve hot straight from the skillet.

COOK'S TIP

Hash is an American term meaning to chop food into small pieces. Therefore a traditional hash dish is made from chopped fresh ingredients, such as bell peppers, onion, and celery.

Kidney Bean Kiev

This is a vegetarian version of chicken Kiev — the bean patties are topped with garlic and herb butter, and coated in breadcrumbs.

NUTRITIONAL INFORMATION

Calories 688   Sugars 8g
Protein . . . . .17g   Fat 49g
Carbohydrate . . .49g   Saturates 20g

 25 MINS   20 MINS

SERVES 4

INGREDIENTS

GARLIC BUTTER

7 tbsp butter

3 garlic cloves, crushed

1 tbsp chopped parsley

BEAN PATTIES

1½ lb canned red kidney beans

1¼ cups fresh white breadcrumbs

2 tbsp butter

1 leek, chopped

1 celery stalk, chopped

1 tbsp chopped parsley

1 egg, beaten

salt and pepper

vegetable oil, for shallow frying

1 To make the garlic butter, put the butter, garlic, and parsley in a bowl and blend together with a wooden spoon. Place the garlic butter on to a sheet of baking parchment, roll into a cigar shape and wrap in the baking parchment. Chill in the refrigerator until required.

2 Using a potato masher, mash the red kidney beans in a mixing bowl and stir in ¾ cup of the breadcrumbs until thoroughly blended.

3 Melt the butter in a heavy-bottomed skillet. Add the leek and celery and sauté over a low heat, stirring constantly, for 3–4 minutes.

4 Add the bean mixture to the pan, together with the parsley, season with salt and pepper to taste and mix thoroughly. Remove the pan from the heat and set aside to cool slightly.

5 Divide the kidney bean mixture into 4 equal portions and shape them into ovals.

6 Slice the garlic butter into 4 pieces and place a slice in the center of each bean patty. With your hands, mold the bean mixture around the garlic butter to encase it completely.

7 Dip each bean patty into the beaten egg to coat and then roll in the remaining breadcrumbs.

8 Heat a little oil in a skillet and fry the patties, turning once, for 7–10 minutes, or until golden brown. Serve immediately.

Bubble & Squeak

Bubble and squeak is best known as fried mashed potato and leftover greens served as an accompaniment.

NUTRITIONAL INFORMATION

Calories 301   Sugars 5g
Protein . . . . .11g   Fat 18g
Carbohydrate . . .24g   Saturates 2g

15 MINS   40 MINS

SERVES 4

INGREDIENTS

1 lb mealy potatoes, diced

8 oz Savoy cabbage, shredded

5 tbsp vegetable oil

2 leeks, chopped

1 garlic clove, crushed

8 oz smoked tofu, cubed

salt and pepper

shredded cooked leek, to garnish

1 Cook the diced potatoes in a saucepan of lightly salted boiling water for 10 minutes, until tender. Drain and mash the potatoes.

2 Meanwhile, in a separate saucepan, blanch the cabbage in boiling water for 5 minutes. Drain well and add to the potato.

COOK'S TIP

This vegetarian version is a perfect main meal, as the smoked tofu cubes added to the basic bubble and squeak mixture make it very substantial and nourishing.

3 Heat the oil in a heavy-bottomed skillet. Add the leeks and garlic and fry gently for 2-3 minutes. Stir into the potato and cabbage mixture.

4 Add the smoked tofu and season well with salt and pepper. Cook over a moderate heat for 10 minutes.

5 Carefully turn the whole mixture over and continue to cook over a moderate heat for a further 5-7 minutes, until crispy underneath. Serve immediately, garnished with shredded leek.

Cheese Potato Cakes

Make these tasty potato cakes for a quick and simple supper dish. Serve them with scrambled eggs if you're very hungry.

NUTRITIONAL INFORMATION

Calories 766	Sugars 7g	
Protein 22g	Fat 50g	
Carbohydrate ...60g	Saturates 20g	

25 MINS   35 MINS

SERVES 4

INGREDIENTS

2 lb 4 oz potatoes

4 tbsp milk

¼ cup butter or margarine

2 leeks, finely chopped

1 onion, finely chopped

1½ cups grated sharp
   hard cheese

1 tbsp chopped parsley or chives

1 egg, beaten

2 tbsp water

1½ cups fresh white or
   brown breadcrumbs

vegetable oil, for shallow frying

salt and pepper

fresh flat leaf parsley sprigs, to garnish

mixed greens, to serve

1 Cook the potatoes in lightly salted boiling water until tender. Drain and mash them with the milk and the butter or margarine.

2 Cook the leeks and onion in a small quantity of lightly salted boiling water for about 10 minutes until tender. Drain well.

3 In a large mixing bowl, combine the leeks and onion with the mashed potato, cheese, and parsley or chives. Season to taste with salt and pepper.

4 Beat together the egg and water in a shallow bowl. Sprinkle the breadcrumbs into a separate shallow bowl. Shape the potato mixture into 12 even-sized cakes, brushing each with the egg mixture, then coating all over with the breadcrumbs.

5 Heat the oil in a large skillet. Add the potato cakes, in batches if necessary, and fry over a low heat for about 2–3 minutes on each side, until light golden brown. Garnish with flat leaf parsley and serve with mixed greens.

Stir-fried Summer Vegetables

The freshness of lightly cooked summer vegetables is enhanced by the aromatic flavor of a tarragon and white wine dressing.

NUTRITIONAL INFORMATION

Calories 217   Sugars 8g
Protein . . . . .2g   Fat 18g
Carbohydrate . . . .9g   Saturates 9g

🍲 10 MINS   🕐 10–15 MINS

SERVES 4

I N G R E D I E N T S

8 oz baby carrots, scrubbed

4½ oz string beans

2 zucchini, trimmed

1 bunch large scallions

1 bunch radishes

½ cup butter

2 tbsp light olive oil

2 tbsp white wine vinegar

4 tbsp dry white wine

1 tsp superfine sugar

1 tbsp chopped tarragon

salt and pepper

tarragon sprigs, to garnish

1 Cut the carrots in half lengthways, slice the beans and zucchini, and halve the scallions and radishes, so that all the vegetables are cut to even-size pieces.

2 Melt the butter in a large, heavy-bottomed skillet or wok. Add all the vegetables and fry them over a medium heat, stirring frequently, until they are tender, but still crisp and firm to the bite.

3 Heat the olive oil, vinegar, white wine, and sugar in a small saucepan over a low heat, stirring until the sugar has dissolved. Remove from the heat and add the chopped tarragon.

4 When the vegetables are just cooked, pour over the 'dressing'. Stir through, tossing the vegetables well to coat, and then transfer to a warmed serving dish. Garnish with sprigs of fresh tarragon and serve at once.

Cashew Nut Paella

Paella traditionally contains chicken and fish, but this recipe is packed with vegetables and nuts for a truly delicious and simple vegetarian dish.

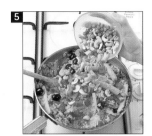

NUTRITIONAL INFORMATION

Calories 406	Sugars 8g
Protein 10g	Fat 22g
Carbohydrate ...44g	Saturates 6g

15 MINS · 35 MINS

SERVES 4

I N G R E D I E N T S

2 tbsp olive oil

1 tbsp butter

1 red onion, chopped

1 cup arborio rice

1 tsp ground turmeric

1 tsp ground cumin

½ tsp cayenne pepper

3 garlic cloves, crushed

1 green chili, sliced

1 green bell pepper, seeded, and diced

1 red bell pepper, seeded, and diced

2¾ oz baby-corn-on-the-cobs,
   halved lengthways

2 tbsp pitted black olives

1 large tomato, seeded, and diced

2 cups vegetable stock

¾ cup unsalted cashew nuts

¼ cup frozen peas

2 tbsp chopped parsley

pinch of cayenne pepper

salt and pepper

herbs, to garnish

1 Heat the olive oil and butter in a large skillet or paella pan until the butter has melted.

2 Add the chopped onion to the pan and sauté over a medium heat, stirring constantly, for 2–3 minutes, until the onion has softened.

3 Stir in the rice, ground turmeric, ground cumin, cayenne pepper, garlic, sliced chili, bell peppers, corn cobs, black olives, and diced tomato and cook over a medium heat, stirring occasionally, for 1–2 minutes.

4 Pour in the stock and bring the mixture to a boil. Reduce the heat and cook, stirring constantly, for 20 minutes.

5 Add the cashew nuts and peas and cook, stirring occasionally, for 5 minutes. Season to taste with salt and pepper and sprinkle with parsley and cayenne pepper. Transfer to warm serving plates, garnish, and serve immediately.

Vegetable Medley

Serve this as a crisp and colorful dish, with pocket bread, chapattis, or naan, or as an accompaniment to baked pasta dishes.

15 MINS   10 MINS

SERVES 4

I N G R E D I E N T S

5½ oz green beans

8 baby carrots

6 baby turnips

½ small cauliflower

2 tbsp vegetable oil

2 large onions, sliced

2 garlic cloves, finely chopped

1¼ cups unsweetened yogurt

1 tbsp cornstarch

2 tbsp tomato paste

pinch of chili powder

salt

1 Top and tail the beans and snap them in half. Cut the carrots in half and the turnips in quarters. Divide the cauliflower into florets, discarding the thick stalk.

2 Steam the vegetables over boiling, salted water for 3 minutes, then turn them into a colander and plunge them at once in a large bowl of cold water to prevent further cooking.

3 Heat the oil in a skillet and fry the onions over a medium heat until they are translucent. Stir in the garlic and cook for 1 minute.

4 Mix together the yogurt, cornstarch and tomato paste to form a smooth paste. Stir this paste into the onions and cook for 1–2 minutes, until the sauce is thoroughly blended.

5 Drain the vegetables well, then gradually stir them into the sauce,

taking care not to break them up. Season with salt and chili powder to taste, cover and simmer over a low heat for 5 minutes, until the vegetables are just tender. Taste and adjust the seasoning if necessary. Serve immediately.

Vegetable Pasta Stir-Fry

East meets West in this delicious dish. Prepare all the vegetables and cook the pasta in advance, then the dish can be cooked in a few minutes.

NUTRITIONAL INFORMATION

Calories	383	Sugars	........18g
Protein	........14g	Fat	..........23g
Carbohydrate	...32g	Saturates	.......8g

  20 MINS   30 MINS

SERVES 4

I N G R E D I E N T S

4⅔ cups dried wholewheat pasta shells, or other short pasta shapes

1 tbsp olive oil

2 carrots, thinly sliced

4 oz baby-corn-on-the-cobs

3 tbsp peanut oil

1-inch piece fresh gingerroot, thinly sliced

1 large onion, thinly sliced

1 garlic clove, thinly sliced

3 celery stalks, thinly sliced

1 small red bell pepper, seeded and sliced into matchstick strips

1 small green bell pepper, seeded and sliced into matchstick strips

salt

steamed snow peas, to serve

S A U C E

1 tsp cornstarch

2 tbsp water

3 tbsp soy sauce

3 tbsp dry sherry

1 tsp clear honey

dash of hot pepper sauce (optional)

1 Cook the pasta in a large pan of boiling, lightly salted water, adding the tablespoon of olive oil. When tender, but still firm to the bite, drain the pasta in a colander, return to the pan, cover and keep warm.

2 Cook the carrots and baby-corn-on-the-cobs in boiling, salted water for 2 minutes. Drain them in a colander, plunge into cold water to prevent further cooking and drain again.

3 Heat the peanut oil in a large skillet over medium heat. Add the ginger and stir-fry for 1 minute, to flavor the oil. Remove with a draining spoon and discard.

4 Add the onion, garlic, celery, and bell peppers to the oil and stir-fry over a medium heat for 2 minutes. Add the carrots and baby-corn-on-the-cobs, and stir-fry for a further 2 minutes, then stir in the reserved pasta.

5 Put the cornstarch in a small bowl and mix to a smooth paste with the water. Stir in the soy sauce, sherry, and honey.

6 Pour the sauce into the pan, stir well and cook for 2 minutes, stirring once or twice. Taste the sauce and season with hot pepper sauce if wished. Serve with a steamed green vegetable, such as snow peas.

Sweet & Sour Vegetables

Serve this dish with plain noodles or fluffy white rice for a filling, and flavorsome oriental meal.

NUTRITIONAL INFORMATION

Calories	401	Sugars 16g
Protein	........14g	Fat 9g
Carbohydrate	...70g	Saturates 2g

 10 MINS   15 MINS

SERVES 4

I N G R E D I E N T S

1 tbsp peanut oil

2 garlic cloves, crushed

1 tsp grated gingerroot

1¾ oz baby-corn-on-the-cobs

1¾ oz snow peas

1 carrot, cut into matchsticks

1 green bell pepper, seeded and cut
    into matchsticks

8 scallions

1¾ oz canned bamboo shoots

8 oz marinated firm tofu, cubed

2 tbsp dry sherry or Chinese rice wine

2 tbsp rice vinegar

2 tbsp clear honey

1 tbsp light soy sauce

⅔ cup vegetable stock

1 tbsp cornstarch

noodles or boiled rice, to serve

1 Heat the oil in a preheated wok until almost smoking. Add the garlic and grated gingerroot and cook over a medium heat, stirring frequently, for 30 seconds.

2 Add the baby-corn-on-the-cobs, snow peas, carrot, and bell pepper matchsticks and stir-fry for about 5 minutes, or until the vegetables are tender, but still crisp.

3 Add the scallions, bamboo shoots and tofu and cook for 2 minutes.

4 Stir in the sherry or Chinese rice wine, rice vinegar, honey, soy sauce, vegetable stock, and cornstarch and bring to the boil. Reduce the heat to low and simmer for 2 minutes, until heated through. Transfer to warmed serving dishes and serve immediately.

Feta Cheese Patties

Grated carrots, zucchini, and feta cheese are combined with cumin seeds, poppy seeds, curry powder, and chopped fresh parsley.

NUTRITIONAL INFORMATION

Calories 217	Sugars 6g
Protein 6g	Fat 16g
Carbohydrate . . .12g	Saturates 7g

 15 MINS   20 MINS

SERVES 4

INGREDIENTS

2 large carrots

1 large zucchini

1 small onion

2 oz feta cheese

½ cup all-purpose flour

¼ tsp cumin seeds

½ tsp poppy seeds

1 tsp medium curry powder

1 tbsp chopped fresh parsley

1 egg, beaten

2 tbsp butter

2 tbsp vegetable oil

salt and pepper

herb sprigs, to garnish

1 Grate the carrots, zucchini, onion, and feta cheese coarsely, either by hand or process in a food processor.

2 Mix together the flour, cumin seeds, poppy seeds, curry powder, and parsley in a large bowl. Season to taste with salt and pepper.

3 Add the carrot mixture to the seasoned flour, tossing well to combine. Stir in the beaten egg.

4 Heat the butter and oil in a large, heavy-bottomed skillet. Place heaped tablespoonfuls of the carrot mixture in the pan, flattening them slightly with the back of the spoon. Fry gently for about 2 minutes on each side, until crisp and golden brown. Drain on paper towels and keep warm until all the mixture is used.

5 Serve immediately, garnished with sprigs of fresh herbs.

Casseroles & Bakes

Anyone who ever thought that vegetarian meals were dull will be proved wrong by the rich variety of dishes in this chapter. You'll recognize influences from Mexican and

Chinese cooking, but there are also traditional stews and casseroles, as well as hearty bakes and roasts. They all make exciting meals, at any time of year, and for virtually any occasion. Don't be afraid to substitute your own personal favorite ingredients where appropriate. There is no reason why you cannot enjoy experimenting and adding your own touch to these imaginative ideas.

Lentil & Rice Casserole

This is a really hearty dish, perfect for cold days when a filling hot dish is just what you need.

NUTRITIONAL INFORMATION

Calories 312   Sugars 9g
Protein . . . . .20g   Fat 2g
Carbohydrate . . .51g   Saturates 0.4g

15 MINS   40 MINS

SERVES 4

INGREDIENTS

1 cup split red lentils

⅓ cup long grain white rice

5 cups vegetable stock

1 leek, cut into chunks

3 garlic cloves, crushed

14 oz can chopped tomatoes

1 tsp ground cumin

1 tsp chili powder

1 tsp garam masala

1 red bell pepper, seeded and sliced

3½ oz small broccoli florets

8 baby-corn-on-the-cobs,
    halved lengthways

1¾ oz green beans, halved

1 tbsp shredded basil

salt and pepper

fresh basil sprigs, to garnish

VARIATION

You can vary the rice in this recipe — use brown or wild rice, if you prefer.

1 Place the lentils, rice, and vegetable stock in a large flameproof casserole and cook over a low heat, stirring occasionally, for 20 minutes.

2 Add the leek, garlic, tomatoes, and their can juice, ground cumin, chili powder, garam masala, sliced bell pepper, broccoli, corn-on-the-cobs, and green beans to the pan.

3 Bring the mixture to a boil, reduce the heat, cover, and simmer for a further 10–15 minutes, or until the vegetables are tender.

4 Add the shredded basil and season with salt and pepper to taste.

5 Garnish with fresh basil sprigs and serve immediately.

Winter Vegetable Casserole

This hearty supper dish is best served with plenty of warm crusty bread to mop up the delicious juices.

NUTRITIONAL INFORMATION

Calories 211	Sugars 6g	
Protein 11g	Fat 6g	
Carbohydrate . . .26g	Saturates 0.8g	

 10 MINS 40 MINS

SERVES 4

I N G R E D I E N T S

1 tbsp olive oil

1 red onion, halved and sliced

3 garlic cloves, crushed

8 oz spinach

1 fennel bulb, cut into eight

1 red bell pepper, seeded and cubed

1 tbsp all-purpose flour

1¾ cups vegetable stock

6 tbsp dry white wine

14 oz can garbanzo beans, drained

1 bay leaf

1 tsp ground coriander

½ tsp paprika

salt and pepper

fennel fronds, to garnish

1 Heat the olive oil in a large flameproof casserole. Add the onion and garlic and sauté over a low heat, stirring frequently, for 1 minute. Add the spinach and cook, stirring occasionally, for 4 minutes, or until wilted.

2 Add the fennel pieces and red bell pepper and cook, stirring constantly, for 2 minutes.

3 Stir in the flour and cook, stirring constantly, for 1 minute.

4 Add the vegetable stock, white wine, garbanzo beans, bay leaf, ground coriander, and paprika, cover and simmer for 30 minutes. Season to taste with salt and pepper, garnish with fennel fronds, and serve immediately straight from the casserole.

COOK'S TIP

Use other canned legumes or mixed beans instead of the garbanzo beans, if you prefer.

Winter Vegetable Cobbler

Seasonal fresh vegetables are casseroled with lentils, then topped with a ring of fresh cheese biscuits to make this tasty cobbler.

NUTRITIONAL INFORMATION

Calories	734	Sugars	.......22g
Protein	........27g	Fat	..........30g
Carbohydrate	...96g	Saturates	......16g

20 MINS   40 MINS

SERVES 4

I N G R E D I E N T S

1 tbsp olive oil

1 garlic clove, crushed

8 small onions, halved

2 celery stalks, sliced

8 oz rutabaga, chopped

2 carrots, sliced

½ small cauliflower, broken into florets

8 oz mushrooms, sliced

14 oz can chopped tomatoes

¼ cup red lentils

2 tbsp cornstarch

3–4 tbsp water

1¼ cups vegetable stock

2 tsp Tabasco sauce

2 tsp chopped oregano

oregano sprigs, to garnish

C O B B L E R   T O P P I N G

2 cups self-rising flour

¼ cup butter

1 cup grated sharp hard cheese

2 tsp chopped oregano

1 egg, beaten

⅔ cup milk

salt

1 Heat the oil in a large saucepan. Fry the garlic and onions for 5 minutes. Add the celery, rutabaga, carrots, and cauliflower and fry for 2–3 minutes. Add the mushrooms, tomatoes, and lentils.

2 Mix the cornstarch and water and add to the pan with the stock, Tabasco, and oregano. Bring to a boil, stirring. Transfer to an ovenproof dish, cover and bake in a preheated oven, 350°F, for 20 minutes.

3 To make the topping, sift the flour and salt into a bowl. Rub in the butter, then stir in most of the cheese and the chopped herbs. Beat together the egg and milk and add enough to the dry ingredients to make a soft dough. Knead lightly, roll out to ½ inch thick, and cut into 2 inch rounds.

4 Remove the dish from the oven and increase the temperature to 400°F. Arrange the rounds around the edge of the dish, brush with the remaining egg and milk, and sprinkle with the reserved cheese. Cook for a further 10–12 minutes, until the topping is risen and golden. Garnish and serve.

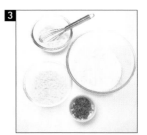

Lentil Roast

The perfect dish to serve for Sunday lunch. Roast vegetables make a succulent accompaniment.

NUTRITIONAL INFORMATION

Calories	400	Sugars	.........2g
Protein	........26g	Fat	..........20g
Carbohydrate	...32g	Saturates	......10g

15 MINS   1 HR 20 MINS

SERVES 6

I N G R E D I E N T S

1 cup red lentils

2 cups vegetable stock

1 bay leaf

1 tbsp butter or margarine, softened

2 tbsp dried whole wheat breadcrumbs

2 cups grated sharp hard cheese

1 leek, finely chopped

4½ oz button mushrooms,
    finely chopped

1½ cups fresh whole wheat breadcrumbs

2 tbsp chopped parsley

1 tbsp lemon juice

2 eggs, lightly beaten

salt and pepper

flat leaf parsley sprigs, to garnish

mixed roast vegetables, to serve

1 Put the lentils, stock and bay leaf in a saucepan. Bring to a boil, cover, and simmer gently for 15–20 minutes, until all the liquid is absorbed and the lentils have softened. Discard the bay leaf.

2 Base-line a 2 lb 4 oz loaf pan with baking parchment. Grease with the butter or margarine and sprinkle with the dried breadcrumbs.

3 Stir the cheese, leek, mushrooms, fresh breadcrumbs, and parsley into the lentils.

4 Bind the mixture together with the lemon juice and eggs. Season with salt and pepper. Spoon into the prepared loaf pan and smooth the top.

5 Bake in a preheated oven, 375°F, for about 1 hour, until golden.

6 Loosen the loaf with a spatula and turn on to a warmed serving plate. Garnish with parsley and serve sliced, with roast vegetables.

Almond & Sesame Nut Roast

Toasted almonds are combined with sesame seeds, rice, and vegetables in this tasty roast. Serve it with a delicious onion and mushroom sauce.

NUTRITIONAL INFORMATION

Calories 612   Sugars 7g
Protein . . . . .22g   Fat 46g
Carbohydrate . . .29g   Saturates 13g

30–40 MINS   35 MINS

SERVES 4

I N G R E D I E N T S

2 tbsp sesame or olive oil

1 small onion, finely chopped

scant ¼ cup risotto rice

1¼ cups vegetable stock

1 large carrot, grated

1 large leek, finely chopped

2 tsp sesame seeds, toasted

¾ cup chopped almonds, toasted

½ cup ground almonds

¾ cup grated sharp hard cheese

2 eggs, beaten

1 tsp dried mixed herbs

salt and pepper

flat leaf parsley sprigs, to garnish

fresh vegetables, to serve

S A U C E

2 tbsp butter

1 small onion, finely chopped

1½ cups finely chopped mushrooms

¼ cup all-purpose flour

1½ cups vegetable stock

1 Heat the oil in a large skillet and fry the onion gently for 2–3 minutes. Add the rice and cook gently for 5–6 minutes, stirring frequently.

2 Add the stock, bring to a boil, lower the heat, and simmer for 15 minutes, or until the rice is tender. Add a little extra water if necessary. Remove from the heat and transfer to a large mixing bowl.

3 Add the carrot, leek, sesame seeds, almonds, cheese, beaten eggs, and herbs. Mix well and season with salt and pepper. Transfer the mixture to a greased 1 lb 2 oz loaf pan, leveling the surface.

Bake in a preheated oven, 350°F, for 1 hour, until set and firm. Leave in the pan for 10 minutes.

4 To make the sauce, melt the butter in a small saucepan, and fry the onion until dark golden brown. Add the mushrooms and cook for 2 minutes. Stir in the flour, cook gently for 1 minute, then gradually add the stock. Bring to a boil, stirring constantly, until thickened and blended. Season to taste.

5 Turn out the nut roast, slice, and serve, garnished with parsley, and fresh vegetables, accompanied by the sauce.

Potato-Topped Lentil Bake

A wonderful mixture of red lentils, tofu, and vegetables is cooked beneath a crunchy potato topping for a really hearty meal.

NUTRITIONAL INFORMATION

Calories	627	Sugars	.........7g
Protein	........26g	Fat	..........30g
Carbohydrate	...66g	Saturates	......13g

🍲 10 MINS   🕐 1½ HOURS

SERVES 4

I N G R E D I E N T S

T O P P I N G

1½ lb mealy potatoes, diced

2 tbsp butter

1 tbsp milk

½ cup chopped pecan nuts

2 tbsp chopped thyme

thyme sprigs, to garnish

F I L L I N G

1 cup red lentils

½ cup butter

1 leek, sliced

2 garlic cloves, crushed

1 celery stalk, chopped

4½ oz broccoli florets

6 oz smoked tofu, cubed

2 tsp tomato paste

salt and pepper

1 To make the topping, cook the potatoes in a saucepan of boiling water for 10–15 minutes, or until cooked through. Drain well, add the butter and milk, and mash thoroughly. Stir in the pecan nuts and chopped thyme and set aside.

2 Cook the lentils in boiling water for 20–30 minutes, or until tender. Drain and set aside.

3 Melt the butter in a skillet. Add the leek, garlic, celery, and broccoli. Fry over a medium heat, stirring frequently, for 5 minutes, until softened. Add the tofu cubes. Stir in the lentils, together with the tomato paste. Season with salt and pepper to taste, then turn the mixture into the base of a shallow ovenproof dish.

4 Spoon the mashed potato on top of the lentil mixture, spreading to cover it completely.

5 Cook in a preheated oven, 400°F, for about 30–35 minutes, or until the topping is golden. Garnish with sprigs of fresh thyme and serve hot.

VARIATION

You can use almost any combination of your favorite vegetables in this dish.

Mexican Chili Corn Pie

This bake of corn and kidney beans, flavored with chili and fresh cilantro, is topped with crispy cheese cornbread.

NUTRITIONAL INFORMATION

Calories	519	Sugars	. . . . .17g
Protein	. . . . .22g	Fat	. . . . .22g
Carbohydrate	. . .61g	Saturates	. . . . . . .9g

25 MINS   20 MINS

SERVES 4

INGREDIENTS

1 tbsp corn oil

2 garlic cloves, crushed

1 red bell pepper, seeded and diced

1 green bell pepper, seeded and diced

1 celery stalk, diced

1 tsp hot chili powder

14 oz can chopped tomatoes

11½ oz can corn, drained

7½ oz can kidney beans,
   drained and rinsed

2 tbsp chopped cilantro

salt and pepper

cilantro sprigs, to garnish

tomato and avocado salad, to serve

TOPPING

⅔ cup cornmeal

1 tbsp all-purpose flour

½ tsp salt

2 tsp baking powder

1 egg, beaten

6 tbsp milk

1 tbsp corn oil

1 cup grated sharp hard cheese

1 Heat the oil in a large skillet and gently fry the garlic, bell peppers, and celery for 5–6 minutes until just softened.

2 Stir in the chili powder, tomatoes, sweetcorn, beans, and seasoning. Bring to a boil and simmer for 10 minutes. Stir in the cilantro and spoon into an ovenproof dish.

3 To make the topping, mix together the cornmeal, flour, salt, and baking powder. Make a well in the center, add the egg, milk, and oil and beat until a smooth batter is formed.

4 Spoon over the bell pepper and corn mixture and sprinkle with the cheese. Bake in a preheated oven, at 425°F, for 25–30 minutes until golden and firm.

5 Garnish with cilantro sprigs and serve immediately with a tomato and avocado salad.

Vegetable Hot Pot

In this recipe, a variety of vegetables are cooked under a layer of potatoes, topped with cheese, and cooked until golden brown.

NUTRITIONAL INFORMATION

Calories	279	Sugars	........12g
Protein	........10g	Fat	...........11g
Carbohydrate	...34g	Saturates	.......4g

🕙 25 MINS   🕐 1 HOUR

SERVES 4

I N G R E D I E N T S

2 large potatoes, thinly sliced

2 tbsp vegetable oil

1 red onion, halved and sliced

1 leek, sliced

2 garlic cloves, crushed

1 carrot, cut into chunks

3½ oz broccoli florets

3½ oz cauliflower florets

2 small turnips, quartered

1 tbsp all-purpose flour

3 cups vegetable stock

⅔ cup dry cider

1 eating apple, cored and sliced

2 tbsp chopped sage

pinch of cayenne pepper

½ cup grated hard cheese

salt and pepper

1 Cook the potato slices in a saucepan of boiling water for 10 minutes. Drain thoroughly and reserve.

2 Heat the oil in a flameproof casserole. Add the onion, leek, and garlic and sauté, stirring occasionally, for 2–3 minutes. Add the remaining vegetables and cook, stirring constantly, for a further 3–4 minutes.

3 Stir in the flour and cook for 1 minute. Gradually add the stock and cider and bring to a boil. Add the apple, sage, and cayenne pepper and season well. Remove from the heat and transfer the vegetables to an ovenproof dish.

4 Arrange the potato slices on top of the vegetable mixture to cover.

5 Sprinkle the cheese on top of the potato slices and cook in a preheated oven, 375°F, for 30–35 minutes or until the potato is golden brown and beginning to crispen around the edges. Serve immediately.

Brazil Nut & Mushroom Pie

The button mushrooms give this wholesome vegan pie a wonderful aromatic flavor. The pie can be frozen uncooked and baked from frozen.

NUTRITIONAL INFORMATION

Calories ....530 Sugars 4g
Protein ....12g Fat 38g
Carbohydrate ...38g Saturates 8g

1 HOUR   50 MINS

SERVES 6

INGREDIENTS

PASTRY

1¾ cups all-purpose
   whole wheat flour

⅓ cup margarine, cut into small pieces

4 tbsp water

soya milk, to glaze

FILLING

2 tbsp margarine

1 onion, chopped

1 garlic clove, finely chopped

4½ oz button mushrooms, sliced

1 tbsp all-purpose flour

⅔ cup vegetable stock

6 oz Brazil nuts

1 tbsp tomato paste

2¾ oz fresh whole wheat breadcrumbs

2 tbsp chopped parsley

½ tsp pepper

1 To make the pastry, place the flour in a mixing bowl and rub in the margarine with your fingertips until the mixture resembles fine breadcrumbs. Stir in the water and bring together to form a smooth dough. Knead lightly, then wrap and chill in the refrigerator for 30 minutes.

2 To make the filling, melt half of the margarine in a pan. Add the onion, garlic, and mushrooms and fry over a medium heat, stirring occasionally, for 5 minutes, until softened. Add the flour and cook for 1 minute, stirring frequently. Gradually add the stock, stirring until the sauce is smooth and beginning to thicken. Chop the Brazil nuts. Stir in the tomato paste, nuts, breadcrumbs, parsley and pepper. Set aside to cool slightly.

3 On a lightly floured surface, roll out two-thirds of the pastry and use to line a 8 inch loose-based flan pan or pie dish. Spread the filling in the pastry case. Brush the edges of the pastry with soya milk. Roll out the remaining pastry to fit the top of the pie. Seal the edges, make a slit in the top of the pastry, and brush with soya milk to glaze.

4 Bake in a preheated oven, 400°F, for 30–40 minutes, until golden brown. Serve immediately.

Layered Pies

These individual pies of layered potato, eggplant and zucchini baked in a tomato sauce can be made in advance.

NUTRITIONAL INFORMATION

Calories 427	Sugars 8g	
Protein 22g	Fat 21g	
Carbohydrate ...41g	Saturates 8g	

40 MINS   1 HR 20 MINS

SERVES 4

INGREDIENTS

3 large waxy potatoes, thinly sliced

1 small eggplant, thinly sliced

1 zucchini, sliced

3 tbsp vegetable oil

1 onion, diced

1 green bell pepper, seeded and diced

1 tsp cumin seeds

2 tbsp chopped basil

7 oz can chopped tomatoes

6 oz mozzarella cheese, sliced

8 oz tofu, sliced

2 oz/1 cup fresh white breadcrumbs

2 tbsp grated Parmesan cheese

salt and pepper

basil leaves, to garnish

1 Cook the sliced potatoes in a saucepan of boiling water for 5 minutes. Drain and set aside.

2 Put the eggplant slices on a plate, sprinkle with salt, and leave for 20 minutes. Meanwhile, blanch the zucchini in a saucepan of boiling water for 2-3 minutes. Drain and set aside.

3 Heat 2 tbsp of the oil in a skillet. Add the onion and fry over a low heat, stirring occasionally, for 2-3 minutes, until softened. Add the bell pepper, cumin seeds, basil, and canned tomatoes. Season to taste with salt and pepper and simmer for 30 minutes.

4 Rinse the eggplant slices and pat dry. Heat the remaining oil in a large skillet and fry the eggplant slices for 3-5 minutes, turning to brown both sides. Drain and set aside.

5 Arrange half of the potato slices in the base of 4 small loose-based flan pans. Cover with half of the zucchini slices, half of the eggplant slices, and half of the mozzarella slices. Lay the tofu on top and spoon over the tomato sauce. Repeat the layers of vegetables and cheese in the same order.

6 Mix the breadcrumbs and Parmesan together and sprinkle over the top. Cook in a preheated oven, 375°F, for 25-30 minutes, or until golden. Garnish with basil leaves.

Curry Turnovers

These turnovers, which are suitable for vegans, are a delicious combination of vegetables and spices.

NUTRITIONAL INFORMATION

Calories	455	Sugars	.........5g
Protein	.........8g	Fat	..........27g
Carbohydrate	...48g	Saturates	.......5g

1 HOUR   1 HOUR

SERVES 4

I N G R E D I E N T S

2 cups all-purpose whole wheat flour

⅓ cup margarine, cut into small pieces

4 tbsp water

2 tbsp oil

8 oz diced root vegetables, such as
    potatoes, carrots, and parsnips

1 small onion, chopped

2 garlic cloves, finely chopped

½ tsp curry powder

½ tsp ground turmeric

½ tsp ground cumin

½ tsp wholegrain mustard

5 tbsp vegetable stock

soya milk, to glaze

1 Place the flour in a mixing bowl and rub in the margarine with your fingertips until the mixture resembles breadcrumbs. Stir in the water and bring together to form a soft dough. Wrap and set aside to chill in the refrigerator for 30 minutes.

2 To make the filling, heat the oil in a large saucepan. Add the diced root vegetables, chopped onion, and garlic and fry, stirring occasionally, for 2 minutes. Stir in all of the spices, turning the vegetables to coat them thoroughly. Fry the vegetables, stirring constantly, for a further 1 minute.

3 Add the stock to the pan and bring to a boil. Cover and simmer, stirring occasionally, for about 20 minutes, until the vegetables are tender and the liquid has been absorbed. Leave to cool.

4 Divide the pastry into 4 portions. Roll each portion into a 6 inch round. Place the filling on one half of each round.

5 Brush the edges of each round with soya milk, then fold over and press the edges together to seal. Place on a baking sheet. Bake in a preheated oven, 400°F, for 25–30 minutes until golden brown.

Mushroom Vol-au-Vent

A simple mixture of creamy, tender mushrooms filling a crisp,
rich pastry case, this dish will make an impression at any dinner party.

NUTRITIONAL INFORMATION

Calories	688	Sugars	.........2g
Protein	........10g	Fat	..........52g
Carbohydrate	...45g	Saturates	......22g

🧊 25 MINS 🕐 50 MINS

SERVES 4

I N G R E D I E N T S

1 lb 2 oz puff pastry, thawed if frozen

1 egg, beaten, for glazing

FILLING

2 tbsp butter or margarine

1 lb 10 oz mixed mushrooms, such
   as open cup, field, button, crimini,
   shiitake, pied de mouton, sliced

6 tbsp dry white wine

4 tbsp heavy cream

2 tbsp chopped chervil

salt and pepper

chervil sprigs, to garnish

1 Roll out the pastry on a lightly floured
surface to a 8 inch square.

2 Using a sharp knife, mark a square
1 inch from the pastry edge, cutting
halfway through the pastry.

3 Score the top in a diagonal pattern.
Knock up the edges with a kitchen
knife and put on a baking sheet. Brush the
top with beaten egg, taking care not to let
the egg run into the cut. Bake in a
preheated oven, 425°F, for 35 minutes.

4 Cut out the central square. Discard
the soft pastry inside the case, leaving
the base intact. Return to the oven, with
the square, for 10 minutes.

5 Meanwhile, make the filling. Melt the
butter or margarine in a skillet and
stir-fry the mushrooms over a high heat
for 3 minutes.

6 Add the wine and cook, stirring
occasionally, for 10 minutes, until the
mushrooms have softened. Stir in the
cream and chervil and season to taste
with salt and pepper.

7 Pile into the pastry case. Top with the
pastry square, garnish with sprigs of
chervil, and serve.

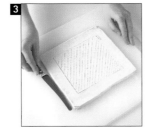

Green Vegetable Gougère

A tasty, simple supper dish of choux pastry and crisp green vegetables.
The choux pastry ring can be filled with all kinds of vegetables.

NUTRITIONAL INFORMATION

Calories	672	Sugars	.........6g
Protein	........19g	Fat	..........51g
Carbohydrate	...36g	Saturates	......14g

30 MINS   40 MINS

SERVES 4

I N G R E D I E N T S

1¼ cups all-purpose flour

½ cup butter

1¼ cups water

4 eggs, beaten

¾ cup grated Gruyère cheese

1 tbsp milk

salt and pepper

FILLING

2 tbsp garlic and herb butter or margarine

2 tsp olive oil

2 leeks, shredded

8 oz green cabbage, finely shredded

2 cups beansprouts

½ tsp grated lime rind

1 tbsp lime juice

celery salt and pepper

lime slices, to garnish

1 Sift the flour on to a piece of baking parchment. Cut the butter into dice and put in a saucepan with the water. Heat until the butter has melted.

2 Bring the butter and water to a boil, then tip in the flour all at once. Beat until the mixture becomes thick. Remove from the heat and beat until the mixture is glossy and comes away from the sides of the saucepan.

3 Transfer to a mixing bowl and cool for 10 minutes. Gradually beat in the eggs, a little at a time, making sure they are thoroughly incorporated after each addition. Stir in ½ cup of the cheese and season with salt and pepper.

4 Place spoonfuls of the mixture in a 9 inch circle on a dampened baking sheet. Brush with milk and sprinkle with the remaining cheese. Bake in a preheated oven, 425°F, for 30–35 minutes, until golden and crisp. Transfer to a warmed serving plate.

5 Meanwhile, make the filling. Heat the butter or margarine and the oil in a large skillet and stir-fry the leeks and cabbage for 2 minutes. Add the beansprouts, lime rind, and juice and stir-fry for 1 minute. Season to taste.

6 Pile into the center of the pastry ring. Garnish with lime slices and serve.

Vegetable & Tofu Strudels

These strudels look really impressive and are perfect if friends are coming round or for a more formal dinner party dish.

NUTRITIONAL INFORMATION

Calories . . . . . . .485 Sugars 5g
Protein . . . . .16g Fat 27g
Carbohydrate . . .47g Saturates 5g

25 MINS   30 MINS

SERVES 4

INGREDIENTS

FILLING

2 tbsp vegetable oil

2 tbsp butter

⅓ cup potatoes, finely diced

1 leek, shredded

2 garlic cloves, crushed

1 tsp garam masala

½ tsp chili powder

½ tsp turmeric

1¾ oz okra, sliced

1¼ cups sliced button mushrooms

2 tomatoes, diced

8 oz firm tofu, diced

12 sheets phyllo pastry

2 tbsp butter, melted

salt and pepper

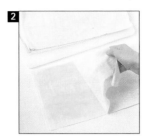

1 To make the filling, heat the oil and butter in a skillet. Add the potatoes and leek and fry, stirring constantly, for 2–3 minutes. Add the garlic and spices, okra, mushrooms, tomatoes, and tofu, and season to taste with salt and pepper. Cook, stirring, for 5–7 minutes, or until tender.

2 Lay the pastry out on a chopping board and brush each individual sheet with melted butter. Place 3 sheets on top of one another; repeat to make 4 stacks.

3 Spoon a quarter of the filling along the center of each stack and brush the edges with melted butter. Fold the short edges in and roll up lengthways to form a cigar shape. Brush the outside with melted butter. Place the strudels on a greased baking sheet.

4 Cook in a preheated oven, 375°F, for 20 minutes, or until golden brown and crisp. Transfer to a warm serving dish and serve immediately.

Mushroom & Spinach Puffs

These puff pastry packets, filled with garlic, mushrooms, and spinach are easy to make and simply melt in the mouth.

NUTRITIONAL INFORMATION

Calories	467	Sugars	.........4g
Protein	.........8g	Fat	..........38g
Carbohydrate	...24g	Saturates	......18g

 20 MINS   30 MINS

SERVES 4

INGREDIENTS

2 tbsp butter

1 red onion, halved and sliced

2 garlic cloves, crushed

3 cups sliced open-cap mushrooms

6 oz baby spinach

pinch of nutmeg

4 tbsp heavy cream

8 oz puff pastry

1 egg, beaten

salt and pepper

2 tsp poppy seeds

1 Melt the butter in a skillet. Add the onion and garlic and sauté over a low heat, stirring, for 3–4 minutes, until the onion has softened.

2 Add the mushrooms, spinach, and nutmeg and cook over a medium heat, stirring occasionally, for 2–3 minutes.

3 Stir in the heavy cream, mixing thoroughly. Season with salt and pepper to taste and remove the pan from the heat.

4 Roll the pastry out on a lightly floured surface and cut into four 6 inch rounds.

5 Put a quarter of the filling on to one half of each round and fold the pastry over to encase it. Press down to seal the edges and brush with the beaten egg. Sprinkle with the poppy seeds.

6 Place the packets on a dampened baking sheet and cook in a preheated oven, 400°F, for 20 minutes, until risen and golden brown in color.

7 Transfer the mushroom and spinach puffs to warmed serving plates and serve immediately.

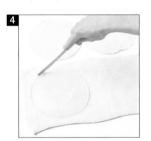

COOK'S TIP

The baking sheet is dampened so that steam forms with the heat of the oven, which helps the pastry to rise and set.

Italian Vegetable Tart

This mouthwateringly attractive tart is full of Mediterranean flavors — spinach, red bell peppers, ricotta cheese, and pine nuts.

NUTRITIONAL INFORMATION

Calories ....488 Sugars 7g
Protein ....13g Fat 40g
Carbohydrate ...21g Saturates 19g

  30 MINS   30 MINS

SERVES 6

I N G R E D I E N T S

8 oz frozen phyllo pastry, thawed

½ cup butter, melted

12 oz frozen spinach, thawed

2 eggs

⅔ cup thin cream

1 cup ricotta cheese

1 red bell pepper, seeded and
    sliced into strips

½ cup pine nuts

salt and pepper

  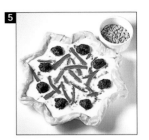 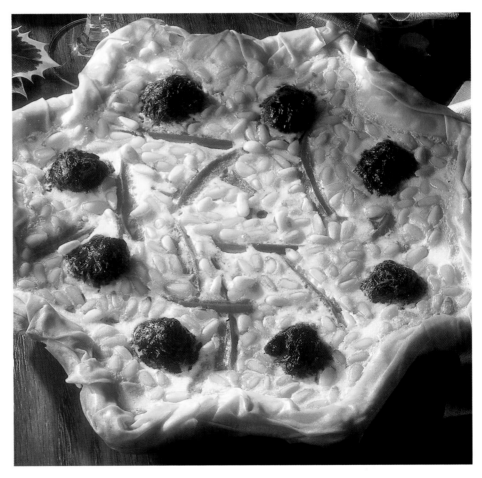

1 Use the sheets of phyllo pastry to line an 8 inch flan pan, brushing each layer with melted butter.

2 Put the spinach into a strainer or colander and squeeze out the excess moisture with the back of a spoon or your hand. Form the spinach into 8–9 small balls and arrange them in the prepared flan pan.

3 Beat the eggs, cream, and ricotta cheese together until thoroughly blended. Season to taste with salt and pepper and pour over the spinach.

4 Put the remaining butter into a saucepan. Add the red bell pepper strips and sauté over a low heat, stirring frequently, for about 4–5 minutes, until softened. Arrange the strips on the flan.

5 Scatter the pine nuts over the surface and bake in a preheated oven at 375°F for about 20–25 minutes, until the filling has set and the pastry is golden brown. Serve immediately or allow to cool completely and serve at room temperature.

VARIATION

If you are not fond of bell peppers, you could use mushrooms instead. Wild mushrooms would be especially delicious. Add a few sliced sun-dried tomatoes for extra color and flavor.

Mushroom & Pine Nut Tarts

Different varieties of mushroom are becoming more widely available in supermarkets, so use this recipe to make the most of them.

NUTRITIONAL INFORMATION

Calories 494	Sugars 2g
Protein 9g	Fat 35g
Carbohydrate ...38g	Saturates 18g

15 MINS   20 MINS

SERVES 4

INGREDIENTS

1 lb 2 oz phyllo pastry

½ cup butter, melted

1 tbsp hazelnut oil

¼ cup pine nuts

12 oz mixed mushrooms, such as
    button, crimini, oyster,
    and shiitake

2 tsp chopped parsley

1 cup soft goat's cheese

salt and pepper

parsley sprigs to garnish

lettuce, tomatoes, cucumber, and
    scallions, to serve

1 Cut the sheets of phyllo pastry into pieces about 4 inches square and use them to line 4 individual tart pans, brushing each layer of pastry with melted butter. Line the pans with foil or baking parchment and baking beans. Bake in a preheated oven at 400°F for about 6–8 minutes, or until light golden brown.

2 Remove the tarts from the oven and carefully take out the foil or parchment and baking beans. Reduce the oven temperature to 350°F.

3 Put any remaining butter into a large saucepan with the hazelnut oil and fry the pine nuts gently until golden brown. Lift them out with a draining spoon and drain on paper towels.

4 Add the mushrooms to the saucepan and cook them gently, stirring frequently, for about 4–5 minutes. Add the chopped parsley and season to taste with salt and pepper.

5 Spoon one quarter of the goat's cheese into the base of each cooked phyllo tart. Divide the mushrooms equally between them and scatter the pine nuts over the top.

6 Return the tarts to the oven for 5 minutes to heat through, and then serve them, garnished with sprigs of parsley. Serve with lettuce, tomatoes, cucumber, and scallions.

Vegetable Cake

This is a savory version of a cheesecake with a layer of fried potatoes as a delicious base. Use frozen mixed vegetables for the topping, if liked.

NUTRITIONAL INFORMATION

Calories 502   Sugars 8g
Protein . . . . .16g   Fat 31g
Carbohydrate . . .41g   Saturates 14g

20 MINS   45 MINS

SERVES 4

I N G R E D I E N T S

BASE

2 tbsp vegetable oil, plus extra for brushing

4 large waxy potatoes, thinly sliced

TOPPING

1 tbsp vegetable oil

1 leek, chopped

1 zucchini, grated

1 red bell pepper, seeded and diced

1 green bell pepper, seeded and diced

1 carrot, grated

2 tsp chopped parsley

1 cup full-fat soft cheese

¼ cup grated sharp cheese

2 eggs, beaten

salt and pepper

shredded cooked leek, to garnish

salad, to serve

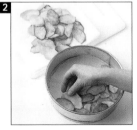  

1 Brush a 8 inch springform cake pan with oil.

2 To make the base, heat the oil in a skillet. Cook the potato slices until softened and browned. Drain on paper towels and place in the base of the pan.

3 To make the topping, heat the oil in a separate skillet. Add the leek and fry over a low heat, stirring frequently, for 3-4 minutes, until softened.

4 Add the zucchini, bell peppers, carrot, and parsley to the pan and cook over a low heat for 5-7 minutes, or until the vegetables have softened.

5 Meanwhile, beat the cheeses and eggs together in a bowl. Stir in the vegetables and season to taste with salt and pepper. Spoon the mixture evenly over the potato base.

6 Cook in a preheated oven, 375°F, for 20–25 minutes, until the cake is set.

7 Remove the vegetable cake from the pan, transfer to a warm serving plate, garnish with shredded leek, and serve with a crisp salad.

Spinach Pancake Layer

Nutty-tasting buckwheat pancakes are combined with a cheese and spinach mixture and baked with a crispy topping.

NUTRITIONAL INFORMATION

Calories 467   Sugars 10g
Protein . . . . .29g   Fat 26g
Carbohydrate . . .31g   Saturates 7g

45 MINS   1 HR 5 MINS

SERVES 4

INGREDIENTS

1 cup buckwheat flour

1 egg, beaten

1 tbsp walnut oil

1¼ cups milk

2 tsp vegetable oil

FILLING

2 lb 4 oz young spinach leaves

2 tbsp water

1 bunch scallions, white
    and green parts, chopped

2 tsp walnut oil

1 egg, beaten

1 egg yolk

1 cup cottage cheese

½ tsp grated nutmeg

¼ cup grated sharp hard cheese

¼ cup walnut pieces

salt and pepper

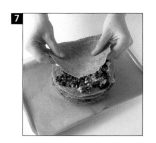

1   Sift the flour into a bowl and add any husks that remain in the strainer.

2   Make a well in the center and add the egg and walnut oil. Gradually whisk in the milk to make a smooth batter. Leave to stand for 30 minutes.

3   To make the filling, wash the spinach and pack into a saucepan with the water. Cover tightly and cook on a high heat for 5–6 minutes, until soft.

4   Drain well and leave to cool. Gently fry the scallions in the walnut oil for 2–3 minutes, until just soft. Drain on paper towels and set aside.

5   Whisk the batter. Brush a small skillet with oil, heat until hot and pour in enough batter just to cover the base. Cook for 1–2 minutes, until set, flip over and cook for 1 minute, until golden on the underside. Turn on to a warmed plate.

Repeat to make 8–10 pancakes, layering them with baking parchment.

6   Chop the spinach and dry with paper towels. Mix with the scallions, beaten egg, egg yolk, cottage cheese, and nutmeg and season to taste with salt and pepper.

7   Layer the pancakes and spinach mixture on a baking sheet lined with baking parchment, finishing with a pancake. Sprinkle with hard cheese and bake in a preheated oven, 375°F, for 20–25 minutes, until firm and golden. Sprinkle with the walnuts and serve immediately.

Leek & Herb Soufflé

Hot soufflés look very impressive if served as soon as they come out of the oven, otherwise they will sink quite quickly.

NUTRITIONAL INFORMATION

Calories 182   Sugars 4g
Protein . . . . .8g   Fat 15g
Carbohydrate . . . .5g   Saturates 2g

15 MINS   50 MINS

SERVES 4

I N G R E D I E N T S

12 oz baby leeks

1 tbsp olive oil

½ cup vegetable stock

½ cup walnuts

2 eggs, separated

2 tbsp chopped mixed herbs

2 tbsp unsweetened yogurt

salt and pepper

1 Using a sharp knife, chop the leeks finely. Heat the oil in a skillet. Add the leeks and sauté over a medium heat, stirring occasionally, for 2–3 minutes.

2 Add the vegetable stock to the pan, lower the heat and simmer gently for a further 5 minutes.

3 Place the walnuts in a food processor and process until finely chopped. Add the leek mixture to the nuts and process briefly to form a paste. Transfer to a mixing bowl.

4 Mix together the egg yolks, herbs, and yogurt until thoroughly combined. Pour the egg mixture into the leek paste. Season with salt and pepper to taste and mix well.

5 In a separate mixing bowl, whisk the egg whites until firm peaks form.

6 Fold the egg whites into the leek mixture. Spoon the mixture into a lightly greased 3¾ cup soufflé dish and place on a warmed baking sheet.

7 Cook in a preheated oven, 350°F, for 35–40 minutes, or until risen and set. Serve the soufflé immediately.

COOK'S TIP

Placing the soufflé dish on a warm baking sheet helps to cook the soufflé from the bottom, thus aiding its cooking and lightness.

Jacket Potatoes with Beans

Baked jacket potatoes, topped with a tasty mixture of beans in a spicy sauce, provide a deliciously filling, high-fiber dish.

NUTRITIONAL INFORMATION

Calories 378   Sugars 9g
Protein ....15g   Fat 9g
Carbohydrate ...64g   Saturates 1g

 15 MINS   1¼ HOURS

SERVES 6

I N G R E D I E N T S

6 large potatoes

4 tbsp vegetable ghee or oil

1 large onion, chopped

2 garlic cloves, crushed

1 tsp ground turmeric

1 tbsp cumin seeds

2 tbsp mild or medium curry paste

12 oz cherry tomatoes

14 oz can black-eyed peas,
    drained and rinsed

14 oz can red kidney beans,
    drained and rinsed

1 tbsp lemon juice

2 tbsp tomato paste

⅔ cup water

2 tbsp chopped fresh mint or cilantro

salt and pepper

VARIATION

Instead of cutting the potatoes in half, cut a cross in each and squeeze gently to open out. Spoon some of the prepared filling into the cross and place any remaining filling to the side.

1 Scrub the potatoes and prick several times with a fork. Place in a preheated oven, 350°F, and cook for 1–1¼ hours, or until the potatoes feel soft when gently squeezed.

2 About 20 minutes before the end of cooking time, prepare the topping. Heat the ghee or oil in a saucepan, add the onion and cook over a low heat, stirring frequently, for 5 minutes. Add the garlic, turmeric, cumin seeds, and curry paste and cook gently for 1 minute.

3 Stir in the tomatoes, black-eyed peas and red kidney beans, lemon juice, tomato paste, water and chopped mint. Season to taste with salt and pepper, then cover and simmer over a low heat, stirring frequently, for 10 minutes.

4 When the potatoes are cooked, cut them in half and mash the flesh lightly with a fork. Spoon the prepared bean mixture on top, place on warming serving plates and serve immediately.

Four-Cheese & Potato Layer

This is a quick dish to prepare and it can be left to cook in the oven without requiring any further attention.

NUTRITIONAL INFORMATION

Calories	766	Sugars	........14g
Protein	........44g	Fat	..........40g
Carbohydrate	...60g	Saturates	......23g

25 MINS   45 MINS

SERVES 4

I N G R E D I E N T S

2 lb unpeeled waxy potatoes,
   cut into wedges

2 tbsp butter

1 red onion, halved and sliced

2 garlic cloves, crushed

¼ cup all-purpose flour

2½ cups milk

14 oz can artichoke hearts in brine,
   drained and halved

5½ oz frozen mixed
   vegetables, thawed

1 cup grated Gruyère cheese

1 cup grated sharp cheese

½ cup crumbled Gorgonzola

⅓ cup grated Parmesan cheese

8 oz tofu, sliced

2 tbsp chopped thyme

salt and pepper

thyme sprigs, to garnish

1 Cook the potato wedges in a saucepan of boiling water for 10 minutes. Drain thoroughly.

2 Meanwhile, melt the butter in a saucepan. Add the sliced onion and garlic and fry over a low heat, stirring frequently, for 2–3 minutes.

3 Stir the flour into the pan and cook for 1 minute. Gradually add the milk and bring to a boil, stirring constantly.

4 Reduce the heat and add the artichoke hearts, mixed vegetables, half of each of the 4 cheeses, and the tofu to the pan, mixing well. Stir in the chopped thyme and season with salt and pepper to taste.

5 Arrange a layer of parboiled potato wedges in the base of a shallow ovenproof dish. Spoon the vegetable mixture over the top and cover with the remaining potato wedges. Sprinkle the rest of the 4 cheeses over the top.

6 Cook in a preheated oven, 400°F, for 30 minutes or until the potatoes are cooked and the top is golden brown. Serve the bake garnished with fresh thyme sprigs.

Potato & Cheese Soufflé

This soufflé is very simple to make, yet it has a delicious flavor and melts in the mouth. Choose three alternative cheeses, if preferred.

NUTRITIONAL INFORMATION

Calories	447	Sugars	.........1g
Protein	........22g	Fat	..........23g
Carbohydrate	...41g	Saturates	......11g

🍞 🍞

🥔 10 MINS   🕐 55 MINS

SERVES 4

I N G R E D I E N T S

2 tbsp butter

2 tsp all-purpose flour

2 lb mealy potatoes

8 eggs, separated

¼ cup grated Gruyère cheese

¼ cup crumbled blue cheese

¼ cup grated sharp hard cheese

salt and pepper

1 Butter a 2½ quart soufflé dish and dust with the flour. Set aside.

2 Cook the potatoes in a saucepan of boiling water until tender. Mash until very smooth and then transfer to a mixing bowl to cool.

3 Beat the egg yolks into the potato and stir in the Gruyère cheese, blue cheese, and hard cheese, mixing well. Season to taste with salt and pepper.

4 Whisk the egg whites until standing in peaks, then gently fold them into the potato mixture with a metal spoon until fully incorporated.

5 Spoon the potato mixture into the prepared soufflé dish.

6 Cook in a preheated oven, 425°F, for 35–40 minutes, until risen and set. Serve immediately.

COOK'S TIP

Insert a fine skewer into the center of the soufflé; it should come out clean when the soufflé is fully cooked through.

Creamy Baked Fennel

Fennel tastes fabulous in this creamy sauce, flavored with caraway seeds. A crunchy breadcrumb topping gives an interesting texture.

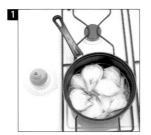

NUTRITIONAL INFORMATION

Calories	292	Sugars	. . . . .5g
Protein	. . . . .10g	Fat	. . . . .23g
Carbohydrate	. . .12g	Saturates	. . . . . .14g

 10 MINS   45 MINS

SERVES 4

I N G R E D I E N T S

2 tbsp lemon juice

2 fennel bulbs, thinly sliced

¼ cup butter, plus extra for greasing

¼ cup low-fat soft cheese

⅔ cup light cream

⅔ cup milk

1 egg, beaten

2 tsp caraway seeds

1 cup fresh white breadcrumbs

salt and pepper

parsley sprigs, to garnish

1 Bring a saucepan of water to a boil and add the lemon juice and fennel. Cook for 2–3 minutes to blanch, drain, and place in a greased ovenproof dish.

2 Beat the soft cheese in a bowl until smooth. Add the cream, milk, and beaten egg, and whisk together until combined. Season with salt and pepper and pour the mixture over the fennel.

3 Melt 1 tbsp of the butter in a small skillet and fry the caraway seeds gently for 1–2 minutes, until they release their aroma. Sprinkle them over the fennel.

4 Melt the remaining butter in a skillet. Add the breadcrumbs and fry over a low heat, stirring frequently, until lightly browned. Sprinkle them evenly over the surface of the fennel.

5 Place in a preheated oven, 350°F, and bake for 25–30 minutes, or until the fennel is tender. Serve immediately, garnished with sprigs of parsley.

Lentil & Vegetable Shells

These stuffed eggplants are delicious served hot or cold, topped with unsweetened yogurt or cucumber raita.

NUTRITIONAL INFORMATION

Calories	386	Sugars	.........9g
Protein	........14g	Fat	..........24g
Carbohydrate	...30g	Saturates	.......3g

25 MINS   1 HOUR

SERVES 6

INGREDIENTS

1⅓ cup European lentils

3¾ cups water

2 garlic cloves, crushed

3 well-shaped eggplants

⅔ cup vegetable oil, plus
    extra for brushing

2 onions, chopped

4 tomatoes, chopped

2 tsp cumin seeds

1 tsp ground cinnamon

2 tbsp mild curry paste

1 tsp ground chili

2 tbsp chopped mint

salt and pepper

unsweetened yogurt and
    mint sprigs, to serve

1 Rinse the lentils under cold running water. Drain and place in a saucepan with the water and garlic. Cover and simmer for 30 minutes.

2 Cook the eggplants in a saucepan of boiling water for 5 minutes. Drain, then plunge into cold water for 5 minutes. Drain again, then cut the eggplants in half lengthways and scoop out most of the flesh and reserve, leaving a ½ inch thick border to form a shell.

3 Place the eggplant shells in a shallow greased ovenproof dish, brush with a little oil, and sprinkle with salt and pepper. Cook in a preheated oven, 375°F, for 10 minutes. Meanwhile, heat half the remaining oil in a skillet, add the onions and tomatoes, and fry gently for 5 minutes. Chop the reserved eggplant flesh, add to the pan with the spices and cook gently for 5 minutes. Season with salt.

4 Stir in the lentils, most of the remaining oil, reserving a little for later, and the mint. Spoon the mixture into the shells. Drizzle with remaining oil and bake for 15 minutes. Serve hot or cold, topped with a spoonful of unsweetened yogurt and mint sprigs.

COOK'S TIP

Choose nice plump eggplants, rather than thin tapering ones, as they retain their shape better when filled and baked with a stuffing.

Potato & Vegetable Gratin

Similar to a simple moussaka, this recipe is made up of layers of eggplant, tomato, and potato baked with a yogurt topping.

NUTRITIONAL INFORMATION

Calories	409	Sugars	........17g
Protein	........28g	Fat	..........14g
Carbohydrate	...45g	Saturates	.......3g

25 MINS   1¼ HOURS

SERVES 4

I N G R E D I E N T S

1 lb 2 oz waxy potatoes, sliced

1 tbsp vegetable oil

1 onion, chopped

2 garlic cloves, crushed

1 lb 2 oz tofu, diced

2 tbsp tomato paste

2 tbsp all-purpose flour

1¼ cups vegetable stock

2 large tomatoes, sliced

1 eggplant, sliced

2 tbsp chopped fresh thyme

scant 2 cups unsweetened yogurt

2 eggs, beaten

salt and pepper

salad, to serve

VARIATION

You can use marinated or smoked tofu for extra flavor, if you wish.

1 Cook the sliced potatoes in a saucepan of boiling water for 10 minutes, until tender, but not breaking up. Drain and set aside.

2 Heat the oil in a skillet. Add the onion and garlic and fry, stirring occasionally, for 2-3 minutes.

3 Add the tofu, tomato paste, and flour and cook for 1 minute. Gradually stir in the stock and bring to a boil, stirring. Reduce the heat and simmer for 10 minutes.

4 Arrange a layer of the potato slices in the base of a deep ovenproof dish.

Spoon the tofu mixture evenly on top. Layer the sliced tomatoes, then the eggplant and finally, the remaining potato slices on top of the tofu mixture, making sure that it is completely covered. Sprinkle with thyme.

5 Mix the yogurt and beaten eggs together in a bowl and season to taste with salt and pepper. Spoon the yogurt topping over the sliced potatoes to cover them completely.

6 Bake in a preheated oven, 375°F, for about 35–45 minutes or until the topping is browned. Serve with a crisp salad.

Potato-Topped Vegetables

This is a very colorful and nutritious dish, packed full of crunchy vegetables in a tasty white wine sauce.

NUTRITIONAL INFORMATION

Calories 413	Sugars 11g	
Protein 19g	Fat 18g	
Carbohydrate . . .41g	Saturates 11g	

20 MINS   1¼ HOURS

SERVES 4

I N G R E D I E N T S

1 carrot, diced

6 oz cauliflower florets

6 oz broccoli florets

1 fennel bulb, sliced

2¾ oz green beans, halved

2 tbsp butter

¼ cup all-purpose flour

⅔ cup vegetable stock

⅔ cup dry white wine

⅔ cup milk

6 oz crimini mushrooms, quartered

2 tbsp chopped sage

T O P P I N G

4 mealy potatoes, diced

2 tbsp butter

4 tbsp unsweetened yogurt

4 tbsp grated Parmesan cheese

1 tsp fennel seeds

salt and pepper

1 Cook the carrot, cauliflower, broccoli, fennel, and beans in a large saucepan of boiling water for 10 minutes, until just tender. Drain the vegetables thoroughly and set aside.

2 Melt the butter in a saucepan. Stir in the flour and cook for 1 minute. Remove from the heat and stir in the stock, wine, and milk. Return to the heat and bring to a boil, stirring until thickened. Stir in the reserved vegetables, mushrooms and sage.

3 Meanwhile, make the topping. Cook the diced potatoes in a pan of boiling water for 10-15 minutes. Drain and mash with the butter, yogurt, and half the cheese. Stir in the fennel seeds.

4 Spoon the vegetable mixture into a 1 quart pie dish. Spoon the potato over the top and sprinkle with the remaining cheese. Cook in a preheated oven, 375°F, for 30–35 minutes, or until golden. Serve hot.

Vegetable Jalousie

This is a really easy dish to make, but looks impressive. The mixture of vegetables gives the dish a wonderful color and flavor.

NUTRITIONAL INFORMATION

Calories . . . . . . .660 Sugars 7g
Protein . . . . .11g Fat 45g
Carbohydrate . . .53g Saturates 15g

25 MINS   45 MINS

SERVES 4

I N G R E D I E N T S

1 lb 2 oz puff pastry

1 egg, beaten

F I L L I N G

2 tbsp butter or margarine

1 leek, shredded

2 garlic cloves, crushed

1 red bell pepper, seeded and sliced

1 yellow bell pepper, seeded and sliced

½ cup sliced mushrooms

2¾ oz small asparagus spears

2 tbsp all-purpose flour

6 tbsp vegetable stock

6 tbsp milk

4 tbsp dry white wine

1 tbsp chopped oregano

salt and pepper

1 Melt the butter or margarine in a skillet and sauté the leek and garlic, stirring frequently, for 2 minutes. Add the remaining vegetables and cook, stirring, for 3–4 minutes.

2 Add the flour and cook for 1 minute. Remove the pan from the heat and stir in the vegetable stock, milk, and white wine. Return the pan to the heat and bring to a boil, stirring, until thickened.

Stir in the oregano and season with salt and pepper to taste.

3 Roll out half of the pastry on a lightly floured surface to form a rectangle 15 x 6 inches.

4 Roll out the other half of the pastry to the same shape, but a little larger all round. Put the smaller rectangle on a baking sheet lined with dampened baking parchment.

5 Spoon the filling evenly on top of the smaller rectangle, leaving a ½ inch clear margin around the edges.

6 Using a sharp knife, cut parallel diagonal slits across the larger rectangle to within 1 inch of each of the long edges.

7 Brush the edges of the smaller rectangle with beaten egg and place the larger rectangle on top, pressing the edges firmly together to seal.

8 Brush the whole jalousie with egg to glaze and bake in a preheated oven, 400°F, for about 30–35 minutes, until risen, and golden. Transfer to a warmed serving dish and serve immediately.

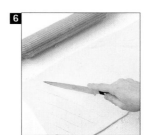

Spicy Potato Casserole

This is based on a Moroccan dish in which potatoes are spiced with cilantro and cumin and cooked in a lemon sauce.

NUTRITIONAL INFORMATION

Calories ....338 Sugars 8g
Protein ....5g Fat 23g
Carbohydrate ...29g Saturates 2g

 15 MINS   🕐 35 MINS

SERVES 4

I N G R E D I E N T S

½ cup olive oil

2 red onions, cut into eight

3 garlic cloves, crushed

2 tsp ground cumin

2 tsp ground coriander

pinch of cayenne pepper

1 carrot, thickly sliced

2 small turnips, quartered

1 zucchini, sliced

1 lb 2 oz potatoes, thickly sliced

juice and rind of 2 large lemons

1¼ cups vegetable stock

2 tbsp chopped cilantro

salt and pepper

COOK'S TIP

Check the vegetables while they are cooking, as they may begin to stick to the pan. Add a little more boiling water or stock if necessary.

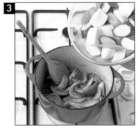  

1 Heat the olive oil in a flameproof casserole. Add the onion and sauté over a medium heat, stirring frequently, for 3 minutes.

2 Add the garlic and cook for 30 seconds. Stir in the spices and cook, stirring constantly, for 1 minute.

3 Add the carrot, turnips, zucchini, and potatoes and stir to coat in the oil.

4 Add the lemon juice and rind and the vegetable stock. Season to taste with salt and pepper. Cover and cook over a medium heat, stirring occasionally, for 20–30 minutes, until tender.

5 Remove the lid, sprinkle in the cilantro and stir well. Serve immediately.

Indian Curry Feast

This vegetable curry is quick and easy to prepare and it tastes superb. A colorful Indian salad and mint raita make perfect accompaniments.

NUTRITIONAL INFORMATION

Calories ....473 Sugars 18g
Protein ....19g Fat 9g
Carbohydrate ...84g Saturates 1g

25-30 MINS   55 MINS

SERVES 4

INGREDIENTS

1 tbsp vegetable oil

2 garlic cloves, crushed

1 onion, chopped

3 celery stalks, sliced

1 apple, cored and chopped

1 tbsp medium-strength curry powder

1 tsp ground ginger

14 oz can garbanzo beans

4½ oz thin beans, sliced

8 oz cauliflower, broken into florets

8 oz potatoes, cut into cubes

2 cups sliced mushrooms

2½ cups vegetable stock

1 tbsp tomato paste

1 oz golden raisins

scant 1 cup basmati rice

1 tbsp garam masala

MINT RAITA

⅔ cup unsweetened yogurt

1 tbsp chopped mint

1 Heat the oil in a large saucepan. Add the garlic, onion, celery, and apple and fry over a medium heat, stirring frequently, for 3–4 minutes. Add the curry powder and ginger, and cook gently for 1 more minute.

2 Drain the garbanzo beans and add to the onion mixture, together with the thin beans, cauliflower, potatoes, mushrooms, stock, tomato paste, and golden raisins. Bring to the boil, then reduce the heat. Cover and simmer for 35–40 minutes.

3 Meanwhile, make the raita. Mix the yogurt and mint together. Transfer to a small serving bowl, then cover and chill in the refrigerator.

4 Cook the rice in a large saucepan of boiling, lightly salted water for about 12 minutes, or until just tender. Drain, rinse with boiling water and drain again.

5 Just before serving, stir the garam masala into the curry. Divide between four warmed serving plates and serve with the rice. Garnish the raita with fresh mint and hand the bowl separately.

Coconut Vegetable Curry

A mildly spiced, but richly flavored Indian-style dish full of different textures and flavors. Serve with naan bread to soak up the tasty sauce.

NUTRITIONAL INFORMATION

Calories 159   Sugars 8g
Protein . . . . .8g   Fat 6g
Carbohydrate . . .19g   Saturates 1g

45 MINS   35 MINS

SERVES 6

INGREDIENTS

1 large eggplant, cut into 1 inch cubes

2 tbsp salt

2 tbsp vegetable oil

2 garlic cloves, crushed

1 fresh green chili,
   seeded and finely chopped

1 tsp grated gingerroot

1 onion, finely chopped

2 tsp garam masala

8 cardamom pods

1 tsp ground turmeric

1 tbsp tomato paste

3 cups vegetable stock

1 tbsp lemon juice

8 oz potatoes, diced

8 oz small cauliflower florets

8 oz okra, trimmed

8 oz frozen peas

⅔ cup coconut milk

salt and pepper

flaked coconut, to garnish

naan bread, to serve

1 Layer the eggplant in a bowl, sprinkling with salt as you go. Set aside for 30 minutes.

2 Rinse well under cold running water to remove all the salt. Drain and pat dry with paper towels. Set aside.

3 Heat the oil in a large saucepan. Add the garlic, chili, ginger, onion, and spices and fry over a medium heat, stirring occasionally, for 4–5 minutes, until lightly browned.

4 Stir in the tomato paste, stock, lemon juice, potatoes, and cauliflower and mix well. Bring to the boil, lower the heat, cover and simmer for 15 minutes.

5 Stir in the eggplant, okra, peas, and coconut milk and season to taste with salt and pepper. Return to the boil and continue to simmer, uncovered, for a further 10 minutes, or until tender. Remove and discard the cardamom pods.

6 Pile on to a warmed serving platter, garnish with flaked coconut and serve immediately with naan bread.

Bread & Butter Savory

Quick, simple, nutritious, and a pleasure to eat — what more could you ask for an inexpensive midweek meal?

NUTRITIONAL INFORMATION

Calories	472	Sugars	.........7g
Protein	........22g	Fat	..........33g
Carbohydrate	...25g	Saturates	......20g

30 MINS   45 MINS

SERVES 4

I N G R E D I E N T S

¼ cup butter or margarine

1 bunch scallions, sliced

6 slices of white or brown bread,
   crusts removed

1½ cups grated sharp hard cheese

2 eggs

scant 2 cups milk

salt and pepper

flat leaf parsley sprigs, to garnish

1 Grease a 1½ quart ovenproof dish with a little of the butter or margarine.

2 Melt the remaining butter or margarine in a small saucepan. Add the scallions and fry over a medium heat, stirring occasionally, until softened and golden.

3 Meanwhile, cut the bread into triangles and place half of them in the base of the dish. Cover with the spring onions (scallions) and top with half the grated cheese.

4 Beat together the eggs and milk and season to taste with salt and pepper. Layer the remaining triangles of bread in the dish and carefully pour over the milk mixture. Leave to soak for 15–20 minutes.

5 Sprinkle the remaining cheese over the soaked bread. Bake in a preheated oven, 375°F, for 35–40 minutes, until puffed up and golden brown. Garnish with flat leaf parsley and serve immediately.

VARIATION

You can vary the vegetables used in this savory bake, depending on what you have to hand. Shallots, mushrooms, or tomatoes are all suitable.

White Nut Phyllo Packets

These crisp, buttery packets, filled with nuts and pesto, would make an interesting break with tradition for Sunday lunch.

NUTRITIONAL INFORMATION

Calories	1100	Sugars	. . . . .9g
Protein	. . . . .29g	Fat	. . . . .80g
Carbohydrate	. . .73g	Saturates	. . . . . .15g

🕐 15 MINS   ⏱ 25 MINS

SERVES 4

INGREDIENTS

3 tbsp butter or margarine

1 large onion, finely chopped

2¼ cups mixed white nuts, such as
   pine nuts, unsalted cashew nuts,
   blanched almonds, unsalted peanuts,
   finely chopped

1½ cups fresh white breadcrumbs

½ tsp ground mace

1 egg, beaten

1 egg yolk

3 tbsp pesto sauce

2 tbsp chopped basil

½ cup butter or margarine, melted

16 sheets phyllo pastry

salt and pepper

basil sprigs to garnish

TO SERVE

cranberry sauce

steamed vegetables

1 Melt the butter or margarine in a skillet and gently fry the onion for 2–3 minutes, until just softened but not browned.

2 Remove from the heat and stir in the nuts, two-thirds of the breadcrumbs, the mace, and beaten egg. Season to taste with salt and pepper. Set aside.

3 Place the remaining breadcrumbs in a bowl and stir in the egg yolk, pesto sauce, basil, and 1 tablespoon of the melted butter or margarine. Mix well.

4 Brush 1 sheet of phyllo with melted butter or margarine. Fold in half and brush again. Repeat with a second sheet and lay it on top of the first one so that it forms a cross.

5 Put one-eighth of the nut mixture in the center of the pastry. Top with one-eighth of the pesto mixture. Fold over the edges, brushing with more butter or margarine, to form a packet. Brush the top with butter or margarine and transfer to a baking sheet. Make eight packets in the same way and brush with the remaining butter or margarine.

6 Bake in a preheated oven at 425°F for 15–20 minutes, until golden. Transfer to serving plates, garnish with basil sprigs and serve with cranberry sauce and steamed vegetables.

Root Croustades

This colorful combination of grated root vegetables and mixed bell peppers would make a stunning dinnerparty dish.

NUTRITIONAL INFORMATION

Calories . . . . . . .304 Sugars 17g
Protein . . . . .6g Fat 19g
Carbohydrate . . .28g Saturates 3g

🥘 2½ HOURS 🕐 1¼ HOURS

SERVES 4

INGREDIENTS

1 orange bell pepper

1 red bell pepper

1 yellow bell pepper

3 tbsp olive oil

2 tbsp red wine vinegar

1 tsp French mustard

1 tsp clear honey

salt and pepper

flat leaf parsley sprigs, to garnish

green vegetables, to serve

CROUSTADES

8 oz potatoes, coarsely grated

8 oz carrots, coarsely grated

12 oz celeriac, coarsely grated

1 garlic clove, crushed

1 tbsp lemon juice

2 tbsp butter or margarine, melted

1 egg, beaten

1 tbsp vegetable oil

1 Place the bell peppers on a baking sheet and bake in a preheated oven, 375°F, for 35 minutes, turning after 20 minutes.

2 Cover with a dish cloth and leave to cool for 10 minutes.

3 Peel the skin from the cooked bell peppers; cut in half and discard the seeds. Thinly slice the flesh into strips and place in a shallow dish.

4 Put the oil, vinegar, mustard, honey, and seasoning in a small screw-top jar and shake well to mix. Pour over the bell pepper strips, mix well and set aside to marinate for 2 hours.

5 To make the croustades, put the potatoes, carrots, and celeriac in a mixing bowl and toss in the garlic and lemon juice.

6 Mix in the melted butter or margarine and the egg. Season to taste with salt and pepper. Divide the mixture into 8 and pile on to 2 baking sheets lined with baking parchment, forming each into a 4 inch round. Brush with oil.

7 Bake in a preheated oven, 425°F, for 30–35 minutes, until the croustades are crisp around the edges and golden. Carefully transfer to a warmed serving dish. Heat the bell peppers and the marinade for 2–3 minutes until warmed through. Spoon the bell peppers over the croustades, garnish with flat leaf parsley and serve immediately with green vegetables.

Mushroom & Nut Crumble

A filling, tasty dish that is ideal for a warming family supper. The crunchy topping is flavored with three different types of nuts.

NUTRITIONAL INFORMATION

Calories	779	Sugars	.........5g
Protein	........16g	Fat	..........59g
Carbohydrate	...48g	Saturates	......14g

20 MINS   55 MINS

SERVES 4

I N G R E D I E N T S

5 cups sliced open-cup mushrooms

5 cups sliced crimini mushrooms, sliced

1¾ cups vegetable stock

¼ cup butter or margarine

1 large onion, finely chopped

1 garlic clove, crushed

½ cup all-purpose flour

4 tbsp heavy cream

2 tbsp chopped parsley

salt and pepper

herbs, to garnish

C R U M B L E   T O P P I N G

¾ cup medium oatmeal

¾ cup whole wheat flour

¼ cup ground almonds

¼ cup finely chopped walnuts

½ cup finely chopped unsalted
   shelled pistachio nuts

1 tsp dried thyme

⅓ cup butter or margarine, softened

1 tbsp fennel seeds

1 Put the mushrooms and stock in a large saucepan, bring to a boil, cover and simmer for 15 minutes, until tender. Drain, reserving the stock.

2 In another saucepan, melt the butter or margarine and fry the onion and garlic for 2–3 minutes, until just soft. Stir in the flour and cook for 1 minute.

3 Remove from the heat and gradually stir in the reserved mushroom stock. Return to the heat and cook, stirring, until thickened. Stir in the mushrooms, seasoning, cream, and parsley and spoon into a shallow ovenproof dish.

4 To make the topping, in a bowl, mix together the oatmeal, flour, nuts, thyme, and plenty of salt and pepper to taste.

5 Using a fork, mix in the butter or margarine until the topping resembles coarse breadcrumbs.

6 Sprinkle the topping mixture evenly over the mushrooms and then sprinkle with the fennel seeds. Bake in a preheated oven, at 375°F, for about 25–30 minutes, or until the topping is golden and crisp. Garnish with fresh herbs and serve immediately.

Spinach Roulade

A delicious savory roll, stuffed with mozzarella and broccoli. Serve as a main course or as an appetizer, in which case it would easily serve six.

NUTRITIONAL INFORMATION

Calories 287   Sugars 8g
Protein . . . . .23g   Fat 12g
Carbohydrate . . . .8g   Saturates 6g

15 MINS   25 MINS

SERVES 4

INGREDIENTS

1 lb 2 oz small spinach leaves

2 tbsp water

4 eggs, separated

½ tsp ground nutmeg

salt and pepper

1¼ cups sugocasa, to serve

FILLING

6 oz small broccoli florets

¼ cup freshly grated
   Parmesan cheese

1½ cups grated
   mozzarella cheese

1 Wash the spinach and pack, still wet, into a large saucepan. Add the water. Cover with a tight-fitting lid and cook over a high heat for 4–5 minutes, until reduced and soft. Drain thoroughly, squeezing out excess water. Chop finely and pat dry.

2 Mix the spinach with the egg yolks, seasoning, and nutmeg. Whisk the egg whites until very frothy but not too stiff, and fold into the spinach mixture.

3 Grease and line a 13 x 9 inch jelly roll pan. Spread the mixture in the pan and smooth the surface. Bake in a preheated oven, 425°F, for about 12–15 minutes, until firm to the touch and golden.

4 Meanwhile, cook the broccoli florets in lightly salted boiling water for 4–5 minutes, until just tender. Drain and keep warm.

5 Sprinkle Parmesan on a sheet of baking parchment. Turn the base on to it and peel away the lining paper. Sprinkle with mozzarella and top with broccoli.

6 Hold one end of the paper and roll up the spinach base like a jelly roll. Heat the sugocasa and spoon on to warmed serving plates. Slice the roulade and place on top of the sugocasa.

Roast Bell Pepper Tart

This tastes truly delicious, the flavor of roasted vegetables being entirely different from that of boiled or fried.

NUTRITIONAL INFORMATION

Calories ....237 Sugars 3g
Protein ....6g Fat 15g
Carbohydrate ...20g Saturates 4g

25 MINS   40 MINS

SERVES 8

INGREDIENTS

PASTRY

1½ cups all-purpose flour

pinch of salt

6 tbsp butter or margarine

2 tbsp green pitted olives,
    finely chopped

3 tbsp cold water

FILLING

1 red bell pepper

1 green bell pepper

1 yellow bell pepper

2 garlic cloves, crushed

2 tbsp olive oil

1 cup grated mozzarella cheese

2 eggs

⅔ cup milk

1 tbsp chopped basil

salt and pepper

1 To make the pastry, sift the flour and salt into a bowl. Rub in the butter or margarine until the mixture resembles breadcrumbs. Add the olives and cold water, bringing the mixture together to form a dough.

2 Roll the dough out on a floured surface and use to line a 8 inch loose-based flan pan. Prick the base with a fork and leave to chill.

3 Cut all the bell peppers in half lengthways, seed, and place them, skin side uppermost, on a baking sheet. Mix the garlic and oil and brush over the bell peppers. Cook in a preheated oven, 400°F, for 20 minutes, or until beginning to char slightly. Let the bell peppers cool slightly and thinly slice. Arrange in the base of the pastry case, layering with the mozzarella.

4 Beat the egg and milk and add the basil. Season and pour over the bell peppers. Put the tart on a baking sheet and return to the oven for 20 minutes, or until set. Serve hot or cold.

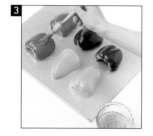

Cauliflower Bake

The red of the tomatoes is a great contrast to the cauliflower and herbs, making this dish appealing to both the eye and the palate.

NUTRITIONAL INFORMATION

Calories 305	Sugars 9g	
Protein 15g	Fat 14g	
Carbohydrate ...31g	Saturates 6g	

🍲 10 MINS 🕐 40 MINS

SERVES 4

I N G R E D I E N T S

1 lb 2 oz cauliflower, broken into florets

2 large potatoes, cubed

3½ oz cherry tomatoes

S A U C E

2 tbsp butter or margarine

1 leek, sliced

1 garlic clove, crushed

3 tbsp all-purpose flour

1¼ cups milk

¾ cup mixed grated cheese, such as
    vegetarian Cheddar, Parmesan
    and Gruyère

½ tsp paprika

2 tbsp chopped flat leaf parsley

salt and pepper

chopped parsley, to garnish

VARIATION

This dish could be made
with broccoli instead of the
cauliflower as an alternative.

1 Cook the cauliflower in a saucepan of boiling water for 10 minutes. Drain well and reserve. Meanwhile, cook the potatoes in a pan of boiling water for 10 minutes, drain and reserve.

2 To make the sauce, melt the butter or margarine in a saucepan and sauté the leek and garlic for 1 minute. Stir in the flour and cook, stirring constantly, for 1 minute. Remove the pan from the heat and gradually stir in the milk, ½ cup of the cheese, the paprika, and parsley. Return the pan to the heat and bring to a boil, stirring constantly. Season with salt and pepper to taste.

3 Spoon the cauliflower into a deep ovenproof dish. Add the cherry tomatoes and top with the potatoes. Pour the sauce over the potatoes and sprinkle on the remaining cheese.

4 Cook in a preheated oven, 350°F, for 20 minutes, or until the vegetables are cooked through and the cheese is golden brown and bubbling. Garnish and serve immediately.

Cauliflower & Broccoli Flan

This really is a tasty flan, the pastry case for which may be made in advance and frozen until required.

NUTRITIONAL INFORMATION

Calories	252	Sugars	........3g
Protein	.........7g	Fat	..........16g
Carbohydrate	...22g	Saturates	.......5g

  15 MINS   50 MINS

SERVES 8

INGREDIENTS

PASTRY

1½ cups all-purpose flour

pinch of salt

½ tsp paprika

1 tsp dried thyme

6 tbsp margarine

3 tbsp water

FILLING

3½ oz cauliflower florets

3½ oz broccoli florets

1 onion, cut into eight

2 tbsp butter or margarine

1 tbsp all-purpose flour

6 tbsp vegetable stock

½ cup milk

¾ cup grated hard cheese

salt and pepper

paprika, to garnish

1 To make the pastry, sift the flour and salt into a bowl. Add the paprika and thyme and rub in the margarine. Stir in the water and bind to form a dough.

2 Roll out the pastry on a floured surface and use to line a 7 inch loose-based flan pan. Prick the base with a fork and line with baking parchment. Fill with baking beans and bake in a preheated oven, 375°F, for 15 minutes. Remove the parchment and beans and return the pastry case to the oven for 5 minutes.

3 To make the filling, cook the vegetables in a pan of lightly salted boiling water for 10–12 minutes, until tender. Drain and reserve.

4 Melt the butter in a pan. Add the flour and cook, stirring constantly, for 1 minute. Remove from the heat, stir in the stock and milk and return to the heat. Bring to a boil, stirring, and add ½ cup of the cheese. Season to taste with salt and pepper.

5 Spoon the cauliflower, broccoli, and onion into the pastry case. Pour over the sauce and sprinkle with the cheese. Return to the oven for 10 minutes, until the cheese is bubbling. Dust with paprika, garnish, and serve.

Spicy Potato & Nut Terrine

This delicious baked terrine has a base of mashed potato which is flavored with nuts, cheese, herbs, and spices.

NUTRITIONAL INFORMATION

Calories 1100	Sugars 13g	
Protein 34g	Fat 93g	
Carbohydrate ...31g	Saturates 22g	

15 MINS 🕐 1½ HOURS

SERVES 4

I N G R E D I E N T S

8 oz mealy potatoes, diced

8 oz pecan nuts

8 oz unsalted cashew nuts

1 onion, finely chopped

2 garlic cloves, crushed

1½ cups diced open-cap mushrooms

2 tbsp butter

2 tbsp chopped mixed herbs

1 tsp paprika

1 tsp ground cumin

1 tsp ground coriander

4 eggs, beaten

½ cup full-fat soft cheese

⅔ cup grated Parmesan cheese

salt and pepper

S A U C E

3 large tomatoes, peeled, seeded, and chopped

2 tbsp tomato paste

⅓ cup red wine

1 tbsp red wine vinegar

pinch of superfine sugar

1 Lightly grease a 2 lb loaf pan and line with baking parchment.

2 Cook the potatoes in a large pan of lightly salted boiling water for 10 minutes, or until cooked through. Drain and mash thoroughly.

3 Finely chop the pecan and cashew nuts or process in a food processor. Mix the nuts with the onion, garlic, and mushrooms. Melt the butter in a skillet and cook the nut mixture for 5-7 minutes. Add the herbs and spices. Stir in the eggs, cheeses, and potatoes and season to taste with salt and pepper.

4 Spoon the mixture into the prepared loaf pan, pressing down firmly. Cook in a preheated oven, 375°F, for 1 hour, or until set.

5 To make the sauce, mix the tomatoes, tomato paste, wine, wine vinegar, and sugar in a pan and bring to a boil, stirring. Cook for 10 minutes, or until the tomatoes have reduced. Press the sauce through a strainer or process in a food processor for 30 seconds. Turn the terrine out of the pan on to a serving plate and cut into slices. Serve with the tomato sauce.

Vegetable Roast Wellington

This is a vegetarian version of the classic 'Beef Wellington'. Served with sherry sauce and roast vegetables it is a tasty and impressive main dish.

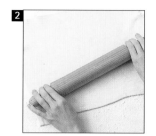

NUTRITIONAL INFORMATION

Calories	821	Sugars	.........8g
Protein	........23g	Fat	..........51g
Carbohydrate	...64g	Saturates	......10g

🥪 20 MINS   🕑 45 MINS

SERVES 4

INGREDIENTS

1 lb can garbanzo beans, drained

1 tsp yeast extract

1¼ cups chopped walnuts

1¼ cups fresh breadcrumbs

1 onion, finely chopped

1¼ cups mushrooms, sliced

⅓ cup canned corn, drained

2 garlic cloves, crushed

2 tbsp dry sherry

2 tbsp vegetable stock

1 tbsp chopped cilantro

8 oz puff pastry

1 egg, beaten

2 tbsp milk

salt and pepper

SAUCE

1 tbsp vegetable oil

1 leek, thinly sliced

4 tbsp dry sherry

⅔ cup vegetable stock

1 Process the garbanzo beans, yeast extract, nuts, and breadcrumbs in a food processor for 30 seconds. In a skillet, sauté the onion and mushrooms in their own juices for 3–4 minutes. Stir in the garbanzo bean mixture, corn, and garlic. Add the sherry, stock, cilantro, and seasoning and bind the mixture together. Remove from the heat and allow to cool.

2 Roll out the pastry out on a floured surface to form a 14 x12 inch rectangle. Shape the garbanzo bean mixture into a loaf shape and wrap the pastry around it, sealing the edges. Place seam side down on a dampened baking sheet and score the top in a criss-cross pattern. Mix the egg and milk and brush over the pastry. Cook in a preheated oven, 400°F, for 25–30 minutes.

3 Heat the oil for the sauce in a pan and sauté the leek for 5 minutes. Add the sherry and stock and bring to the boil. Simmer for 5 minutes and serve the sauce with the roast.

Chili Tofu

A tasty Mexican-style dish with a melt-in-the-mouth combination of tofu and avocado served with a tangy tomato sauce.

🍴 30 MINS   🕐 35 MINS

SERVES 4

I N G R E D I E N T S

½ tsp chili powder

1 tsp paprika

2 tbsp all-purpose flour

8 oz tofu, cut into ½ inch pieces

2 tbsp vegetable oil

1 onion, finely chopped

1 garlic clove, crushed

1 large red bell pepper, seeded and
    finely chopped

1 large ripe avocado

1 tbsp lime juice

4 tomatoes, peeled, seeded, and chopped

1 cup grated hard cheese

8 soft flour tortillas

⅔ cup soured cream

salt and pepper

cilantro sprigs to garnish

pickled green jalapeño chilies, to serve

S A U C E

3¾ cups sugocasa

3 tbsp chopped parsley

3 tbsp chopped cilantro

1 Mix the chili powder, paprika, flour, and salt and pepper on a plate and coat the tofu pieces.

2 Heat the oil in a skillet and gently fry the tofu for 3–4 minutes, until golden. Remove with a draining spoon, drain on paper towels and set aside.

3 Add the onion, garlic, and bell pepper to the oil and fry for 2–3 minutes, until just softened. Drain and set aside.

4 Halve the avocado, peel, and remove the pit. Slice lengthways, put in a bowl with the lime juice and toss to coat.

5 Add the tofu and onion mixture and gently stir in the tomatoes and half the cheese. Spoon one-eighth of the filling down the center of each tortilla, top with soured cream and roll up. Arrange the tortillas in a shallow ovenproof dish in a single layer.

6 To make the sauce, mix together all the ingredients. Spoon the sauce over the tortillas, sprinkle with the remaining grated cheese and bake in a preheated oven, 375°F, for 25 minutes, until golden and bubbling. Garnish with cilantro sprigs and serve immediately with pickled jalapeño chilies.

Salads

A salad makes a refreshing accompaniment or side dish, but can also make a substantial main course meal. Salads are also a very good source of vitamins and minerals; always use the freshest possible ingredients for maximum flavor, texture, and goodness. Salads are quick to 'rustle up' and good for times when you need to prepare a meal-

in-a-moment and have to use store-cupboard ingredients. A splash of culinary inspiration and you will find that you have prepared a fantastic salad that you had no idea was lurking in your kitchen! Experiment with new ingredients in order to add taste and interest to ordinary salad leaves. The only limit is your imagination!

Mexican Salad

This is a colorful salad with a Mexican theme, using beans, tomatoes, and avocado. The chili dressing adds a little kick.

NUTRITIONAL INFORMATION

Calories	307	Sugars	7g
Protein	5g	Fat	26g
Carbohydrate	13g	Saturates	5g

10-15 MINS • 0 MINS

SERVES 4

INGREDIENTS

lollo rosso lettuce

2 ripe avocados

2 tsp lemon juice

4 medium tomatoes

1 onion

2 cups mixed canned beans, drained

DRESSING

4 tbsp olive oil

drop of chili oil

2 tbsp garlic wine vinegar

pinch of superfine sugar

pinch of chili powder

1 tbsp chopped parsley

 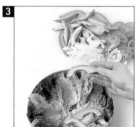 

COOK'S TIP

The lemon juice is sprinkled on to the avocados to prevent discoloration when in contact with the air. For this reason the salad should be prepared, assembled and served quite quickly.

1 Line a large serving bowl with the lettuce leaves.

2 Using a sharp knife, cut the avocados in half and remove the pits. Thinly slice the flesh and sprinkle with the lemon juice.

3 Thinly slice the tomatoes and onion and push the onion out into rings. Arrange the avocado, tomatoes, and onion around the salad bowl, leaving a space in the center.

4 Spoon the beans into the center of the salad and whisk the dressing ingredients together. Pour the dressing over the salad and serve.

Moroccan Salad

Couscous is a type of semolina made from durum wheat. It is wonderful in salads, as it readily takes up the flavor of the dressing.

NUTRITIONAL INFORMATION

Calories	195	Sugars	........15g
Protein	.........8g	Fat	..........2g
Carbohydrate	...40g	Saturates	.....0.3g

30-35 MINS   0 MINS

SERVES 6

INGREDIENTS

2 cups couscous

1 bunch scallions, finely chopped

1 small green bell pepper, seeded
  and chopped

4 inch piece of cucumber, chopped

6 oz can garbanzo beans, rinsed
  and drained

⅔ cup golden raisins or raisins

2 oranges

salt and pepper

mint sprigs, to garnish

lettuce leaves, to serve

DRESSING

finely grated rind of 1 orange

1 tbsp chopped fresh mint

⅔ cup natural yogurt

1 Put the couscous into a bowl and cover with boiling water. Leave it to soak for about 15 minutes to swell the grains, then stir gently with a fork to separate them.

2 Add the scallions, green bell pepper, cucumber, garbanzo beans, and golden raisins or raisins to the couscous, stirring to combine. Season well with salt and pepper.

3 To make the dressing, place the orange rind, mint, and yogurt in a bowl and mix together until well combined. Pour over the couscous mixture and stir to mix well.

4 Using a sharp serrated knife, remove the peel and pith from the oranges. Cut the flesh into segments, removing all the membrane.

5 Arrange the lettuce leaves on 4 serving plates. Divide the couscous mixture between the plates and arrange the orange segments on top. Garnish with sprigs of fresh mint and serve.

Salad with Yogurt Dressing

This is a very quick and refreshing salad, using a whole range of colorful ingredients which make it look as good as it tastes.

NUTRITIONAL INFORMATION

Calories	100	Sugars	.........8g
Protein	.........3g	Fat	...........6g
Carbohydrate	....8g	Saturates	.......1g

 20 MINS 0 MINS

SERVES 4

INGREDIENTS

2¾ oz cucumber, cut into sticks

6 scallions, halved

2 tomatoes, seeded and cut into eight

1 yellow bell pepper, cut into strips

2 celery stalks, cut into strips

4 radishes, quartered

1 bunch arugula

1 tbsp chopped mint, to serve

DRESSING

2 tbsp lemon juice

1 garlic clove, crushed

⅔ cup unsweetened yogurt

2 tbsp olive oil

salt and pepper

1 Mix the cucumber, scallions, tomatoes, bell pepper, celery, radishes, and arugula together in a large serving bowl.

2 To make the dressing, stir the lemon juice, garlic, unsweetened yogurt, and olive oil together. Season well with salt and pepper.

3 Spoon the dressing over the salad and toss to mix.

4 Sprinkle the salad with chopped mint and serve.

COOK'S TIP

Do not toss the dressing into the salad until just before serving, otherwise it will turn soggy.

Mixed Bean Salad

You can use a mixture of any canned beans in this crunchy, very filling salad.

NUTRITIONAL INFORMATION

Calories 198	Sugars 6g	
Protein 10g	Fat 6g	
Carbohydrate ...26g	Saturates 1g	

 30 MINS   15-20 MINS

SERVES 8

INGREDIENTS

14 oz can small navy beans, drained

14 oz can red kidney beans, drained

14 oz can butter beans, drained

1 small red onion, thinly sliced

6 oz dwarf green beans,
   topped and tailed

1 red bell pepper, halved and seeded

salt

DRESSING

4 tbsp olive oil

2 tbsp sherry vinegar

2 tbsp lemon juice

1 tsp light muscovado sugar

1 tsp chili sauce (optional)

VARIATION

Use any combination of beans in this salad. For a distinctive flavor, add 1 teaspoon of curry paste instead of the chili sauce.

1 Put the canned beans in a large mixing bowl. Add the sliced onion and mix together.

2 Cut the dwarf green beans in half and cook in lightly salted boiling water for about 8 minutes until just tender. Refresh under cold water and drain again. Add to the mixed beans and onions.

3 Place the bell pepper halves, cut side down, on a broiler rack and cook until the skin blackens and chars. Leave to cool slightly then pop them into a plastic bag for about 10 minutes. Peel away the skin from the bell peppers and discard. Roughly chop the bell pepper flesh and add it to the beans.

4 To make the dressing, place the oil, sherry vinegar, lemon juice, sugar, and chili sauce (if using) in a screw-top jar and shake vigorously.

5 Pour the dressing over the mixed bean salad and toss well. Leave to chill in the refrigerator until required.

Middle Eastern Salad

This attractive-looking salad can be served with a couple of vegetable kabobs for a delicious light lunch or an informal supper.

NUTRITIONAL INFORMATION

Calories 163	Sugars 12g
Protein 8g	Fat 3g
Carbohydrate ...27g	Saturates 0.4g

 15 MINS   0 MINS

SERVES 4

INGREDIENTS

14 oz can garbanzo beans

4 carrots

1 bunch scallions

1 medium cucumber

½ tsp salt

½ tsp pepper

3 tbsp lemon juice

1 red bell pepper, sliced

1 Drain the garbanzo beans and place them in a large salad bowl.

2 Using a sharp knife, thinly slice the carrots. Cut the scallions into small pieces. Thickly slice the cucumber and then cut the slices into quarters.

3 Add the carrot slices, scallions, and cucumber to the garbanzo beans and mix.

4 Season to taste with the salt and pepper and sprinkle with the lemon juice. Toss the salad ingredients together gently, using 2 serving spoons.

5 Using a sharp knife, thinly slice the red bell pepper. Arrange the slices of red bell pepper decoratively on top of the

garbanzo bean salad. Serve the salad immediately or chill in the refrigerator and serve when required.

VARIATION

This salad would also be delicious made with *ful medames*. If they are not available canned, use 1 cup dried, soaked for 5 hours and then simmered for 2½ hours. Another alternative would be canned gunga beans.

Sweet Potato & Nut Salad

Pecan nuts with their slightly bitter flavor are mixed with sweet potatoes to make a sweet and sour salad with an interesting texture.

NUTRITIONAL INFORMATION

Calories 330   Sugars 5g
Protein . . . . .4g   Fat 20g
Carbohydrate . . .36g   Saturates 2g

🥔 25 MINS   🕐 10 MINS

SERVES 4

INGREDIENTS

1 lb 2 oz sweet potatoes, diced

2 celery stalks, sliced

4½ oz celeriac, grated

2 scallions, sliced

½ cup pecan nuts, chopped

2 heads chicory, separated

1 tsp lemon juice

thyme sprigs, to garnish

DRESSING

4 tbsp vegetable oil

1 tbsp garlic wine vinegar

1 tsp soft light brown sugar

2 tsp chopped thyme

1 Cook the sweet potatoes in a large saucepan of boiling water for 5 minutes, until tender. Drain thoroughly and set aside to cool.

2 When cooled, stir in the celery, celeriac, scallions, and pecan nuts.

3 Line a salad plate with the chicory leaves and sprinkle with lemon juice.

4 Spoon the sweet potato mixture into the center of the leaves.

5 In a small bowl, whisk the dressing ingredients together.

6 Pour the dressing over the salad and serve at once, garnished with fresh thyme sprigs.

COOK'S TIP

Sweet potatoes do not store as well as ordinary potatoes. It is best to store them in a cool, dark place (not the refrigerator) and use within 1 week of purchase.

Gado Gado

This is a well-known and very popular Indonesian salad of mixed vegetables with a peanut dressing.

NUTRITIONAL INFORMATION

Calories	392	Sugars	.........8g
Protein	.........9g	Fat	..........35g
Carbohydrate	....11g	Saturates	.......5g

🍲 10 MINS   🕐 25 MINS

SERVES 4

I N G R E D I E N T S

1 cup shredded white cabbage

3½ oz green beans, cut into three

3½ oz carrots, cut into matchsticks

3½ oz cauliflower florets

3½ oz beansprouts

D R E S S I N G

½ cup vegetable oil

1 cup unsalted peanuts

2 garlic cloves, crushed

1 small onion, finely chopped

½ tsp chili powder

½ tsp light brown sugar

2 cups water

juice of ½ lemon

salt

sliced scallions, to garnish

1 Cook the vegetables separately in a saucepan of salted boiling water for 4–5 minutes, drain well and chill.

2 To make the dressing, heat the oil in a skillet and fry the peanuts, tossing frequently, for 3–4 minutes.

3 Remove from the pan with a draining spoon and drain on paper towels. Process the peanuts in a food processor or crush with a rolling pin until a fine mixture is formed.

4 Pour all but 1 tablespoon of the oil from the pan and fry the garlic and onion for 1 minute. Add the chili powder, sugar, a pinch of salt, and the water and bring to a boil.

5 Stir in the peanuts. Reduce the heat and simmer for 4–5 minutes. until the sauce thickens. Add the lemon juice and set aside to cool.

6 Arrange the vegetables in a serving dish and spoon the peanut dressing into the center. Garnish and serve.

Three-Bean Salad

Fresh thin beans are combined with soya beans and red kidney beans in a chive and tomato dressing to make a tasty salad.

NUTRITIONAL INFORMATION

Calories	276	Sugars	.........7g
Protein	........18g	Fat	..........15g
Carbohydrate	...18g	Saturates	.......4g

15 MINS   10 MINS

SERVES 6

INGREDIENTS

3 tbsp olive oil

1 tbsp lemon juice

1 tbsp tomato paste

1 tbsp light malt vinegar

1 tbsp chopped chives

6 oz thin beans

14 oz can soya beans,
    rinsed and drained

14 oz can red kidney beans, rinsed
    and drained

2 tomatoes, chopped

4 scallions, chopped

4½ oz feta cheese, cut into cubes

salt and pepper

mixed salad greens, to serve

chopped chives, to garnish

1 Put the olive oil, lemon juice, tomato paste, light malt vinegar, and chopped chives into a large bowl and whisk together well until thoroughly combined. Set aside.

2 Cook the thin beans in boiling, lightly salted water for 4–5 minutes, until just cooked. Drain, refresh under cold running water, and drain again. Pat dry with paper towels.

3 Add the thin beans, soya beans, and red kidney beans to the dressing, stirring to mix.

4 Add the tomatoes, scallions, and feta cheese to the bean mixture, tossing gently to coat in the dressing. Season well with salt and pepper.

5 Arrange the mixed salad greens on 6 serving plates. Pile the bean salad on to the plates and garnish with chopped chives.

Warm Goat's Cheese Salad

This delicious salad combines soft goat's cheese with walnut halves, served on a bed of mixed salad greens.

NUTRITIONAL INFORMATION

Calories 408	Sugars 8g	
Protein 9g	Fat 38g	
Carbohydrate 8g	Saturates 8g	

5 MINS   5 MINS

SERVES 4

INGREDIENTS

¾ cup walnut halves

mixed salad greens

4½ oz soft goat's cheese

snipped chives, to garnish

DRESSING

6 tbsp walnut oil

3 tbsp white wine vinegar

1 tbsp clear honey

1 tsp Dijon mustard

pinch of ground ginger

salt and pepper

1 To make the dressing, whisk together the walnut oil, wine vinegar, honey, mustard, and ginger in a small saucepan. Season to taste with salt and pepper.

2 Heat the dressing gently, stirring occasionally, until warm. Add the walnut halves and continue to heat for 3–4 minutes.

3 Arrange the salad greens on 4 serving plates and place spoonfuls of goat's cheese on top. Lift the walnut halves from the dressing with a draining spoon, and scatter them over the salads.

4 Transfer the warm dressing to a small jug. Sprinkle chives over the salads and serve with the dressing.

VARIATION

You could also use a ewe's milk cheese, such as feta, in this recipe for a sharper flavor.

Red Cabbage & Pear Salad

Red cabbage is much underused — it is a colorful and tasty ingredient which is perfect with fruits, such as pears and apples.

NUTRITIONAL INFORMATION

Calories	143	Sugars	........14g
Protein	.........2g	Fat	...........9g
Carbohydrate	...15g	Saturates	.......1g

  15 MINS   0 MINS

SERVES 4

I N G R E D I E N T S

4 cups finely shredded red cabbage

2 Conference pears, cored and thinly sliced

4 scallions, sliced

1 carrot, grated

chives, to garnish

lollo biondo leaves, to serve

D R E S S I N G

4 tbsp pear juice

1 tsp wholegrain mustard

3 tbsp olive oil

1 tbsp garlic wine vinegar

1 tbsp chopped chives

salt and pepper

1 Put the cabbage, pears, and scallions in a bowl and mix together well.

2 Line a serving dish with lettuce leaves and spoon the cabbage and pear mixture into the center.

3 Sprinkle the carrot into the center of the cabbage to form a domed pile.

4 To make the dressing, mix together the pear juice, wholegrain mustard, olive oil, garlic wine vinegar, and chives. Season to taste with salt and pepper.

5 Pour the dressing over the salad, garnish and serve immediately.

COOK'S TIP
Mix the salad just before serving to prevent the color from the red cabbage bleeding into the other ingredients.

Potato & Radish Salad

The radishes and the herb and mustard dressing give this colorful salad a mild mustard flavor which complements the potatoes perfectly.

NUTRITIONAL INFORMATION

Calories 140   Sugars 3g
Protein ....3g   Fat 6g
Carbohydrate ...20g   Saturates 1g

50 MINS   20 MINS

SERVES 4

INGREDIENTS

500 g/1 lb 2 oz new potatoes, scrubbed
  and halved

½ cucumber, thinly sliced

2 tsp salt

1 bunch radishes, thinly sliced

DRESSING

1 tbsp Dijon mustard

2 tbsp olive oil

1 tbsp white wine vinegar

2 tbsp mixed chopped herbs

1 Cook the potatoes in a saucepan of boiling water for 10–15 minutes, or until tender. Drain and set aside to cool.

2 Meanwhile, spread out the cucumber slices on a plate and sprinkle with the salt. Leave to stand for 30 minutes, then rinse under cold running water and pat dry with kitchen paper (paper towels).

3 Arrange the cucumber and radish slices on a serving plate in a decorative pattern and pile the cooked potatoes in the center of the slices.

4 In a small bowl, mix all the dressing ingredients together, whisking until thoroughly combined. Pour the dressing over the salad, tossing well to coat all of the ingredients. Chill in the refrigerator before serving.

COOK'S TIP

The cucumber adds not only color, but also a real freshness to the salad. It is salted and left to stand to remove the excess water, which would make the salad soggy. Wash the cucumber well to remove all of the salt, before adding to the salad.

Three-Way Potato Salad

Small new potatoes, served warm in a delicious dressing. The nutritional information is for the potato salad with the curry dressing only.

NUTRITIONAL INFORMATION

Calories 310   Sugars 12g
Protein . . . . .6g   Fat 19g
Carbohydrate . . .31g   Saturates 4g

 15-20 MINS 20 MINS

SERVES 4

I N G R E D I E N T S

1 lb 2 oz new potatoes (for each
    dressing)

herbs, to garnish

LIGHT CURRY DRESSING

1 tbsp vegetable oil

1 tbsp medium curry paste

1 small onion, chopped

1 tbsp mango chutney, chopped

6 tbsp unsweetened yogurt

3 tbsp light cream

2 tbsp mayonnaise

salt and pepper

1 tbsp light cream, to garnish

VINAIGRETTE DRESSING

6 tbsp hazelnut oil

3 tbsp cider vinegar

1 tsp wholegrain mustard

1 tsp superfine sugar

few basil leaves, torn

PARSLEY CREAM

⅔ cup soured cream

3 tbsp light mayonnaise

4 scallions, finely chopped

1 tbsp chopped fresh parsley

1 To make the Light Curry Dressing, heat the vegetable oil in a saucepan, add the curry paste and onion, and fry, stirring frequently, until the onion is soft. Remove from the heat and set aside to cool slightly.

2 Mix together the mango chutney, yogurt, cream, and mayonnaise. Add the curry mixture and blend together. Season with salt and pepper.

3 To make the Vinaigrette Dressing, whisk the oil, vinegar, mustard, sugar, and basil together in a small jug or bowl. Season with salt and pepper.

4 To make the Parsley Cream, combine the mayonnaise, soured cream, scallions, and parsley, mixing well. Season with salt and pepper.

5 Cook the potatoes in lightly salted boiling water until just tender. Drain well and set aside to cool for 5 minutes, then add the chosen dressing, tossing to coat. Serve, garnished with fresh herbs, spooning a little light cream on to the potatoes if you have used the curry dressing.

Mexican Potato Salad

The flavors of Mexico are echoed in this dish where potato slices are topped with tomatoes and chilies, and served with guacamole.

NUTRITIONAL INFORMATION

Calories 260	Sugars 6g
Protein 6g	Fat 9g
Carbohydrate ...41g	Saturates 2g

20 MINS   20 MINS

SERVES 4

INGREDIENTS

4 large waxy potatoes, sliced

1 ripe avocado

1 tsp olive oil

1 tsp lemon juice

1 garlic clove, crushed

1 onion, chopped

2 large tomatoes, sliced

1 green chili, chopped

1 yellow bell pepper, seeded and sliced

2 tbsp chopped cilantro

salt and pepper

lemon wedges, to garnish

1 Cook the potato slices in a saucepan of boiling water for 10–15 minutes, or until tender. Drain and set aside to cool.

2 Meanwhile, cut the avocado in half and remove the pit. Mash the avocado flesh with a fork (you could also scoop the avocado flesh from the 2 halves using a spoon and then mash it).

3 Add the olive oil, lemon juice, garlic, and chopped onion to the avocado flesh and stir to mix. Cover the bowl with plastic wrap, to minimize discoloration, and set aside.

4 Mix the tomatoes, chili, and yellow bell pepper together and transfer to a salad bowl with the potato slices.

5 Arrange the avocado mixture on top of the salad and sprinkle with the cilantro. Season to taste with salt and pepper and serve garnished with lemon wedges.

VARIATION

You can omit the green chili from this salad if you do not like hot dishes.

Potato & Banana Salad

This hot fruity salad combines sweet potato and fried bananas with colorful mixed bell peppers, tossed in a honey-based dressing.

NUTRITIONAL INFORMATION

Calories 424   Sugars 29g
Protein . . . . .5g   Fat 17g
Carbohydrate . . .68g   Saturates 8g

15 MINS   20 MINS

SERVES 4

INGREDIENTS

1 lb 2 oz sweet potatoes, diced

4 tbsp butter

1 tbsp lemon juice

1 garlic clove, crushed

1 red bell pepper, seeded and diced

1 green bell pepper, seeded and diced

2 bananas, thickly sliced

2 thick slices white bread, crusts
   removed, diced

salt and pepper

DRESSING

2 tbsp clear honey

2 tbsp chopped chives

2 tbsp lemon juice

2 tbsp olive oil

1 Cook the sweet potatoes in a saucepan of boiling water for 10–15 minutes, until tender. Drain thoroughly and reserve.

2 Meanwhile, melt the butter in a skillet. Add the lemon juice, garlic, and bell peppers and cook, stirring constantly for 3 minutes.

3 Add the banana slices to the pan and cook for 1 minute. Remove the bananas from the pan with a draining spoon and stir into the potatoes.

4 Add the bread cubes to the skillet and cook, stirring frequently, for 2 minutes, until they are golden brown on all sides.

5 Mix the dressing ingredients together in a small saucepan and heat until the honey is runny.

6 Spoon the potato mixture into a serving dish and season to taste with salt and pepper. Pour the dressing over the potatoes and sprinkle the croûtons over the top. Serve immediately.

COOK'S TIP

Use firm, slightly underripe bananas in this recipe as they won't turn soft and mushy when they are fried.

Potato, Bean, & Apple Salad

Use any mixture of beans you have to hand in this recipe, but the wider the variety, the more colorful the salad.

NUTRITIONAL INFORMATION

Calories 183   Sugars 8g
Protein ....6g   Fat 7g
Carbohydrate ...26g   Saturates 1g

 20 MINS   20 MINS

SERVES 4

I N G R E D I E N T S

8 oz new potatoes, scrubbed
   and quartered

8 oz mixed canned beans, such as
   red kidney beans, flageolet, and borlotti
   beans, drained and rinsed

1 red eating apple, diced and tossed
   in 1 tbsp lemon juice

1 yellow bell pepper, seeded and diced

1 shallot, sliced

½ fennel bulb, sliced

oak leaf lettuce leaves

D R E S S I N G

1 tbsp red wine vinegar

2 tbsp olive oil

½ tbsp American mustard

1 garlic clove, crushed

2 tsp chopped fresh thyme

VARIATION

Use Dijon or wholegrain
mustard in place of American
mustard for a different flavor.

1 Cook the quartered potatoes in a saucepan of boiling water for 15 minutes, until tender. Drain and transfer to a mixing bowl.

2 Add the mixed beans to the potatoes, together with the apple, bell pepper, shallots, and fennel. Mix well, taking care not to break up the cooked potatoes.

3 To make the dressing, whisk all the dressing ingredients together until thoroughly combined, then pour it over the potato salad.

4 Line a serving plate or salad bowl with the oak leaf lettuce leaves and spoon the potato mixture into the center. Serve immediately.

Garden Salad

This chunky salad includes tiny new potatoes tossed in a minty dressing, and has a mustard dip for dunking.

NUTRITIONAL INFORMATION

Calories	227	Sugars	.........6g
Protein	.........4g	Fat	..........17g
Carbohydrate	...16g	Saturates	.......4g

🥔 15-20 MINS   🕐 20 MINS

SERVES 8

I N G R E D I E N T S

1 lb 2 oz tiny new or salad potatoes

8 oz broccoli florets

4½ oz sugar snap peas

2 large carrots

4 celery stalks

1 yellow or orange bell pepper, seeded

1 bunch scallions

1 head chicory

D R E S S I N G

3 tbsp olive oil

1 tbsp white wine vinegar

1 tsp Dijon mustard

2 tbsp chopped mint

M U S T A R D   D I P

6 tbsp soured cream

3 tbsp thick mayonnaise

2 tsp balsamic vinegar

1½ tsp coarse-grain mustard

½ tsp creamed horseradish

pinch of brown sugar

salt and pepper

1 Cook the potatoes in boiling salted water for about 10 minutes, until just tender. While they cook, combine the dressing ingredients.

2 Drain the potatoes thoroughly, add to the dressing while hot, toss well, and set aside until cold, giving them an occasional stir.

3 To make the dip, combine the soured cream, mayonnaise, vinegar, mustard, horseradish, and sugar and season to taste with salt and pepper. Transfer to a small serving bowl, cover and refrigerate until ready to serve.

4 Cut the broccoli into bite-sized florets and blanch for 2 minutes in boiling water. Drain and toss immediately in cold water; when cold, drain thoroughly.

5 Blanch the sugar snap peas in boiling water for 1 minute. Drain, rinse in cold water and drain again.

6 Cut the carrots and celery into matchsticks about 2½ x ½ inches. Slice the bell pepper or cut it into small cubes. Cut off some of the green parts of the scallions and separate the chicory leaves.

7 Arrange the vegetables attractively in a fairly shallow bowl with the potatoes piled up in the center. Serve accompanied with the mustard dip.

Marinated Vegetable Salad

Lightly steamed vegetables taste superb served slightly warm in a marinade of olive oil, white wine, vinegar, and fresh herbs.

NUTRITIONAL INFORMATION

Calories 114   Sugars 4g
Protein . . . . .3g   Fat 9g
Carbohydrate . . . .5g   Saturates 1g

🍲 10 MINS   🕐 10 MINS

SERVES 6

I N G R E D I E N T S

6 oz baby carrots

2 celery hearts, cut into 4 pieces

4½ oz sugar snap peas or snow peas

1 fennel bulb, sliced

6 oz small asparagus spears

1½ tbsp sunflower seeds

dill sprigs, to garnish

D R E S S I N G

4 tbsp olive oil

4 tbsp dry white wine

2 tbsp white wine vinegar

1 tbsp chopped dill

1 tbsp chopped parsley

salt and pepper

1 Put the carrots, celery, sugar snap peas or snow peas, fennel, and asparagus into a steamer and cook over gently boiling water until just tender. It is important that they retain a little 'bite'.

2 Meanwhile, make the dressing. Mix together the olive oil, wine, vinegar, and chopped herbs, whisking until thoroughly combined. Season to taste with salt and pepper.

3 When the vegetables are cooked, transfer them to a serving dish and pour over the dressing at once. The hot vegetables will absorb the flavor of the dressing as they cool.

4 Spread out the sunflower seeds on a baking sheet and toast them under a preheated broiler for 3-4 minutes or until lightly browned. Sprinkle the toasted sunflower seeds over the vegetables.

5 Serve the salad while the vegetables are still slightly warm, garnished with sprigs of fresh dill.

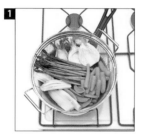

Melon & Strawberry Salad

This refreshing fruit-based salad is perfect for a hot summer's day and would go well with a barbecued food.

NUTRITIONAL INFORMATION

Calories 112	Sugars 22g
Protein 5g	Fat 1g
Carbohydrate . . .22g	Saturates 0.3g

 15 MINS   0 MINS

SERVES 4

INGREDIENTS

½ iceberg lettuce, shredded

1 small honeydew melon

1½ cups sliced strawberries

2 inch piece of cucumber, thinly sliced

mint sprigs to garnish

DRESSING

scant 1 cup unsweetened yogurt

2 inch piece of cucumber, peeled

a few mint leaves

½ tsp finely grated lime or lemon rind

pinch of superfine sugar

3–4 ice cubes

 1 Arrange the shredded lettuce on 4 serving plates.

VARIATION

Omit the ice cubes in the dressing if you prefer, but make sure that the ingredients are well-chilled. This will ensure that the finished dressing is really cool.

2 Cut the melon lengthways into quarters. Scoop out the seeds and cut through the flesh down to the skin at 1 inch intervals. Cut the melon close to the skin and detach the flesh.

3 Place the chunks of melon on the beds of lettuce with the strawberries and cucumber slices.

4 To make the dressing, put the yogurt, cucumber, mint leaves, lime or lemon rind, superfine sugar, and ice cubes into a blender or food processor. Blend together for about 15 seconds, until smooth. Alternatively, chop the cucumber and mint finely, crush the ice cubes, and combine with the other ingredients.

5 Serve the salad with a little dressing poured over it. Garnish with sprigs of fresh mint.

Melon & Mango Salad

A little freshly grated gingerroot mixed with creamy yogurt and clear honey makes a perfect dressing for this refreshing melon salad.

NUTRITIONAL INFORMATION

Calories ....189 Sugars 30g
Protein ....5g Fat 7g
Carbohydrate ...30g Saturates 1g

 15-20 MINS   0 MINS

SERVES 4

I N G R E D I E N T S

1 cantaloupe melon

½ cup black grapes, halved
   and seeded

½ cup seedless green grapes

1 large mango

1 bunch of watercress

iceberg lettuce leaves, shredded

2 tbsp olive oil

1 tbsp cider vinegar

1 passion fruit

salt and pepper

D R E S S I N G

¾ cup unsweetened thick yogurt

1 tbsp clear honey

1 tsp grated gingerroot

1 First, make the dressing for the melon. Mix together the yogurt, honey, and ginger in a small bowl, stirring to combine.

2 Halve the melon and scoop out the seeds. Slice, peel, and cut into chunks. Mix with the grapes.

3 Slice the mango on each side of its large flat pit. On each mango half, slash the flesh into a criss-cross pattern down to, but not through the skin. Push the skin from underneath to turn the mango halves inside out. Now remove the flesh and add to the melon mixture.

4 Arrange the watercress and lettuce on 4 serving plates. Make the dressing for the salad greens. Whisk together the olive oil and cider vinegar and season to taste with salt and pepper. Drizzle the dressing over the watercress and lettuce.

5 Divide the melon mixture equally between the 4 plates and spoon over the yogurt dressing. Scoop the seeds out of the passion fruit and sprinkle them over the salads. Serve immediately.

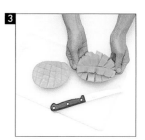

COOK'S TIP

Grated gingerroot gives a marvellous flavor to this recipe, but if you can't get fresh ginger, substitute ½ teaspoon of ground ginger instead.

Grapefruit & Coconut Salad

This salad is quite deceptive — it is, in fact, surprisingly filling, even though it looks very light.

NUTRITIONAL INFORMATION

Calories 201   Sugars 13g
Protein . . . . .3g   Fat 15g
Carbohydrate . . .14g   Saturates 9g

    10 MINS   10 MINS

SERVES 4

I N G R E D I E N T S

1 cup grated coconut

2 tsp light soy sauce

2 tbsp lime juice

2 tbsp water

2 tsp sunflower oil

1 garlic clove, halved

1 onion, finely chopped

2 large ruby grapefruits, peeled
   and segmented

1½ cups alfalfa sprouts

1 Toast the coconut in a dry skillet over a low heat, stirring constantly, for about 3 minutes, or until golden brown. Transfer the toasted coconut to a bowl.

2 Add the light soy sauce, lime juice, and water to the toasted coconut and mix together well.

3 Heat the oil in a saucepan and fry the garlic and onion until soft. Stir the onion into the coconut mixture. Remove and discard the garlic.

4 Divide the grapefruit segments between 4 plates. Sprinkle each with a quarter of the alfalfa sprouts and spoon over a quarter of the coconut mixture.

COOK'S TIP

Alfalfa sprouts can be bought in trays or packets from most supermarkets, but you can easily grow your own, if you like to have a constant and cheap supply.

Alfalfa & Spinach Salad

This is a really refreshing salad that must be assembled just before serving to prevent everything being colored by the beet.

NUTRITIONAL INFORMATION

Calories 139	Sugars 7g
Protein 2g	Fat 11g
Carbohydrate 8g	Saturates 2g

10 MINS   0 MINS

SERVES 4

INGREDIENTS

3½ oz baby spinach

1⅓ cups alfalfa sprouts

2 celery stalks, sliced

4 cooked beet, cut into eight

DRESSING

4 tbsp olive oil

4½ tsp garlic wine vinegar

1 garlic clove, crushed

2 tsp clear honey

1 tbsp chopped chives

1 Place the spinach and alfalfa sprouts in a large bowl and mix together.

2 Add the celery to the bowl and mix together well.

3 Toss in the beet and mix until well combined.

4 To make the dressing, mix the oil, wine vinegar, garlic, honey, and chopped chives.

5 Pour the dressing over the salad, toss well, and serve immediately.

VARIATION

Add the segments of 1 large orange to the salad to make it even more colorful and refreshing. Replace the garlic wine vinegar with a different flavored oil such as chili or herb, if you prefer.

Green Vegetable Salad

This salad uses lots of greencolored ingredients which look and taste wonderful with the minty yogurt dressing.

  10-15 MINS 🕐 10 MINS

SERVES 4

I N G R E D I E N T S

2 zucchini, cut into sticks

3½ oz green beans, cut into three

1 green bell pepper, seeded and cut
 into strips

2 celery stalks, sliced

1 bunch watercress

D R E S S I N G

¾ cup unsweetened yogurt

1 garlic clove, crushed

2 tbsp chopped mint

pepper

COOK'S TIP

The salad must be served as soon as the yogurt dressing has been added — the dressing will start to separate if kept for any length of time.

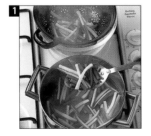  

1 Cook the zucchini and green beans in a saucepan of salted boiling water for 7–8 minutes. Drain and set aside to cool completely.

2 Mix the zucchini and green beans with the bell pepper, celery, and watercress in a large serving bowl.

3 To make the dressing, mix together the unsweetened yogurt, garlic, and chopped mint in a bowl. Season with pepper to taste.

4 Spoon the dressing on to the salad and serve immediately.

Green & White Salad

This potato, arugula, and apple salad is flavored with creamy, salty goat's cheese — perfect with salad greens.

NUTRITIONAL INFORMATION

Calories 282	Sugars 10g	
Protein 8g	Fat 17g	
Carbohydrate ...26g	Saturates 5g	

 15 MINS   20 MINS

SERVES 4

INGREDIENTS

2 large potatoes, unpeeled and sliced

2 green eating apples, diced

1 tsp lemon juice

¼ cup walnut pieces

4½ oz goat's cheese, cubed

2–3 bunches arugula leaves

salt and pepper

DRESSING

2 tbsp olive oil

1 tbsp red wine vinegar

1 tsp clear honey

1 tsp fennel seeds

COOK'S TIP

Serve this salad immediately to prevent the apple from discoloring. Alternatively, prepare all of the other ingredients in advance and add the apple at the last minute.

1 Cook the potatoes in a pan of boiling water for 15 minutes, until tender. Drain and set aside to cool. Transfer the cooled potatoes to a serving bowl.

2 Toss the diced apples in the lemon juice, drain and stir them into the cold potatoes.

3 Add the walnut pieces, cheese cubes, and arugula leaves, then toss the salad to mix.

4 In a small bowl, whisk the dressing ingredients together until well combined and pour the dressing over the salad. Serve immediately.

Multicolored Salad

The beet adds a rich color to this dish, tinting the potato an appealing pink. Mixed with cucumber it is a really vibrant salad.

NUTRITIONAL INFORMATION

Calories ....174 Sugars 8g
Protein ....4g Fat 6g
Carbohydrate ...27g Saturates 1g

15–20 MINS   20 MINS

SERVES 4

INGREDIENTS

1 lb 2 oz waxy potatoes, diced

4 small cooked beets, sliced

½ small cucumber, thinly sliced

2 large dill pickles, sliced

1 red onion, halved and sliced

dill sprigs, to garnish

DRESSING

1 garlic clove, crushed

2 tbsp olive oil

2 tbsp red wine vinegar

2 tbsp chopped fresh dill

salt and pepper

1 Cook the diced potatoes in a saucepan of boiling water for about 15 minutes, or until just tender. Drain and set aside to cool.

2 When cool, mix the potato and beets together in a bowl and set aside.

3 To make the dressing, whisk together the garlic, olive oil, vinegar, and dill and season to taste with salt and pepper.

4 When ready to serve, line a large serving platter with the slices of cucumber, dill pickles, and red onion. Spoon the potato and beet mixture into the center of the platter.

5 Pour the dressing over the salad and serve immediately, garnished with fresh dill sprigs.

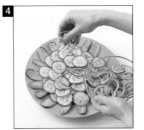

VARIATION

Line the salad platter with 2 heads of chicory, separated into leaves, and arrange the cucumber, dill pickle, and red onion slices on top of the leaves.

Carrot & Nut Coleslaw

This simple salad has a dressing made from poppy seeds pan-fried in sesame oil to bring out their flavor and aroma.

NUTRITIONAL INFORMATION

Calories ....220 Sugars 7g
Protein ....4g Fat 19g
Carbohydrate ...10g Saturates 3g

 15 MINS   5–10 MINS

SERVES 4

I N G R E D I E N T S

1 large carrot, grated

1 small onion, finely chopped

2 celery stalks, chopped

¼ small hard white cabbage, shredded

1 tbsp chopped parsley

4 tbsp sesame oil

½ tsp poppy seeds

½ cup cashew nuts

2 tbsp white wine vinegar or cider vinegar

salt and pepper

parsley sprigs, to garnish

1 In a large salad bowl, mix together the carrot, onion, celery, and cabbage. Stir in the chopped parsley and season to taste with salt and pepper.

2 Heat the sesame oil in a saucepan with a lid. Add the poppy seeds and cover the pan. Cook over a medium-high heat until the seeds start to make a popping sound. Remove from the heat and set aside to cool.

3 Spread out the cashew nuts on a baking sheet. Place them under a medium-hot broiler and toast until lightly browned, being careful not to burn them. Leave to cool.

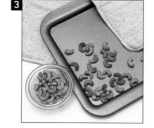

4 Add the vinegar to the oil and poppy seeds, then pour the dressing over the carrot mixture. Add the cooled cashew nuts. Toss together to coat well.

5 Garnish the salad with sprigs of fresh parsley and serve immediately.

Hot Salad

This quickly-made dish is ideal for a cold winter's night. Serve with crusty bread, freshly made rolls, or garlic bread.

NUTRITIONAL INFORMATION

Calories 154   Sugars 13g
Protein ....4g   Fat 9g
Carbohydrate ...14g   Saturates 6g

 10 MINS   10 MINS

SERVES 4

I N G R E D I E N T S

½ medium-sized cauliflower

1 green bell pepper

1 red bell pepper

½ cucumber

4 carrots

2 tbsp butter

salt and pepper

crusty bread, rolls, or garlic bread,
    to serve

D R E S S I N G

3 tbsp olive oil

1 tbsp white wine vinegar

1 tbsp light soy sauce

1 tsp superfine sugar

salt and pepper

1 Cut the cauliflower into small florets, using a sharp knife. Seed the bell peppers and cut the flesh into thin slices. Cut the cucumber into thin slices. Thinly slice the carrots lengthways.

2 Melt the butter in a large heavy-bottomed saucepan. Add the cauliflower florets, bell peppers, cucumber, and carrots and fry over a medium heat, stirring constantly, for 5-7 minutes, until tender, but still firm to the bite. Season

with salt and pepper. Lower the heat, cover with a lid, and simmer for 3 minutes.

3 Meanwhile, make the dressing. Whisk together all the ingredients until thoroughly combined.

4 Transfer the vegetables to a serving dish, pour over the dressing, toss to mix well, and serve immediately.

VARIATION
You can replace the vegetables in this recipe with those of your choice, such as broccoli, scallions, and zucchini.

Index